"*When Bull Elephants Fight* is a [   ]
life. With compassion, intellige [   ]
Roger Youmans tells his story of [   ]
bring hope to a troubled land. You will learn much about modern Africa in these pages, but undoubtedly more about the nature of human kindness."

— Tom Barbash, author of *The Last Good Chance* and *On Top of the World*, a *New York Times* Bestseller

❖

"*When Bull Elephants Fight* is the infectiously fascinating story of a young surgeon's mission to bring medical care to Congo in the 1960s. Driven by heart and soul, Roger Youmans leads his family from the staid world of Eisenhower's America into an exotic realm that most of us access only through daydreams. In prose as limpid as fast-running water, he performs caesareans in the bush, conducts autopsies on bodies three days dead, and survives capture like some latter-day Joseph Conrad. Few of us live lives so deserving of space on the page as this panoramic memoir."

— James D. Sullivan, author of *Over the Moat*

❖

"In a vast country devastated by corruption and handicapped by stressed and limited support system, Roger Youmans was the architect and manager of a ground breaking training program that prepared Congolese doctors to save lives, and offer hope to thousands. Youmans' abiding faith, so evident throughout this memoir, buttresses his superb skill as a surgeon and teacher."

— *William T. Close,* author of the bestselling book *Ebola,* and former personal physician to President Mobutu

❖

"Roger Youmans' story, so well developed in his memoir, reminds me of the service given by Albert Schweitzer and David Livingstone. Dr. Youmans has touched countless lives in his medical missionary work, and it is fascinating to read about his selflessness and that of his family. How fortunate that with this fine book, his experiences will live on in the minds of future generations."

— Edgar F. Puryear, author of *American Generalship,* and *American Admiralship*

When Bull Elephants Fight

An American Surgeon's Chronicle of Congo

When Bull Elephants Fight

An American Surgeon's Chronicle of Congo

To Elsie   *9/28/07*

Roger L. Youmans

Roger L. Youmans

Printed in the United States of America.

Softback ISBN 10: 1-59571-141-4
Softback ISBN 13: 978-1-59571-141-0
Hardback ISBN 10: 1-59571-142-2
Hardback ISBN 13: 978-1-59571-142-7
Library of Congress Number: 2006929356

Cover photograph by Martyn Colbeck
Cover design by Julie Csizmadia.

Word Association Publishers
205 5th Avenue
Tarentum, Pennsylvania 15084
www.wordassociation.com
1-800-827-7903

To

Winkie and Beverly

without whom the events recorded in this book
would never have happened nor would they have
ever been written down or published

Acknowledgments

I want to express my deepest appreciation to my immediate family, Winkie, Grace, Joy, John, and Rogé, who lived the events in this book with me, and to my extended family who preserved the letters and documents that stimulated and supplemented my memory.

I also want to acknowledge my indebtedness to Dr. Otis Simmons, Dr. Frank Allbritten, Emanuel Kimpiatu, Bishop John Wesley Shungu, and Dr. Bill Close, who influenced me at crucial times in my life. I have changed the names of three Congolese doctors to avoid any possible embarrassment to them in as much as I wasn't able to ask their permission to disclose their involvement.

For this book I am indebted to Beverly Youmans, who read and corrected my multiple attempts to express my joy and anguish over living in Congo, and encouraged me when I wanted to give up.

I am deeply grateful to Jeff Kellogg who edited my first draft, and to Dr. Bill Close who graciously reviewed and offered suggestions for the third section of the book. I owe a special debt of gratitude to Tom Barbash for his belief in me, his encouragement to keep writing, and for introducing me to the University of Iowa's Summer Writing Festivals. Thanks also to Tom Costello, the owner of Word Association Publishers, who graciously walked me through the publication process, and to Nan Newell who did the final editing.

Democratic Republic of Congo

Part I

Trampled Grass

"When bull elephants fight, the grass gets trampled."
—Bantu proverb

Prologue

My wife handed me the plain, cream-colored postcard late that evening in early December 1960. It was from the Christian Medical Society. The card said there was an urgent need for American doctors to staff the abandoned hospitals in Congo. The recent riots in Congo, the disappearance of Prime Minister Lumumba, and the collapse of the medical care system had brought on the crisis. The card asked me to write to them if I could go and help, even for as little as six months. My wife, Winkie, had been watching me as I read, and when I looked up she asked, "Why would any American doctor want to go to Congo and get into the middle of that mess?"

"I don't know," I shrugged, tossing the postcard onto the table. I knew Congo was in desperate need of doctors and medical help, but I also knew the country needed a stable government. I wandered into the kitchen and ate leftovers from supper. I was tired and wanted to go to bed. I had to be back at the hospital by 6:30 the next morning.

I had a lot of other things on my mind, and I was tired all the time. A surgical resident in a university medical center works long hours with the constant pressure of new patients, surgical operations, conferences, and never-ending stacks of charts with discharge summaries to be dictated. I was a second-year resident in surgery and hoped to work overseas someday, maybe as a missionary doctor, but had never actually been out of the United States. I had known a girl from India and had thought in terms of going there. I had known a lot of blacks, and I had considered going to Africa someday, maybe to Congo in a few years when my specialty training was finished—if the Congo had settled down by that time.

Things in Congo did not settle down. The newspapers, television, and radio continued to cover the chaos and conflict there. They reported that in the wake of Lumumba's murder, several large tribes that had supported him were now in rebellion against their own government. Tshombe, the governor of one of the provinces that was rich in copper and diamonds, the source of most of the foreign exchange for Congo, had also rebelled against the Kinshasa government. The United Nations sent "peacekeepers" to stop the foreign mercenary soldiers from supporting Tshombe, and to try to hold Congo together as a nation. The newspapers and magazines showed pictures of refugees, mostly skinny women with malnourished babies on their backs and frightened children clinging to their skirts as they fled their destroyed villages. Stories were printed of marauding soldiers killing people and plundering villages in the interior, and of primitive tribesmen arming themselves with spears and magic potions to protect themselves from bullets. They staged horrible ritual killings to terrify their enemies. There was a vivid story of an American woman, a doctor, who was gang-raped at her hospital mission station by a bunch of marauding men. Congo had no trained Congolese physicians, and most of the foreign doctors had already fled the country. Malaria, smallpox, and starvation were the scourge of the villagers. The Congolese people were both helpless and pathetic. I turned away in anguish and tried to push those images out of my mind, but I couldn't.

I sometimes dreamed about the epidemics of exotic diseases that could have been cured with modern medicines had they been available, and of sick mothers with scrawny babies too weak to brush the flies out of their eyes. The reports and images haunted me and I kept thinking about what I could do in one of those abandoned hospitals. I knew I could help, but I was afraid.

One evening a few weeks after Christmas I opened a surgery text to prepare for the next day's operations, and stuck in the pages was that postcard asking for doctors to come to Congo to help. It now seemed like an urgent call for me. When I told Winkie, she sat silently a moment before replying, "At least your children would have a chance to get acquainted with you if we went to Congo."

I hadn't really thought about my family going with me to Congo. How could I possibly take them into such danger, even if I had the money, and of course I didn't. The postcard hadn't mentioned families. If I were to go to Congo, I would have to give notice to the hospital and the chairman of the department of surgery. If my family went with me, we would have to pack up everything we owned and sell or rent our house. There would be immunizations, even for our two little girls. And there would be new languages to learn. How could we do all of this while I continued to work eighty hours a week at the hospital?

Even as these thoughts crossed my mind, I realized the question had subtly changed from *Why would any American doctor want go to Congo and get into that mess?* to *How could we go about doing it?* It was a significant change.

One
Unprepared

"Fools rush in where angels fear to tread."
—Alexander Pope

We departed for Africa on an October day in 1961. We had left Kansas City the day before and flown to New York, where we waited in the airport nearly five hours with our two fussy babies. It had been miserable. Then at midnight we boarded the Pan American flight from New York to Leopoldville, Congo. The sixteen-hour flight to Leopoldville with numerous stops in West African airports was a nightmare. We were red-eyed and irritable, and Winkie and I had splitting headaches by the time we approached the Njili airport outside Leopoldville.

I stood in the aisle to stretch as we began our descent and I caught fragments of a conversation between a Belgian businessman and his British seatmate. "It's only been a year since they got their independence," the thin Englishman was saying, nodding his head for emphasis and raising a trembling finger, "but the future does look bleak. I do hope the trouble is over now. I really didn't think there was any point in my returning, but the board said we ought to salvage what we can."

When Bull Elephants Fight

"It's the damn tribalism," the Belgian said as he tugged his already loosened collar more widely apart. His suit was rumpled from the long flight. Earlier he had told us that Congo was no place for children. Now he said, "They can't keep from killing each other, and the buggers have over two hundred tribes. They go wild, raping and killing. Nuns. Priests. No telling what they might do to us." The Belgian shook his head and turned both palms up in a gesture of helplessness. "Tshombe's the only hope." He then switched to French, and I didn't understand what he said.

I looked at Winkie holding our baby daughter, Joy, on her lap and comforting her while three-year-old Grace turned the pages of a picture book. The conversation had renewed the gnawing anxiety in my stomach, and I was becoming almost certain I had made a mistake by bringing my family, but of course, there was no way to turn back now.

Joy cried as our plane descended, but once we were on the runway she began taking her bottle quietly. Grace put her book back into her small plastic suitcase alongside the crayons, paper, pajamas, and toothbrush. She held her little suitcase impatiently, her shoulder sagging under the weight of the canteen filled with water. Still, her eyes were bright with excitement for this new adventure. She had no idea what lay ahead.

I opened my briefcase to make sure, for the fourth time, that our passports, health cards, and baggage stubs were still there. International travel was new to me, and I was afraid something would go wrong and I wouldn't have the right document or the right answer to a question.

The sun glared out of a cloudless afternoon sky as we walked toward the terminal where a dozen armed Congolese soldiers were standing around, talking and laughing among themselves. I wanted to get my family out of the oppressive heat and into what looked like a modern, cool terminal building, but it was hotter inside the terminal than it was outside. There weren't even any fans to stir the air, and the sour odor of sweating bodies and stale smoke hung heavily in the air. We moved along behind the crowd into a large room where I saw the portly Belgian whose conversation I had overheard in the plane.

He was leaving the immigration officer's desk as I entered the room, and I noticed that sweat had already soaked through his shirt. He glanced at our family, recognized us, and rolled his eyes upward. He shook his head and turned away toward the door. We were at the end of the line waiting to get our passports checked when I realized I couldn't understand what anybody around me was saying. The two weeks I had studied French didn't help me now. I was relieved our passports were in order, and the official stamped and returned them without my saying a word.

By the time I found all four of our large suitcases and dragged them, one by one, to the table where the Congolese customs official could check them, the baggage room was nearly empty. Winkie stood to the side, leaning on a pillar with our carry-on bags and sweaters. She held Grace's hand and still carried Joy on her hip. Her limp hair, damp with perspiration, hung across her face. Dark circles shadowed her eyes. We waited another ten minutes before the customs official got around to examining our suitcases. He had me open each suitcase, even our carry-on sacks, then slowly began going through every item in each suitcase, laying the items on the table one by one. I was irritated and exhausted, and would have asked him to hurry if I had known how. The heat, the humidity, and the stench of human bodies in the room made it difficult to breathe. I was growing increasingly impatient.

A Belgian woman in a neat blue uniform offered advice to the Congolese official about the duty to be charged for various items that he held up for her to evaluate. I found myself becoming inappropriately angry by these delays. The official needed help to evaluate almost every item. The Belgian woman usually just shook her head, which I thought meant, *don't charge anything,* but I didn't understand her French and she never spoke a word in English.

The Congolese official searching through our bags abruptly stopped, looked up at me, and asked a question I couldn't understand. He repeated it, louder this time.

"What do you want?" I asked in English.

He asked again in French.

"I can't understand you. Can't you speak English?" I asked, raising my voice as he had, and with the same result. In each exchange I listened and looked for some word or gesture to clarify for me what he wanted. My ignorance compounded my anger.

With a tired smile Winkie came to my rescue. "He wants to know what you have in your ophthalmoscope case, Roger. Just open it and show him."

I opened the case, picked up my stethoscope and my blood pressure cuff, and laid these on top of the pile by the ophthalmoscope.

"I'm a doctor. I'm here to help your people. I need these things to help."

He looked at the items I had laid out and said something to Winkie.

She answered, *"Oui, monsieur. Il est un médecin, un chirurgien."* Then she said to me, "He wanted to know why you carried those things. He recognized the stethoscope and asked if you were a doctor and I told him you were a surgeon." The corners of her mouth twitched upward in a firm but transient smile. "Stay calm, Roger," she continued. "We'll get through this okay. The children are really hot and thirsty and my canteen is empty." She took the canteen from my shoulder to give a drink to the children.

Finally the customs official was satisfied. He gestured for me to repack the suitcases. I stuffed everything back into them while he and the Belgian woman in the blue uniform watched.

When we finally made it outside, it was cooler and there was now a little breeze. The sun had dipped below the palm trees on the horizon. A large crowd of people stared at us with curiosity. I paused, unsure of what to do next, and several men stepped forward and grabbed our suitcases. I panicked.

"Stop! Come back here," I yelled. In retrospect I realized they were probably just trying to make a tip by carrying our bags, but in that moment I thought they were trying to steal them. I heard a loud voice on my left, but didn't understand what was said. The men must have understood, because they stopped. The voice said something else and the men who had grabbed our suitcases put them down and backed away.

The same voice asked, "Dr. Youmans?"

I saw a sandy-haired, tall white man moving toward us through the crowd. "I'm Dr. Bob Bowers, with the Congo Protestant Relief Agency," he said. A smile animated his weary face. "I've been here waiting for you. They wouldn't let me inside." He led us to his car.

I felt enormously relieved. He would help us and take us where we needed to go. The energy from my anxiety and anger seeped away. I was tired.

As Dr. Bowers drove us away from the airport, I leaned back and closed my eyes. The air blowing through the window was cool and refreshing. "The Union Mission House is full," Dr. Bowers said. I nodded and gazed out the window. He noticed I was looking at the dark hulks of numerous cars and trucks along the side of the road. Some were still blocking part of a lane, but most were in the ditch, and some appeared to have been burned.

"Most of those wrecks are left over from last year when the riots were going on," he explained. "Things are pretty quiet around here now." We drove on in silence until we came to the edge of Leopoldville.

"With so many missionaries leaving the interior of Congo now, our mission housing facilities here in town are full, but I can put you in a small hotel for a few days," Dr. Bowers said just before a huge pothole jarred the car. Joy woke up with a cry and he slowed down and tried to steer around the biggest of the other holes.

"Will a small hotel be okay for your family?" he asked, and then added, "There won't be any Americans around, but if you can handle a little French the Belgian owner will take care of whatever you need."

"Wherever you think best is okay with me," I said sheepishly. I was embarrassed to acknowledge that I had come to Congo without having learned French in advance.

We stopped in front of a two-story building with several lights on, and got out of the car. "This is called the Continental Hotel and this area of Leopoldville is called Limité," he explained. "I know the proprietor. Leave your things in the car; I'll lock it. Let's take a look at the room."

Two of the hotel's windows were boarded over. Three small tables with umbrellas and chairs blocked the sidewalk in front of the hotel. A Congolese man with two skimpily dressed women draped across his arms sat at one table. Inside two couples sat at the bar, talking and drinking beer.

The barkeeper was also the proprietor and he and Dr. Bowers talked in French for several minutes. Then the proprietor led us up a flight of wooden stairs and down a narrow hallway. He opened a door and we entered a rather large room with a sink on one wall and a double bed against the opposite wall.

"He said that he will bring up a mattress for the kids," Dr. Bowers said. "There is a WC, a toilet, over there, through that door."

We looked at the toilet in the little closet. "Seems okay to me," I said, and glanced over at Winkie to get her approval. She nodded and tried to smile, but she was practically asleep on her feet.

Dr. Bowers gave us some Congo francs for breakfast, and paid the proprietor for the room. He and I returned to the car for our bags, leaving Winkie and the girls in the room. Winkie put both girls on the bed, and by the time we got our bags into the room, the promised mattress was on the floor by the bed.

"I'll come by for you about noon tomorrow," Dr. Bowers told us. "I'm sorry about your experience at the airport, and I apologize for rushing off now, but there is another family I've got to help tonight. So many of the missionaries are coming and going these days, mostly going, that I can hardly keep up." He shook my hand and left.

A single bulb hung from the ceiling by its wire in the center of the room. Our things were scattered on the floor. Winkie washed the girls' faces and hands at the sink.

Joy whimpered, but Grace spoke up. "Mommy, I'm thirsty."

Winkie wiped their lips with a little water from the faucet on the sink. "I know, honey," she said to Grace, "but our canteens are empty, and I'm afraid the water here in the sink isn't good for drinking. You stay here with Daddy, and I'll go downstairs and get some water for you to drink." She looked at me, picked up two canteens, and went out, closing the door behind her. Winkie and the children had been well immunized last summer so they would have some resistance to cholera and typhoid just in case the water they drank was contaminated.

Winkie returned a few minutes later with the canteens and a whiskey bottle. A faint smile flickered across her face.

"When I got downstairs I saw there were a lot more Congolese than when we arrived. They were drinking, laughing, and carrying on, but I just asked the barkeeper, *'S'il vous plaît, monsieur, je voudrais un peu d'eau potable.'*

"I'm thirsty, Mommy," Grace piped up, interrupting her story.

"I'm sorry, honey. Here, have a drink." She helped Grace and Joy drink from the canteen in her hand. Both girls lay down and quickly fell asleep.

"When he handed me the whiskey bottle," Winkie resumed, "I objected until he had me taste it. It was just cold water in an old whiskey bottle. I poured it in the canteen and asked for another." She looked at me through her bloodshot eyes and added, "I've got three containers of water, but now I've got to get some sleep."

Winkie began to snore quietly almost as soon as she lay down, and I turned out the light and sat on the bed in the dark listening to the people downstairs and out on the sidewalk laughing and talking in a language I couldn't understand, but it didn't sound like French. A sliver of moon peeked through the trees on the other side of the street. I couldn't sleep. I checked the hook-and-eye lock on the door. It wasn't much, so I pushed a chair against it, then sat down on the bed again. Sometime later I fell asleep. I awoke to a racket downstairs. It sounded as if a chair had been tipped over or even thrown. Some men were shouting and I heard a crashing sound like wood splintering. I couldn't understand what was happening. Somebody ran up the front steps and down the hall toward our room. I held my breath. The runner stopped outside our door. The door handle turned and somebody leaned against the door, but the little hook-and-eye held it shut. Somebody else was running up the stairs. Whoever was at our door raced down the hall. I heard a siren outside. A second person ran by our door without stopping. The siren's scream began to die just below our window and a moment later I heard a car door slam. There were more loud noises of scuffling and shouting. Then it became eerily quiet. Winkie and the girls were still sleeping soundly, but I was wide-awake. Outside, a car started, several doors slammed, and the car drove away. There had been no gunshots. Perhaps it had just been a drunken scuffle, I thought, trying to reassure myself.

I sat there in the dark. The moon was gone. I could hear the quiet breathing of Winkie and the children. We had been in Congo less than a day and I was already scared and helpless. My God, I thought as I struggled to fall back asleep, what have I done to my family?

I opened my eyes to bright sunshine streaming in through the window. Winkie was up and getting dressed. Grace was standing on the mattress, holding Joy's hand. "Drink, Mommy," she pleaded. I looked at my watch.

"Is it really nine already?" I asked Winkie.

She was washing her face now. She dabbed her face dry and smiled at me. Her eyes were bright and I felt relieved. "Yes, honey. We've slept for over twelve hours." She looked more rested than she had for several days. She handed Grace the canteen.

It was morning, and we had survived. I washed and shaved with cold water. By the time I was dressed, Winkie and the girls were ready to go. "Let's see if we can find breakfast," I said as cheerfully as I could. I was feeling so much better than last night, relieved and even optimistic, though there wasn't any reason for my renewed confidence except that I was young and rested. Nothing had really changed.

We all sat around a table on the sidewalk outside the hotel and looked at the menu. It was in French, but with explanations in some African language. I knew what *café* was, and what an *oeuf* was, and I could read the prices. Dr. Bowers had given us plenty of money. I held Joy on my lap, and Winkie ordered our breakfast. It was coffee for the two of us, and toast and eggs all around. We were disappointed that there was no milk for the girls.

After breakfast Winkie and I sat at the small table and talked about the hassle at the airport yesterday, and about the long flight from New York. Grace and Joy were happily exploring the area around our sidewalk table.

"Well," Winkie commented, "we knew it wouldn't be easy. But we're here and we're healthy." In the euphoria of the moment, we had forgotten the anxiety and exhaustion of yesterday. We even laughed at our current helplessness like silly school kids. But we couldn't seem to get over the wonder of our actually being in Leopoldville, Democratic Republic of Congo.

As we sat at the table waiting for Dr. Bowers, Grace shouted,

"Look!" and pointed to a small dog racing across the street. Behind the dog was a tall man carrying a leash and running as he called to the dog in English.

"Stop, Sheba! Come back here, Sheba."

I got up and hurried toward the man as he caught the dog and snapped the leash onto her collar. Grace had run ahead of me, and Winkie scooped up Joy in her arms and followed. As I approached the man, I called out as politely as I could, "You speak English?"

He replied with a definite British accent, "Yes, of course I do."

I introduced myself, extending my hand to shake his. "This is my wife, Winkie, that is, we call her Winkie. Her real name is Mary. These are our two little girls, Grace and Joy. I don't speak much French," I said, adding with a touch of hyperbole, "and I haven't heard English for two days."

"My name is Stewart Wright," he said, shaking hands with Winkie, then shaking my hand again. "My dog jerked free from her leash, the little rascal. Oh, she won't bite," he added, noticing that Grace was petting the dog and trying to keep from being licked in the face by the excited puppy. "Stop that, Sheba. She doesn't want you to lick her face." Both girls were laughing.

"We just arrived last night," Winkie said. "I'm not very good in French either." She smiled. "Roger never really had a chance to study French."

"Really? What brought you to Congo at such a time as this? Everything is falling apart, it seems. I say, I do think Sheba likes your daughters."

I told him we were just here for six months to help out medically, that I was a doctor, and that I would be working in the Sona Bata Hospital.

"Splendid for you," Mr. Wright responded. "There weren't many good doctors here before all of this independence started, and most of the doctors that were here have gone back to Europe. Mostly they were Belgians, you know. These people here are nowhere near ready for independence. It's a shame. There's no order or discipline among them now."

"What kind of work do you do?" I asked.

"Me? I'm responsible for the Coates thread factory. It's dreadfully difficult now. I've almost run out of cotton, and the

Congo cotton fibers are too short to make decent thread. By the way, I don't believe I know Sona Bata. Is it near?"

"I've never been there, but they say it is south, about halfway to Kimpese on the road toward Matadi."

"Oh, yes. I know Matadi and I've heard of Kimpese. Maybe one of these days we can take a drive down there and see your hospital."

"You would be most welcome."

"Oh, I see my wife," Mr. Wright said, looking across the street where an attractive, slender woman was waving her hand. "You must come and meet Fernanda. She speaks English, French, Spanish, and Portuguese."

We crossed the road and met Fernanda, who greeted us warmly. She was from Brazil, but emphasized that there weren't many Brazilians in Congo except with the United Nations peacekeeping unit.

Stooping down to look into Grace's face, Fernanda asked, "How would you like a glass of milk and a cookie?" Grace grinned and nodded her head vigorously, then looked up at her mother for permission. "We live right over there," Frenanda continued. "Come over and have a glass of milk and play with Sheba. I can see she likes you."

As we walked to their house, Grace told Joy about the milk and cookies and playing with the puppy. Joy grinned. Winkie and I were relieved to find a friendly family here in Kinshasa that could speak English, and somebody who cared about our children. Fernanda invited Winkie to give Grace and Joy a bath, if she wanted. The invitation was quickly expanded to make the bath available to Winkie and me.

Two
The Sona Bata Hospital

"Foolishness often precedes wisdom."
—Bakongo proverb

Because of the urgent need for doctors and the confidence of the government officials in the mission leaders, it only required one day to get drivers licenses, extensions on our visas, my work permit, my license to practice medicine, and to complete other paperwork in Leopoldville. It took an additional day for Mabel, the wife of one of the mission administrators, to help us buy a few groceries. The first grocery store we entered had long rows of shelves that were bare except for an occasional can of beans or a can of powdered milk every three or four feet. The second store wasn't much better. The Belgian businessmen who were still in Congo had not been able to import adequate supplies of food to restock their inventories since the riots began a year ago. Mabel said she would see if she could locate some flour, sugar, preserves, and other staples for us in the next week or two. Some of the Belgian merchants knew her and would be able to get these things that weren't otherwise available. In the meantime, she would ask some of the Congolese ladies in our church in Sona Bata to find eggs, pineapples, and bananas for us.

For the first few days we ate with the two missionary teachers at Sona Bata who had already returned after having been evacuated last year. "The lower Congo is more stable now," Mabel assured us. "It's the rest of the country that is in trouble. The teachers will feed you until you get your things settled. They will feed Dr. Weschi too. He is sponsored by the relief agency, just like you are, but he will be transferred to another hospital in a few days. Rev. Orville Chapman and his family have returned to Sona Bata. He will be able to help you with Kikongo and French, Roger." Mabel encouraged Winkie to return to Leopoldville in a few days, when she would help her find additional groceries and supplies. Mabel was optimistic and full of information, and although she talked constantly, her information was relevant. We appreciated her help and confidence in us.

I was overwhelmed by this new culture, the noise of the crowds, the emptiness of the stores, the language difficulties, and the surprising number of Belgian shopkeepers still working in Leopoldville. Mabel introduced us to most of the American and Congolese personnel who worked at the Baptist mission headquarters. Winkie was far less bewildered than I, probably because she knew French. But she also had a clearer knowledge of what she would need to care for the family, and the questions she asked Mabel were specific and practical.

"Will somebody help us with laundry and diapers, or will we have a washing machine?" Winkie asked, laughing at the absurd possibility of having a washer. "Is there a good stove for cooking? Will we have helpers around the house? Running water?"

Mabel reassured her that the doctor's house was the best on the station, and that we would have water and helpers to cook and do laundry. "And don't worry about the language, because Emanuel Kimpiatu speaks excellent English, in addition to Kikongo and French. Kimpiatu is a graduate nurse and has been the director of the mission station since independence. His office is in the hospital, and he'll handle all of the hassles with the government or soldiers, as well as the salaries of the nurses and collection of fees from patients."

She told us arrangements had already been made for us to have a cook, a houseboy to do laundry, a man to cut the grass, and a sentinel who would stay on the porch of our house every night.

Mabel seemed to know what our questions were before we asked, and I was relieved that so many arrangements had already been made for us. Winkie and I both began to relax as Mabel's cheerful stream of explanations continued.

She drove us to Sona Bata three days after our arrival. The highway to Sona Bata was a two-lane asphalt road that had a faded centerline, but no shoulders. We passed several burned-out cars and trucks that were in the ditch at the side of the road. Twice there were trucks blocking an entire lane. There were no warning signs and nobody seemed to be in or around the vehicles. The road had many curves and hills, and the abandoned vehicles were a danger to traffic, but nobody seemed to care. Mabel just swung across to the other side of the road, like all the other drivers.

Soldiers stopped us twice to vaccinate all of us against smallpox, even though we showed them our yellow WHO health cards that verified that we were already vaccinated. Their equipment was a test tube of vaccine and one syringe and needle. There was no evidence of any attempt to keep the vaccine cold, nor evidence of any additional needles. I didn't want their needle touching my family or me. They said they had orders to vaccinate everybody who didn't already have a vaccination scar. Thankfully, we all had obvious scars on our arms, and were allowed to pass on.

About half an hour after our second escape from the soldiers with vaccine and needles, Mabel said the hospital was just over a couple more hills. Suddenly I saw the sun reflecting off the hospital roof on a distant hill, less than a mile ahead of us. I felt a wave of excitement. This would be *my* hospital in Congo for the next six months! But I was also aware of a growing insecurity and fear. I wondered if I could really handle the medical problems there. Would Kimpiatu really take time to help me, to translate the languages, and would I be able to understand his English?

We pulled onto the dirt road of the Sona Bata mission station. Hundreds of Congolese women wearing brightly colored head wraps and blouses with wrap-around skirts were standing around the station buildings, and turned to watch us as we drove in. Many of the women had babies tied onto their backs with a wide piece of cloth they called a *panya*. The women were all barefoot, talking in groups and laughing. Several groups of men, dressed in shirts and

When Bull Elephants Fight

dusty trousers, stood around near the hospital. They kicked the dust idly with their bare feet as they looked at us.

"Are all of these people patients?" I asked.

"Oh, no," Mabel said quickly. "These are the families of patients, *les aides de malades*. They cook the meals and feed the patients. The hospital doesn't provide food service."

"Where do all these people sleep at night?"

"In the hospital. Some sleep on the floor between the beds, or in the corridors, and sometimes in bed with the patient."

As I got out of the car I noticed goats, dozens of chickens, and two dogs in the yard around the hospital. A tall, well-built Congolese man wearing a white coat and appearing to be about forty years old, walked toward us. He was smiling broadly and his eyes were bright, almost laughing. He was wearing shoes.

"You are welcome," he called in a resonating baritone voice.

I stepped toward him, extending my hand. "You must be Kimpiatu," I said.

"*M'bote, Tata,*" he replied in Kikongo, greeting me with respect as though I was his father. He shook my hand vigorously. "We are glad you are here. We have many *malades*."

Winkie had helped both children out of the car, and now they stood timidly, looking at the multitude of strange faces staring at them. "*M'bote*, Mama, we are glad Docteur brought you and his children. You will maybe stay here with us long time." Kimpiatu shook Winkie's hand and bent down, laughing, to shake hands with Grace and Joy. They grinned, accepting his friendly reassurance.

Mabel came around the front of the car and introduced us all, and then turned to Kimpiatu. "We will take their things down to the doctor's house first, then you can show Dr. Youmans around the hospital. I'm in a hurry to get back up to Leopoldville."

Two other neatly dressed Congolese men wearing shoes and white coats came out of the hospital. I assumed correctly that they were also nurses. A crowd of fifteen or so children had gathered around us, and many of them were reaching out and touching Grace and Joy timidly, and then backing away laughing. They felt the girls' soft yellow hair and rubbed their white skin, and giggled some more. Twenty or more adults had also gathered around us, standing back farther than the children, but staring at us with curiosity.

"Come see your house," Kimpiatu said, moving down the wide path toward a house about one hundred yards away. Winkie and I and the girls followed. An entourage of thirty or more people, all of them talking and laughing, followed us to the house. Even though Sona Bata was one of the oldest Baptist mission stations in Congo and there had been white people and doctors here for generations, our arrival still caused quite a stir. I think it was because of the children.

The house was a single-story brick building with a wide, screened-in porch to keep out the mosquitoes. Winkie noticed a fifty-five-gallon drum for collecting rainwater on the open porch.

"Will we use water from the rain barrel for drinking, or just for bathing and flushing the toilet?" she asked.

Mabel quickly spoke up. "You can use rainwater during the rainy season for laundry and bathing like everybody else, but the station has a deep well and an electric pump. The generator is turned on from six to nine o'clock every evening, and water is pumped up to the reservoir in the church tower, and then piped into your house. Of course, you will also have lights at that time. But if you want hot water, you have to heat it on the stove and pour it into the sink or tub."

"Did you live in this house at one time?" Winkie asked.

"No, only the families of the doctors. Dr. Weschi lives here now—he is with the Operation Doctor program, but now that you're here, he will be leaving in a day or so to go to Stanleyville for the rest of his term in Congo. He will use your third bedroom until he leaves."

After we unloaded the car, Mabel returned to Leopoldville. Kimpiatu introduced the three Congolese men who would provide household help for Winkie. Then he encouraged me to stay with my family and help them get settled. I thanked him, but insisted that I would come to the hospital at two o'clock to see the patients. He laughed and agreed, then left.

That afternoon I returned to the ward for male surgical patients. The records for the current patients, five-by-seven inch pieces of stiff paper with dates and a few brief phrases of French mixed with English words were stacked together on the corner of the table. Tata

When Bull Elephants Fight

Nsiala, the senior male nurse responsible for the patients in the hospital, was waiting for me with three young assistant nurses. The five of us began seeing the patients, and I attempted to understand why each was in the hospital and how they were being treated.

At the end of each ward, or pavilion as it was called, were two very small private rooms used mainly for isolation of potentially infectious patients. Beds lined both sides of each pavilion with an aisle about five feet wide running between the rows. Large windows with screens and shutters allowed cross-ventilation during the day, but I later observed that the shutters were always closed at night. The Congolese tolerated heat very well, but were cold if the temperature dropped below seventy degrees. Most of the patients were from the Bakongo tribe, and spoke Kikongo. Only half of the men spoke French, and less than a quarter of the women.

Nsiala handed me the first patient's record, and began talking to the patient in Kikongo. Apparently the notes on the card had been written by Dr. Weschi in Americanized French: *"1/11/61 Fièvre, mal de tête. Dx Malaria Rx CHQ 4,2,2,2. ASA 2, Multi-vit 1."*

I asked Nsiala what the writing meant. When he understood my question, he answered in simplified French, pointing at each phrase. First was the date, then the patient's complaint of fever and headache—Nsiala touched his own forehead. Then came the diagnosis, malaria, which is spelled the same in English and French, and finally the treatment with chloroquine, which he pronounced while he pointed at *"CHQ,"* adding that four tablets were given immediately and two tablets every twelve hours for three doses. I understood the American symbol for aspirin (ASA) and the shorthand for one tablet of a multi-vitamin.

I asked the patient if he was okay now, but he just grinned at me, not understanding what I had said. So I asked Nsiala in English combined with gestures, and he seemed to understand. Nsiala talked to the patient in Kikongo for a moment, then turned to me smiling and said, "Okay."

I didn't see on the chart any indication that the patient's temperature had ever been taken or recorded. I mimed the taking of the temperature, and pointed at a blank spot on the chart. Nsiala spoke to one of the assistant nurses, who then left and returned with a thermometer and took the patient's temperature. It was 99 degrees. I nodded, and wrote on the chart, "Discharge," in English. Nsiala looked at what I wrote and said, "Okay."

There were fifty-nine more patients to see on the medical and surgical wards for men, and my communication problems were embarrassingly obvious. I took out my small notebook and began writing down the symbols that my predecessor had used in the chart, noting how Nsiala interpreted them. We went from patient to patient for the next three hours. The process was pathetic and rudimentary, but I did begin to have some understanding of the diagnoses and treatment plans for all twenty-one of the patients in the men's ward. I had so much to learn and so little time—how could I take care of the patients in this hospital? I was worn out, and all three of the assistants had left us to do other necessary work on the pavilion. I thanked Nsiala, and managed to communicate to him that I would return at eight in the morning. He smiled and thanked me. All the patients were smiling as I left and I took some satisfaction in suspecting that they had been encouraged by my presence and interest. I smiled politely in return, and went home frustrated by my ignorance of their language and culture.

Winkie showed me the bananas, pineapples, peanuts, and eggs that she had bought from women who had come to the house during the afternoon. Grace and Joy had slept for an hour and a half, and had eaten a good snack of bananas and mashed peanuts when they woke up. They had been playing together contentedly for the last hour. Winkie was upbeat. She was in her own home and her children were rested and happy. French was coming back to her more quickly than she had expected.

I sat down and began writing questions and phrases in English: *What is wrong with this patient? Where does he hurt? How many days has he had this? Has he taken any medicine for it?* and so on for twenty more questions. Winkie supplied the French for each question, and I wrote down what she told me, and tried to pronounce the phrases as she had.

I wrote down instructions that a patient would need to understand prior to my doing a physical examination: *Take a deep breath* (so I can listen to your lungs); *Open your mouth* (so I can look at your throat); *Cough* (so I can check for a hernia). I wrote down twenty more instructions that I could have Nsiala translate for a patient before the exam. *Stand up. Bend over.* I then began to memorize the French words that Winkie supplied, but I didn't get very far before it got dark.

That first evening after an afternoon of discouragement, just after dark, I heard the pickup truck arrive with Dr. Weschi. He was nearly six feet tall with disheveled brown hair. He had spent the last two days working in the hospital at Kimpese with the four American doctors. Kimpese was a referral center for patients, especially the Protestant patients in the province of Bakongo. He was a short-term doctor in Congo, just as I was, and wanted to get a position as a resident in surgery when he finished his year here. He was single, had been in Congo for nearly two months, and could speak and understand some French.

"Have you had a chance to visit the hospital at Kimpese yet?" he asked as we stood in front of the house in the darkness.

"No," I replied, "I haven't seen any place except here and Leopoldville. Is it like Sona Bata?"

"It's a little bit like here, but they've got more equipment, more doctors, and American nurses." When he said they had American nurses at the Kimpese Hospital, I immediately wished that I had been assigned there instead of Sona Bata. Dr. Weschi smiled as though he read my mind, and extended his hand to me in an apparent gesture of condolence. "It's bigger, but it's not like any hospital I've ever seen in America. You will have to go down there sometime and see it," he added.

Just talking with another doctor my age, especially an American doctor, was a relief, and after my frustrating rounds that afternoon it encouraged me to believe that I could learn and be of some help to the patients at Sona Bata. If he could care for the patients here, then I began to believe that I could do it, too.

"Don't worry," he advised me, "Kimpiatu and the other nurses will show you. They are very knowledgeable about tropical diseases. When you're in doubt, ask them what to do."

"That's the heart of my problem," I told him. "I can't speak Kikongo and I've never really had a chance to study French. I don't even know how to ask Nsiala or Kimpiatu anything."

He told me he'd go over the common diseases and treatments with me and I'd catch on quickly. He said Kikongo would actually be more helpful here than French because so few of the patients spoke French. When he would go to Stanleyville next week, nobody there would speak Kikongo and very few of the patients would speak or understand French. "No matter," he laughed. "Whatever we do, it will be better than what they had before we came."

I showed him my list of words and phrases and asked his advice. His French was fairly good, but not nearly as good as Winkie's. We hadn't worked on this long before the houseboy from Madeline's house came by with a note explaining that Bob Weschi would join our family for supper at her house tonight, and supper was ready now.

The sun sets at about 6:15 every evening at Sona Bata, followed by about twenty minutes of twilight, and by 6:40 it is very dark unless there is a nearly full moon. There are only three or four evenings a month when the moon provides enough light in the evening so that a flashlight isn't needed. This evening was not one of them.

We took our flashlights to Emily and Madeline's house and stayed for an hour or so after dinner talking and learning more about the hospital and the mission station. There was no end to our questions and the discussions that followed. Within a day or two I would be the only doctor for the entire hospital. My limitations seemed almost overwhelming, so I tried to keep the conversation on medical subjects, but Winkie, Emily and Madeline were talking about the housekeeping and teaching challenges in Sona Bata.

The electric lights in the house suddenly went off, and we were plunged into darkness.

"Must be nine o'clock," Madeline said. A few seconds later the lights came back on and Emily lit a kerosene lantern. Then the lights went off again and we were left in the soft glow of the lantern. Our daughters had grabbed Winkie anxiously when the lights first went off, and now they were wide-eyed, but not frightened.

"I guess it's time for us to go back to our house," Winkie said calmly, still holding both girls by the hand to reassure them. We expressed our gratitude and walked under the light of the stars across the compound to our house.

Winkie put the girls to bed by kerosene lamplight and with a story. Bob stayed on to help me with the French phrases I'd need to communicate with the nurses, and I took notes. He quickly told me the medications used for the common diseases and how to write them on the charts so the nurses would know what and how to give them. By the end of this session I had a handle on their simple record system. Bob was going to operate on a patient with a hernia the next day and asked if I would scrub in with him. I quickly accepted, knowing I had much to learn about what instruments were available and what the Congolese nurses understood about assisting in surgery. I felt a growing confidence as we talked, even though there wasn't any reason to be confident. We stayed up talking until far past midnight.

Three
The Doctor Can Talk

"Better a black man's heart without words than a black man's words without heart."

—Bakongo proverb

I awoke to the sound of singing, loud talking, and laughter in front of our house in the faint light of dawn. Several women dressed in brightly colored *panyas* and blouses were sweeping the path in front of our house with palm branches. Other women stood outside our door calling, "*Ko, ko, ko,*" their way of saying, "Knock, knock, knock." They had bananas, pineapples, yams, palm nuts, peanuts, and eggs to sell and one of the women translated the Kikongo of the other women into French for Winkie, who bought a little of everything.

Three men who were to be our helpers waited on the porch steps. For the next six months our days would start at sunrise with women sweeping the leaves off the path, singing and talking, and others selling us fruit and vegetables. Winkie's three helpers in the house knew what they were to do, but only Tata Tomas could speak French. He would be our cook and translate the Kikongo of the others into French for Winkie. Tata Kilolo indicated that he would wash and iron the clothes. He knew where the charcoal iron was and how to heat and use it. Tata Jumbo would cut the grass, and he knew where to find the curved machete that he needed for that purpose.

Winkie dressed the kids. I used some of the hot water from the teakettle to shave, and then we all sat down for breakfast. Tomas brought us bread, pineapple slices, and hot water for tea. He had borrowed the tea leaves and sugar and a small can of condensed milk from Madeline. Then he asked if we wanted eggs, and we all did. It was an American breakfast except for the tea instead of coffee. Bob and I went to the hospital at eight and prepared the instruments and the patient for surgery.

The light for the operating room came from the large windows that nearly filled three sides of the room. There was a surgical light, but it was not often used. The small hospital generator was too expensive to operate on a routine basis in the daytime, and it needed to be repaired before it could be used at all. The light coming through the large windows was adequate, and besides, the charge for a hernia repair operation was less than the cost of fuel to run the generator for an hour. The hospital policy was to operate by daylight, if possible; otherwise, we scheduled operations for the evening when the larger mission-station generator would be on and there would be no extra expense caused by using the operating room lights. The surgical instruments in the hospital were sterilized and laid out on a sterile towel on the operating room table. After we scrubbed and donned our sterile gowns and gloves, we selected the instruments that we would need and placed them on a sterile towel on the small Mayo table. That way the remaining sterile instruments would be available for a second or third operation on the same day.

I was in favor of being economical, but I thought re-sterilizing the surgical gloves and using them three or more times before discarding them was carrying economy too far. The gloves we used that first morning had several tiny holes due to prior use and multiple sterilizations, but we washed our hands carefully before we started, and used them anyway.

Tata Nsaku was the Congolese graduate nurse who gave the ether anesthesia when necessary, but this morning we used local anesthesia, Xylocaine with epinephrine, for the hernia repair. It was less expensive than a can of ether, probably safer for the patient, and besides, Tata Nsaku was busy with other responsibilities. I assisted while Bob did the surgery. The patient tolerated the procedure well, and afterward we spent the rest of the morning with Nsiala seeing patients in the hospital. Bob continued orienting me on how he treated the various medical conditions.

After lunch I went back to the hospital to see outpatients, and to practice the questions in French that I had worked on. I had one of the assistant nurses helping me, but I had as much trouble understanding what he said in French as he had understanding my French. Even with gestures, I could hardly figure out what he told me the patient was complaining about. The assistant nurse was sufficiently able to understand my notes about the medicines to give them to the patients without difficulty. I gave most of the people worm medicine, vitamins, and iron. I felt as if I were practicing veterinary medicine, but I was applying the basic precept of medicine, "First, do no harm." There was no doubt that all of the patients would benefit from those simple medicines, even if some other conditions were overlooked and left untreated. I didn't finish at the outpatient clinic until six o'clock.

Bob had been looking after several people from a car accident and had admitted two of them for observation overnight. By the time I got home, he was at the house packing his clothes and other belongings. Bob said Dr. Bowers would come by tomorrow on his way to Leopoldville from Kimpese. Bob would fly on to Stanleyville later, and I would then be on my own at the hospital. I thought I could manage the infectious and parasitic diseases that I had learned about in medical school, and my surgery training would probably be adequate for the needs here, but I didn't know much about rare or esoteric tropical diseases. I wondered even then at my audacity in having come to Congo thinking I could run a hospital.

The next morning I tried to set up a schedule at the hospital. I decided I would make rounds on the hospitalized patients on Tuesday, Thursday, and Saturday mornings, and do surgical procedures on Monday, Wednesday, and Friday mornings. I would see outpatients every afternoon. But I would see anybody Tata Nsiala requested me to see, anytime he asked, and emergencies would always take precedence over the schedule. Saturdays were open for whatever Tata Kimpiatu or Tata Nsiala wanted me to do. Sunday was to be a "no workday" according to the mission station rules, unless there was an emergency.

Such simple planning made me feel better, but trying to keep the plan would be much harder than making it. Unless I made some rapid headway on my language learning, all my plans would be inadequate. Tata Nsiala was very patient with my struggle in French, and supplied the French words for which I repeatedly used English. I would write the French and English words together in my notebook and review them each evening. Grammar and correct pronunciation were of secondary importance if I could just communicate with Nsiala and the assistant nurses about each patient's condition from day to day and communicate the diagnosis and specific treatments for each patient to receive. Nsiala could teach me the French names of various common drugs, and how the nurses on the ward were used to writing them. For example, CHQ meant chloroquine, our primary drug against malaria; P-mol meant paracetamol, a drug similar to aspirin but safer to use in the Bantu population; and C-col was chloramphenicol, an effective and inexpensive broad-spectrum antibiotic.

We had a rudimentary laboratory in which we could do malaria blood smears, complete blood counts, urinalysis, stool exams, and blood type and cross-matches, but not much else. There were specific ways to write the abbreviations for these tests, and specific abbreviations were used to report the results. I learned these symbols immediately. We began to take daily temperature readings on the patients in the hospital, at least for those who were seriously ill. The nurses quickly learned to anticipate what I would want to know and what treatment I would order. Within a couple of weeks the nurses were doing the routine things they knew I would order—temperatures, blood pressures, and blood smears for malaria on patients with fevers. That allowed more time for me to focus on the less obvious aspects of the patients' medical care.

Most of the Congolese carried a small residue of malaria parasites in their blood that produced no clinical symptoms unless they got cold at night, or over-fatigued during the day. After a cool, rainy night, dozens of Congolese would come to the hospital, shivering with a fever and headache. The nurses would give them CHQ and P-mol, and tell them to come back the next day if they weren't well. As a result I didn't see most of the patients with malaria symptoms, but there were still ten or twenty patients each week with remaining or recurrent symptoms of malaria after treatment by the nurses. During the first month I ordered blood smears for all of these patients, but I quickly improved my clinical judgments, and if my clinical diagnosis was chloroquine-resistant malaria, I gave them Fansidar. The results were as good as if the blood tests had been done.

I was surprised at how many of the men came to me with symptomatic hernias. The word quickly spread among the nearby villages that there was a doctor at the Sona Bata Hospital who could cure hernias with surgery.

The sterile technique was much less rigid in our operating room at Sona Bata than I was used to in America, but post-operative infections were rare. I concluded that the Congolese patients had a high natural resistance to infection and were better able to overcome contamination of wounds. Even so, I did my best to maintain sterile technique, but supplies were so limited that some compromises had to be made.

The first week I drained two deep muscle abscesses and repaired a long, deep leg laceration. In the second week Tata Nsaku gave a general anesthesia for the first caesarean section that I had ever done alone. It went well, with no problems more serious than my usual difficulty communicating in French and Kikongo. I was soon operating on eight or ten patients each week and the outpatient consultations kept increasing. I was quite encouraged.

I had memorized a number of phrases in Kikongo, and the patients were delighted every time I said a word or phrase. Sometimes I would try to use a Kikongo word or phrase to ask a question, such as *"Mpasi quai, Tata?"* (Where is your pain?) The patients would gesture and talk to me in Kikongo for a minute or so, explaining the location of their pain, and I wouldn't understand a word of what they said. I would ask Nsiala, in French, what the patient had said, and he would tell me. Then the Congolese men within earshot would laugh, and one of them once said in pigeon English, "Doctor talk question. No hear answer." I grinned, acknowledging my linguistic inadequacy in their language.

Tata Kimpiatu did a remarkable job as the administrative director of the hospital, combining his Congolese wisdom and knowledge of people with insights and knowledge of the Congolese government, and the peculiarities of Americans, especially me. Again and again he demonstrated an ability to recognize a problem and act decisively.

One afternoon when I had returned from lunch, the assistant nurse was on the porch registering the patients for my clinic and collecting the registration fee (about twenty-five cents in U.S. currency) from each one. I paused to watch a moment. Another nurse inside the hospital called to the assistant nurse who was doing the registration. The assistant nurse turned around to respond and while his attention was diverted, a muscular young man, shabbily dressed, reached into the open cash box on the table and grabbed a handful of money. He then turned, jumped off the porch, and ran through the crowd toward the main road. The assistant nurse began yelling in Kikongo and immediately many of the Congolese began shouting the same word, which meant "thief."

The thief had run about forty yards when Kimpiatu bolted out of the hospital and ran after him. Kimpiatu was very athletic. He caught the man before he got to the road, and threw him to the ground. There was no fight. The thief got up slowly and Kimpiatu held his arm. I stepped up onto the porch so that I could see better. The thief's head was now bowed, his trousers torn and dirty, and his feet were bare. Kimpiatu walked him back to the hospital, preventing the people who surrounded them from hitting the thief with their fists or with sticks.

I entered Kimpiatu's office behind them and closed the door. Kimpiatu looked at me and said in English, "We take *steal man* to commissariat, ah, um, *le police*, at Madimba. You will come?" In the excitement of chasing and catching the thief, Kimpiatu had more difficulty with English than usual.

"Yes," I said, "if it doesn't take too long."

Tata Nsaku came into the office and told Kimpiatu that the car was ready. The prisoner walked meekly to the car with downcast eyes, his head still bowed. As we drove the five miles to the district police station, I asked Kimpiatu why the thief didn't put up a fight when he was knocked down.

"He knew he could not run away when all the people knew he was a thief. They would beat him if he tried to fight or run, maybe kill him. He knew. Better for him not to fight." He smiled at me in satisfaction.

There was a lot of talking and gesturing at the police station, and some information was written down. Kimpiatu, having recovered all the money, had taken the man to the police station to protect him, knowing that the thief would probably be sternly told to stop stealing, and then released with no further punishment.

While we were at the police station, I was drawn to the sound of rapid typing. There was a clerk in the corner of the office, and with his left hand he pushed the shift key up and down rapidly, making a lot of noise, and with his right hand he typed slowly by the hunt-and-peck method. He wanted to appear busy, even if he could barely type. Efficiency here seemed somewhat irrelevant.

But who was I to judge? I should respect anybody attempting to maintain justice in this troubled society just as Kimpiatu did. I would show them my desire to do the best I could. I'd put in long days treating the sick, and I'd do it courteously and treat these government functionaries with respect. I had a lot to learn.

Four
Cross-Cultural Communication

"Nobody cares how much you know
until they know how much you care."
—An aphorism for physicians

Life on the mission station was peaceful, but we knew that law and order in the Bakongo Province where we lived was tenuous. Rev. Chapman, his wife and two little boys, and the two American women who taught in the secondary school had been evacuated from Sona Bata by helicopter a year before our arrival, but now they had all returned to work.

The children in Sona Bata were curious about how white children lived, and they watched our family through the curtainless windows. Our one-story brick house had large windows on all sides, and cement floors with large cracks through which large ants crawled in and out. Winkie wanted to get some cloth for curtains to provide some privacy, and some kind of mat or rug for the floor so the girls could play without being bitten by ants. Winkie now knew what food we could buy from the women who came by our house each day, and she knew what additional food supplies we needed. At the end of our first week on the Sona Bata mission station, we decided to drive back to Leopoldville to buy cloth for curtains, a rug for the floor, and groceries.

Mabel had agreed to help us find what we needed. We met her in Leopoldville and she drove us in her station wagon to a store where we could buy two large sacks of flour from one of the few Belgian merchants still in town. Printed on the outside of each sack was an American flag and the words "A gift from the American people to Congo."

I didn't understand why a Belgian merchant was selling sacks of flour that were gifts from Americans to the Congolese, but I was discovering there were many things in Congo that I didn't understand.

Winkie wanted to buy some rice, powdered milk, sugar, bread, beans, laundry soap, as well as a rug and curtains. At a grocery store we found a box of Quaker Oats, a ten-pound sack of granulated sugar, and a small one-pound sack of brown sugar. At another shop we bought two cans of Blue Band margarine and several cans of beans, peas, and corned beef. At the butcher shop we bought three pieces of beef. At another store Winkie bought three colorful pieces of the kind of cloth the women used for *panyas*, but that we could use for curtains. At the bakery we bought three loaves of bread. We never found any rice or rugs, but Mabel thought we might find a rug in a store on our way back to Sona Bata. By this time the stores were all closing for a two-hour lunch break and a brief rest. Buying these few items had taken us nearly three hours in the tropical heat and humidity. We, too, were ready for a break.

Mabel took us to her house and gave our daughters a genuine American meal that included the last can of wieners that she had brought back from America. The rest of us had boiled chicken and rice, and a worthwhile conversation.

Mabel wanted to know how we, as newcomers to Congo, were dealing with living in a village. Winkie explained that we had never had servants working for us before, and how they compromised our privacy. We were somewhat embarrassed to have servants now, but Mabel said the Congolese desperately needed jobs. Winkie had been able to instruct our household help with the help of Françoise, our cook. She was delighted with the Congolese women who came to the house every morning to sell us bananas, eggs, and papaya, and her eyes danced as she told Mabel how she and the women bantered and bartered each morning. Mabel was delighted with our progress. I didn't say much, just that the hospital was doing okay and I was learning some Kikongo and French.

After lunch we transferred our food supplies from the station wagon to the bed of our pickup, and headed toward a large store on the outskirts of town where Mabel thought we might be able to find a rug.

We found the large store and I transferred the groceries from the bed of the truck into the cab so they wouldn't get stolen while we were in the store. I locked the truck, since I had been warned repeatedly that the city was full of thieves.

We looked at several room-sized rugs and decided that we should get something inexpensive. Winkie found what she wanted, but we couldn't find a price tag. The value of Congo francs was falling rapidly and merchants had to increase the prices every few weeks so they could stay in business. A dapper young man in a white dress shirt checked the current price on the rug we had picked, and told us it was 12,000 Congo francs (about $80 U.S.). Winkie clearly wanted it, so I gave the money to the man and asked for a receipt.

"Yes, sir. I will get you a receipt immediately," he said and headed to the back of the store where I assumed the cash register was located. When he did not return after ten minutes, we both became concerned.

Winkie found an older Belgian salesman and told him in French, "We were buying this rug from one of your salesmen, and we paid him the money and asked for a receipt. He went to get the receipt, but never came back."

The Belgian salesman laughed gently. "Which salesman did you give the money to, madam?"

"I don't know his name. He was a young Congolese in a white shirt like yours."

"Did he have a name tag with our store's name on it, like I'm wearing?"

"No, I didn't see a name tag," she answered. Her face fell as she realized we had given the money to a Congolese who did not work in the store.

"Madam, if he did not have this kind of name tag, he was not one of our salesmen. The Congolese are thieves, and they come into our store and take money from customers who think they work here. I am so sorry, madam, but these are very hard times."

"What shall I do?" she asked. "What *can* I do?"

The Belgian was sympathetic. "If you want the rug, I can sell it to you. Or, you can do without the rug. This stealing happens here all the time and I cannot put a stop to it. The police will not find the thief."

We had been robbed in spite of our efforts to be alert. Winkie still wanted the rug and I had 16,000 Congo francs left in my wallet, so we paid the Belgian salesman and he wrote us a receipt and accepted our money.

"The rug is yours, madam. I am so sorry that this happened in my store." He shrugged his shoulders, turned the palms of his hands upward, and said, "What can I do?"

Back outside, I took the groceries from the cab and put them in the truck bed, along with the rug. We didn't have much to say as we drove back to Sona Bata. Grace, sensing our concern about unexpected expenses, played quietly on the seat between us. Joy became tired of looking out the window and fell asleep on her mother's lap.

At the end of our second full week at Sona Bata, a delegation of four of the male nurses from the hospital, led by Tata Nsiala, came to our house to talk with Winkie. They had a problem and they thought she could help. I was their problem. They knew that I was struggling with French, and they were unable to communicate with me satisfactorily.

"Mama Youmani," Tata Nsiala began in very polite French, "the doctor has many things to tell us that will help our patients. And we sometimes need to ask him questions. But he cannot understand our French, and we cannot understand his English. Mama, please, would you help us learn to speak and understand English so that we may be of more help to the doctor?"

Winkie had thought that there was some kind of trouble at the hospital, but when she heard their request she laughed. "Yes, yes, of course I will." The nurses had been concerned that she might think they were imposing on her by requesting English lessons, but now they, too, laughed in relief. Winkie continued, "I would like very much to teach you English. Nothing could make the doctor happier than for you to be able to speak to him in English. I know that you are very busy at the hospital. When would you like to have lessons?"

"Please, Mama, we are very busy all day, but maybe in the evening. Could we come to your house in the evening, perhaps at seven o'clock, after we eat and rest a bit?"

"Yes, Tata, that would be very good. What evenings would you like to come?"

"Please, Mama, could we come three times each week? If it is not too much and does not make you too tired."

Winkie was still laughing to herself as she answered, "Could you come every Monday, Wednesday, and Friday at seven o'clock, and stay perhaps until nine o'clock?"

All of the nurses were laughing now, and saying, "*Oui, oui. Merci, merci,* Mama."

Winkie's English classes began with seven students the following Monday. Her curriculum was practical. She asked me what I wanted them to understand, and what they should be able to tell me in English. I gave her the two pages of English and French expressions that I had been working on, and that became their first lesson.

When the nurses were seated in our living room that Monday, Winkie chatted with them in French while I put the girls to bed. "What is this?" she asked in English, patting her head. A few of the nurses said, "Head." Then Winkie would say in English, "My head," and then in French, "*Ma tête.*" Each nurse repeated "My head" several times.

She proceeded with the eye, the ear, the nose, the mouth, etc., teaching the English word for the various parts of the body. They laughed and spoke to each other in English, trying out the new words for the various parts of the body. She moved on to words like hurt, bleed, vomit, diarrhea, urine, etc., giving the French equivalent for each word. They learned rapidly, which shouldn't have surprised me; they had received most of their schooling from American missionaries.

I told Winkie it was important for me to know if a headache was preceded by fever for several hours, which meant that malaria was the likely cause. If the headache came after a fall, the headache was more likely due to trauma than to malaria, and if the headache began several days ago without fever or a bump to the head, then high blood pressure was probably the cause. I wanted the nurses to tell me how severe the patient's pain was, and what part of the body hurt the most. Most of the patients could honestly say that their head hurt or their stomach hurt most of the time. The part of the body that hurt the most, the sequence of symptoms, and their relative severity was important for me to know, and I asked Winkie to teach the nurses to ask the patients these kinds of questions before telling me what the patient was complaining about. This seemed very simple to me, but Winkie told me the nurses resisted such detailed questions, even when Winkie insisted that I needed to know.

Then she discovered that the problem for the nurses in getting a good history of an illness from the Congolese had nothing to do with French or English, but with the Kikongo language and culture. Comparative words in Kikongo were rare, the nurses explained to Winkie, and the illiterate Congolese people did not usually think in terms of comparisons or gradations. For them their head hurt or it didn't. They didn't think in terms of whether their head hurt more or less today than yesterday. And it didn't matter much to them which pain came first or second, or which pain hurt the most. If they'd had a pain since the day before yesterday, they would say only that they had had pain for a long, long time. My problems in communicating were more than just learning words and phrases—I needed to understand their culture and how these people thought.

The nurses finally made it clear that the simple questions to which I wanted answers required extended conversations with the patients in Kikongo. If I could make it clear to the nurses what I wanted to know, they could find the answer from the patient, but it would require time. The nurses could comprehend the limitations of their language and they were relieved when Winkie and I finally understood them, too. In this process of trying to teach the nurses, I was learning some elementary French and a little Kikongo as well.

Winkie's students learned the instructions that I often gave to patients during my examinations. *Cough. Bend over. Squat down on your heels.* Always she would explain why I gave such directions to the patient, and was actually teaching them some of the fundamentals of physical diagnosis.

Winkie liked the students and their enthusiasm, and the students enjoyed mimicking each other and her. She appreciated and respected them and her rapport with the nurses continued to grow as their conversations switched back and forth between English, French, and even Kikongo, and as they laughed they learned together.

Within a few weeks the quality of my communication with the nurses had improved significantly, and consequently our care of the patients also improved. As our care improved, more patients came to our hospital and the nurses had to work even harder.

I was surprised when I learned that nurses at most of the government hospitals were paid twice as much as our nurses, but didn't have to work as many hours each week. I marveled at the commitment of our nurses that kept them working harder for a lower salary. I got a little better understanding of their motivation later when I learned that the government was not always faithful about paying the nurses' salaries regularly, but our nurses could count on the mission's payment every month. We only had five graduate nurses and a dozen assistant nurses to run the hospital, the nurses' school, and the rural dispensaries.

Taking care of a baby in diapers is a significant challenge when there is neither a washing machine nor disposable diapers available. Tata Kilola was Winkie's helper who did our washing, including the diapers, by hand in a tub of water twice a week. When necessary, he would do the laundry three times each week. He was always cheerful, played with the children, and even taught Grace some Kikongo words. Like most of the Congolese men, he had a garden, chickens, and a few goats near his house where he raised most of the food for his family. It was the goats that caused a problem.

Winkie gave him the day off on Thanksgiving so our family could have some privacy on that uniquely American holiday. Tata Kilola used the day off to work in his garden. In the afternoon I was called to the hospital to treat his broken leg. His goats had gotten into his garden, and when he tried to chase them out, he fell over a rock and broke his leg. I asked Nsaku, the only nurse who had been trained to give a general anesthesia, to administer the ether so I could reduce the fracture and apply a plaster cast. It took three hours to get everything organized and done, so I missed most of the Thanksgiving Day with my family.

Kilola recovered well and went home two days later with a walking heel on his cast. After six weeks I removed the cast, enabling him to resume his work as Winkie's laundryman. By Congo law I was obliged to pay Kilola's regular salary as his employer, for the six weeks when he was unable to work. Our finances were very tight because I was supporting my family with the subsistence allowance that I received, but I knew that his family had much less money because his salary was low. I really didn't mind paying him his salary while he was unable to work, but it seemed strange to me that I also had to pay the hospital for his medical expenses for an accident that occurred in his own yard. What bothered me most was that I had to wash out the dirty diapers for six weeks while Kilola was recuperating. I was learning some of the facts of life in Congo.

During the two-week dry season in December, the mission-station water pump, which supplied the well water for the hospital and for our house, broke. We used the rainwater that we had collected in a barrel for bathing during such an emergency, but it only lasted for five days. We stopped taking baths and could not even flush the toilet. We had consumed all of our boiled water and soft drinks, and the pump had not yet been repaired. I didn't realize how much water our family consumed. I had seen the village women go down a path not far from our house, carrying buckets on their heads, then return a half-hour later with the buckets filled with water. I could have paid someone to carry water for us, but I decided to use the occasion to demonstrate my belief that manual labor was as honorable as doctoring. I would carry my own water and set an example for the Congolese men of the American work ethic. The men always left such work to the women. Of course, I couldn't balance a three-gallon bucket of water on my head, but I could carry a bucket of water in each hand.

I took two empty buckets down the path that I believed led to the water. At the bottom of the hill was a broad, shallow stream with three women washing their clothes in the middle. There were two other women standing near the bank with buckets of water. All of them stopped what they were doing and watched me. I thought they'd probably never seen a white man, much less a doctor, come down to the stream and carry his own water. In that assumption I was correct, but I misjudged what their reaction might be.

I went upstream from where the women were washing their clothes, and carefully stepped on the larger stones to keep my shoes dry while I filled each bucket from the middle of the stream. Then, with considerable difficulty, I walked back to shore on the stepping-stones with a bucket of water in each hand. Nobody said anything. They just watched me as I started up the path.

The filled buckets were much heavier than I had expected, and climbing up the hill was much more difficult than the descent. I became short of breath before I was halfway up the hill; pretty soon I was gasping for breath, my heart was pounding, and my arms ached. I had to set the buckets down on the sloping ground to rest and some of the water slopped over the top. Two women several hundred yards away saw me as they nursed their babies. I imagined they were wishing their husbands would carry water for them.

When I set the buckets down to rest, the two women, realizing my distress, quickly took their babies off their breasts and swung them around to their backs, where they bound the babies to themselves with their *panya*. They trotted quickly down to me and said something in Kikongo, gestured toward the buckets, and then pointed toward my house. I nodded, still too short of breath to talk, even if I had known their language. Each woman put a bucket of water on her head and walked gracefully up the hill with a baby on her back while continuing her conversation. The women set the buckets down at our front door, turned, waved to me, and walked casually back to the pastor's house where they sat down and resumed nursing their babies.

I was impressed by the sensitive awareness of my distress, their kindness, and especially the remarkable strength of those women. When I got back to my house, I carried the buckets inside and sat down to rest. Orville Chapman, the American pastor on the station, came to my door and called to me.

"Hey, Roger, what's going on?" He opened the screen door and came in.

"Not much," I answered. "I just went down and got some water, and I'm pooped out."

"I know that," he said. "The pastor's wife just told me. I think we'll have the pump fixed by tomorrow, and there'll be plenty of water. Why didn't you ask your houseboy to get the water for you?"

"The exercise was probably good for me," I said, ignoring his question. "Maybe it will encourage some of the Congolese men around here to help their wives a little more with their work."

"Maybe." Orville was laughing now. "But probably the only thing they will remember is that the white doctor went down to the women's bathing stream. Didn't you know men aren't allowed down there?"

"No," I said with embarrassment, "I didn't know."

Five
A Congo Christmas

"Each lives alone in a world of dark,
Crossing the sky in a lonely arc,
Save when love leaps out like a leaping spark,
Over thousands, ten thousands of miles."
—Maxwell Anderson, *Lost in the Stars*

The surgeon at the Kimpese hospital would have to be away from his post for a week just before Christmas and sent word through the Baptist mission headquarters requesting that I replace him during his absence. Kimpiatu and the nurses at Sona Bata had previously managed the Sona Bata Hospital without a doctor for months at a time during the chaotic year before I arrived, and they assured me they could get along for a week while I helped out at Kimpese. I was thrilled by the opportunity to work in that hospital with the four other American doctors and five American nurses. I was enjoying my work at Sona Bata and had talked with Winkie about returning to this part of Congo after I finished my residency. Kimpese sounded as if it might be our future. This opportunity would give my family and me a realistic idea of what raising a family in a large hospital compound in Congo would be like. And it would also give us an idea about housing, as we would stay in the house of the doctor I was temporarily replacing. Just thinking about this opportunity made me so excited that I could almost forget that it was nearly Christmas.

The house at Kimpese had running water, electric lights, carpets, and even a gas range and an electric refrigerator. But what really surprised us most was the Christmas tree. It was artificial, of course, but there were lights, ornaments, tinsel, and dozens of beautifully wrapped presents under the tree, and a shiny star at the top. Grace, who didn't remember ever having seen a Christmas tree before, stood transfixed. Her mouth hung open, and then softened into an angelic smile. We were glad for our children to see and experience such a wonder, but we were sad that we would be back in Sona Bata for Christmas Eve and Christmas Day, and there would be no tree or presents for our children this year.

After we moved our suitcases into the house at Kimpese, we showed our little girls the room where they would sleep. After lunch Winkie took a nap with the girls, and I went over to the hospital to get oriented.

Winkie was awakened an hour later by the faint sound of rustling paper. When she looked into the living room, she saw Grace sitting on the floor under the Christmas tree, surrounded by mounds of Christmas wrapping paper. She had opened all the Christmas presents. Winkie was horrified. What would Dr. Anderson's family think when they returned and found that all of their presents were already opened?

But Winkie was resourceful and Grace had been careful. She had removed the ribbons without breaking them, and had been careful not to tear the paper in which the presents were wrapped. Winkie explained to Grace that these presents were not for us, but for another family. For the next several hours Winkie and Grace played a wrapping game, trying to wrap the presents so they would look as nearly as possible as though they had never been unwrapped. Of course, our one-year-old woke up and wanted to join the wrapping game. When I came home for supper I had no difficulty seeing that the presents had been opened and rewrapped. Winkie was almost in tears about having no gifts or tree for our children this Christmas.

We returned to our own house in Sona Bata on December 23. The cement floors, the kerosene stove, and the nearly empty rooms seemed depressing after the glamour we had just seen in the homes at Kimpese. Orville came by and gave me a notice from the post office stating that I was to go to Leopoldville and pick up a parcel that required additional postage. Early the next day I drove to Leopoldville and stood in line at the post office for half an hour, then paid the fee of 150 francs for the small package. I returned to Sona Bata just before dark, feeling sorry for Winkie and especially for our children. Winkie, with tears in her eyes, showed me the little Christmas decorations that she and the girls had made from scraps of red cellophane and the green label from a can of peas. There was a plain piece of white paper with a red bow taped to it pinned above the fireplace. "Merry Christmas" was written on it with a red crayon. It was a sweet gesture, but pathetic.

I wanted to support Winkie's efforts to celebrate Christmas, so I went out in the yard and filled an empty can with dirt and stuck a small branch from a locust tree into the dirt. It didn't really look like a Christmas tree, but our imaginations enhanced it. Winkie put the red ribbon on the top of the locust branch.

We all sat down on the floor around the little tree and sang Christmas carols. We missed our families and friends in America, the snow outside and a fire in the fireplace, presents, and a special dinner.

I even built a small fire in the fireplace and told the girls to pretend that it was winter and cold outside. Grace and Joy watched in silence. The fire gave off too much heat and we had to move our tree and sit near a window where it was cooler. We sang more carols—*Hark the Herald Angels Sing, Away in a Manger,* and *Silent Night*—over and over.

"What was at the post office?" Winkie asked. I had forgotten about the small package, but in response to her question I retrieved it and opened it. There were four pieces of chewing gum, four pieces of candy, and a Christmas card with a greeting from our nieces and nephews. There were four tiny Christmas decorations that we put on our makeshift tree, a package of chocolate chips for making cookies, as well as a note from Winkie's sister wishing us a Merry Christmas. We had not been forgotten. We laughed and cried and sang Christmas carols into the night. We survived.

When Bull Elephants Fight

Two weeks after Christmas, a student-nurse came to our house on a Saturday afternoon about five o'clock with the message that a woman had been in labor during the previous day and all night, but was not making progress. The nurse-midwife had tried to use the vacuum extractor without success. She wanted me to come and see the patient immediately.

The fetal heart-sounds had begun to slow and a caesarean section was needed. I called for Nsaku to give the patient anesthesia, but I couldn't find any of the other nurses who could assist me in the operation. Nsaku was the oldest nurse on the station and had never learned to speak or understand English. I was afraid to operate without a nurse who could understand at least a little of my English and translate it into French or Kikongo for Nsaku and my assistant nurse. That's when I decided that Winkie would have to help me. Winkie was aghast.

"I can't help you operate," she protested.

"I'll tell you what to do," I reassured her.

"I'm liable to contaminate everything, Roger."

"I need you to translate what Tata Nsaku says to me during the operation, and then tell him in French what I say." (Tata Nsaku, an older nurse, chose not to come to our house for English lessons.)

"I don't even know how to scrub."

"Don't worry. Come on."

At the hospital I showed her how to scrub her hands and arms. She did exactly as I directed. I put on my surgical gown and gloves and then helped her with her gown and gloves. The student-nurse had already scrubbed the patient's abdomen with soap and disinfectant, and inserted a urinary catheter into her bladder. We draped sterile sheets across the patient's abdomen and legs. Winkie stood across the operating table directly opposite me, and the assistant nurse stood by the tray of instruments. I placed Winkie's hands on the patient's abdomen next to where I would make the incision and asked her to tell the nurse to give me the knife and several hemostats.

The sight of someone bleeding can make a person light-headed, or even cause to faint. To avoid this, Winkie would have to keep her attention focused on what she was doing. Whenever she began to sway, I would tell her to give some instructions to the assistant nurse or to Nsaku, and as she did, her head cleared and she would stop swaying.

I made the incision and exposed the uterus. Winkie's eyes began to glaze and she started to sway, so I quickly gave her two retractors to hold and asked her to pull hard. She did, and her eyes cleared and she stopped swaying. I continued to talk to her as I proceeded with the operation, having her translate my instructions to the nurse and to Nsaku. I opened the uterus and extracted the baby's head, wiped the blood and fluid off her face, and sucked the mucus out of her mouth and nose with a bulb syringe. Then I lifted the baby out of the uterus and laid her on her mother's abdomen while I placed clamps on the umbilical cord and cut between the clamps. The baby hadn't breathed yet, so I held her feet in the air and rubbed her back and gently slapped the soles of her feet. She gasped, breathed, and began crying vigorously.

I turned to lay the baby on the back table and had Winkie tell the nurse to clean the baby up and suck the mucus from her nose again. I had forgotten for a moment that I had left Winkie holding the clamp on the umbilical cord until I heard Winkie say in a weak voice, "Honey, she's running over."

The uterus had contracted and blood was running over the edge of the abdominal incision. The placenta was just separating, but Winkie's eyes were glazed and she was swaying again.

I had her pull harder on the retractors while I removed the placenta. She pulled and her eyes focused again. When the placenta was removed, I instructed Winkie to tell Nsaku to give the woman the ergotomine injection. She relayed my request in clear French. The uterus contracted more firmly and the bleeding stopped as I began closing the uterus and the abdominal incision.

When the mother awoke, her face lit up in a radiant smile when the nurse placed the baby in her arms. Winkie later referred to that patient as the "Congolese Madonna."

Six
A Woman's Value

"It is only with the heart that one can see rightly;
what is essential is invisible to the eye."
—Antoine de Saint-Exupéry

Although I was exhilarated by successful operations and by the patients whom I helped, I was saddened by the misery, poverty, and sickness of the people, especially the refugees who were fleeing into Congo from Angola. The sight of mothers, already weakened by malaria and malnutrition, watching their children die under the scourge of smallpox, measles, and various infections, discouraged me. I wanted the world to know the heroic courage of the people in Congo as they lived and suffered, but when I tried to describe the condition of the refugees, especially the children, I could not communicate it. Some of my friends in America who followed the newspaper reports about Congo wrote letters asking me about the future of Congo. They didn't see much benefit from people like me in little hospitals keeping a few patients alive while armies and tribes were killing so many more. I couldn't explain. I could see the futility of what I was doing, but I could also see that the hopelessness and suffering was mitigated by the labors of the nurses I worked with daily.

When Bull Elephants Fight

Kimpiatu, Nsaku, and Nsiala seemed aware of the enormous problems but they kept doing their work at the hospital and dispensaries every day. They shared what little they had for their own family with relatives who had even less. These men had kept the hospital and nursing school functioning, even after soldiers had overrun the mission station and American helicopters had evacuated all the foreign doctors, teachers, and missionaries.

I wrote home about the hundreds of outpatients I saw in our clinic each month, the scores of babies born in our hospital, the numerous operations I did each month, and the student nurses being trained here. But I sometimes asked myself what was I really doing. It seemed that every day's activities were a mixture of seeing endless lines of patients and struggling with unforeseen emergencies.

Often my day began in the middle of the night with a gentle knock at my door and a student nurse with a lantern whispering in the dark, "*Docteur, Grave malade à l'hôpital.*" I would get up, put on my clothes, walk into the dark Congo night, and see the *grave malade* in the hospital.

On one such moonless night, the clouds covered the stars and my flashlight had little effect on the darkness. As I walked, I heard a muffled scream from the hospital, and assumed it came from the newly arrived patient, or perhaps a member of his or her family. I shined my light on the wide, empty porches as I approached the hospital and noticed how unnatural they looked. In the daytime they were always cluttered with cooking utensils, food, bed mats, and scores of people eating, cooking, talking, or resting. Now, in the dark of night, the porches were empty and silent. When I entered the nurses' station I saw a half-dozen people sleeping on the floor. Two of them lifted their heads and gazed toward me sleepily, then put their heads back onto the floor. These were the families and friends of patients, the *aides de malades* who had accompanied them from their village to prepare the meals and to wash their clothes and dressings.

I was met by Nsaku, who led me to a tiny isolation room at the end of one of the pavilions. I carefully stepped over more of these *aides de malades* sleeping between the beds and in the corridor, as we passed to the new patient's room. The patient was a young woman.

Her husband was leaning over her. He stepped aside and I leaned down to see her better in the dim light of the lantern.

Suddenly her lips curled back from her teeth and her face twisted into a horrible grimace. She arched her back spastically, her arms and legs jerking in extension. A frightening scream pierced the night air. I was paralyzed for a moment, but waited until she relaxed and lay quietly. Nsaku gave me the history of the illness, pausing only when a scream drowned out his voice. She had been convulsing since noon, when the family had taken her from the fetish doctor and carried her to this hospital. She had numerous small cuts on the calloused soles of her feet, any one of which could have been the site of a tetanus infection. I wrote the orders and instructed Nsaku to have her feet and hands scrubbed with antiseptic soap, and to give her penicillin, tetanus antitoxin, and Valium. We had no oxygen, no endotracheal tubes, and no respirator. There wasn't much else I could do for advanced tetanus—I didn't expect her to live.

The next morning when I returned to the hospital to begin the day's operating schedule, the young woman with tetanus was still alive. I was just halfway into the third patient's operation when a student nurse informed me that the midwife wanted me to come quickly to see one of the women in labor. The unborn baby's hand had presented first, and I knew that meant the baby was trying to come out sideways, a transverse lie, making a vaginal delivery impossible. If the baby could not be rotated into a normal position, the woman would require a C-section. I ordered six mg of morphine IV for the mother and had her moved to the operating room. I sent word for Nsaku to give her general anesthesia.

I hurried to finish the operation I was in the process of doing, and was told that Nsaku could not be found. He was the only nurse who could give a general anesthesia and I would have to attempt the version of the baby under a regional block. I injected the pudendal and uterosacral nerves with Xylocaine and obtained a satisfactory regional anesthesia. When I inserted my gloved hand into the vagina, I was able to reduce the baby's hand back into the uterus without difficulty. I then rotated the baby inside the uterus so the head came down to the cervix. In a few minutes the mother had her sixth child. That was my first internal version of a baby with a transverse lie, and I was proud of the result.

When Bull Elephants Fight

I made rounds with Nsiala in the afternoon and saw a new patient, a two-year-old boy with confluent smallpox all over his head and extremities, including his palms and the soles of his feet. I ordered the treatment for him, but knew it would be hopeless. In the mid-afternoon I began my outpatient clinic.

I returned home that night for a late supper. Just before I finished eating, we heard the screams and wails coming from the hospital that announced that somebody had died. In a few minutes the nurses came to our house for their regular class in English with Winkie. The nurses told us the little boy with smallpox had just died, but the woman with tetanus had not had any convulsions since morning. She eventually got well and went home.

Not every day was satisfying or successful. Each day was different from the others. Some days were encouraging and some were depressing. Each was unpredictable.

A few weeks later I was called to the hospital on a Sunday afternoon. There was a noisy crowd around the outpatient ward, and inside nearly thirty patients milled around, moaning in pain from their injuries. Nsiala waved an outstretched hand, palm down, and with his fingers signaled me to come with him to see a patient. She was hardly more than a girl. Her abdomen was very distended and she lay quietly on her back, taking rapid, shallow breaths. When Nsiala spoke to her, she turned her head toward him. Her eyes were wide with fear and her pupils were dilated. She looked as if she were dying. I glanced around the room and saw Kimpiatu supervising eight of our nursing students as they cleaned and dressed the other patients' wounds and abrasions.

These people had been riding in the back of a truck carrying charcoal and farm produce from their gardens in the forest to the city of Leopoldville. The truck went off the highway in a rainstorm and slid down a gully on its side. Another truck had stopped at the accident scene and had brought these people to our hospital.

The truck driver had told Nsiala that the girl with the distended abdomen and rapid pulse was pregnant. She only groaned with pain when I touched her belly. There were no bowel sounds. I was sure that she was bleeding internally and needed emergency surgery.

Nsiala took her into the operating room, and another nurse washed her belly and put a urinary catheter into her bladder while

Nsaku drew some blood, sent it to the laboratory, and prepared to anesthetize her. The nurse in the lab would have to find a relative of the patient or one of our student nurses with a compatible blood type so we could give a blood transfusion.

I scrubbed my hands, donned a sterile gown and gloves, and painted the patient's abdomen with iodine. Nsaku administered ether while an assistant nurse helped me cover the patient with sterile sheets. I made a midline abdominal incision. More than a quart of dark blood burst through the incision and onto the drapes, table, and floor. A dead fetus, three inches long, floated out of the incision with the blood.

I put my hand into the pool of blood that filled her abdomen and felt a weak pulse in her aorta and along the edges of her ruptured uterus. I pressed one hand against the uterus to compress it while I mopped out the blood. When I could see the shattered uterus, I had the assistant nurse place his hands around it and squeeze it to reduce the blood loss. I mopped out more blood and packed the intestines away from the uterus, then inserted a retractor and proceeded with a hysterectomy.

After removing the uterus, I began to remove the packs, and Nsaku said in French, "*Vite! Se presser!*" which I took to mean, "Hurry."

Blood was still running into the operative field from the upper abdomen when the packs were removed. I wanted to avoid looking at the spleen, but my better judgment told me I had to look at it. I extended my incision and saw that indeed the spleen was also ruptured. I removed it and there was no more bleeding. The pulse in her aorta was weak, but still present, and Nsaku had stopped giving her ether. It was a wonder she was still alive. I closed the abdomen. Compatible blood for transfusion was not yet available, but a student was in the process of donating a unit for her. We waited in the operating room until the blood arrived and the transfusion was started before moving the patient to a bed in the surgical ward. She was breathing and a pulse could be palpated in her wrist. Later a second blood transfusion was given. She survived.

This patient began taking fluids by mouth the second day after surgery, and did not develop any complications. She gained strength and went home two weeks after the operation. I was jubilant about the successful outcome. It was the greatest surgical triumph of my short surgical career. The patient was appreciative, but didn't share my enthusiastic joy.

Tata Kimpiatu later explained to me how bleak this Congolese girl's future really was. She would never be able to have any babies, and in the Bakongo culture her husband would be expected to marry another woman who could bear children for him. This girl would be put aside by her husband, and unless her parents would take her back into their home and provide for her as long as she lived, she would have no place to go. If she was a church member, the church might temporarily give her a little financial support. But the Congo church had very little money for such charitable activities.

No matter what temporary help she got, she would lead a life of poverty, unless she turned to prostitution, which might sustain her for a few years, but even that wouldn't last long. Her life had been saved, but in this culture where a woman's value is based on her ability to bear children and to please her husband, her life was now of little value to others. I had done my best for her, and I had to leave it at that. Only the Bakongo people could help, if they would, and it would be a miracle if they did. It was a crushing disappointment for me to realize that what I had considered heroic action on my part only created a life of misery and poverty for this woman.

Seven
The People Are Grass

"Visitors' footfalls are like medicine; they heal the sick."
—Bantu proverb

Tribal loyalties in central Africa were firmly established long before Europeans established the current national boundaries, and the tribes along the southern border of Congo and the northern border of Angola extend into both countries. When Congo became independent, the restive Africans in northern Angola intensified their efforts for independence as well. The war between the native Angolans and the colonial Portuguese erupted with a brutality hardly noticed in America because it was fought in rural villages and small towns instead of cities. The Bakongo people in Angola fled to their relatives in southern Congo in 1961, seeking refuge from the horrors of war as tribes and nations fought for dominance like bull elephants. And the people were trampled like grass.

The doctor at the Sona Bata Hospital prior to Congolese independence had established rural dispensaries in several villages south of Sona Bata, extending near the Angolan border where the Bakongo tribe dominated. But no doctor had visited any of these dispensaries since independence. The nurses there had not received any salary and the dispensaries had not been restocked with medicine for a year and a half. Bakongo families in Angola, driven from their villages, starving and dying, poured across the border into Congo as refugees. Nsaku, the nurse responsible for the supervision of all of the dispensaries of the Sona Bata Hospital, planned to take medicine and overdue salaries to the nurses in these dispensaries. I traveled with him to attend to the sick patients who came to the dispensaries. Messengers from Sona Bata had carried information about our schedule to each of the villages we visited.

On the road south toward the Angolan border, we saw hundreds of refugees—women, children, and old men limping along the side of the road. Many of the women were pregnant, yet they still carried heavy loads on their heads—large pans of *manioc* (cassava), palm nuts, clothes, rolled-up grass mats, and sometimes a machete on the top of the load. Some had a baby tied to their back with a *panya*, a toddler holding their hand, and several older children trailing behind them with smaller loads on their heads. The Congolese women I saw south of Sona Bata were tough and strong, and walked with such an erect posture that they looked absolutely regal. Indeed they were.

The refugees along the roadside were Bakongo people, descendants of the ancient Kongo kingdom that had extended into Angola and had dominated the coastal area adjacent to the Congo River for hundreds of years before the Portuguese discovered it in 1482. This kingdom had stretched from a hundred miles south of the river to fifty miles north, and inland onto the plateau a thousand feet above sea level. But their land had been divided among European nations at the Berlin Conference of 1844. Portugal took most of the land south of the mouth of the Congo River, and France took most of the coastal land to the north. Belgium took a twenty-five-mile strip of coast between the Portuguese and French, plus the Congo River basin on the high plateau farther inland.

The refugees hoped to find relatives in Congo who would help them. It was their only hope for survival. As we drove farther south the stream of humanity fleeing the ravages of war, sickness, and death became a torrent. The refugees looked exhausted, and some seemed hardly able to continue.

At the Kimbatafinda dispensary I found cases of malaria, intestinal worms, anemia and dysentery, and numerous lacerations and gunshot wounds. Scabies and impetigo were common in the malnourished children, and several had the characteristic red hair and potbelly of Kwashiorkor, a disorder caused by severe protein deficiency. Fortunately, the refugees could get food and protein supplements at a UN food station several miles away. It was a temporary project, but life saving for the children.

The Kimbatafinda dispensary at which I would set up the medical clinic had a cement floor and an aluminum roof. Several openings in the walls near the floor allowed the cooler air to flow in, and space between the walls and the roof let the hot air flow out. The building had been carefully planned and built. At first I attached no significance to the bare ground around the dispensary, but I was told this was to allow the people to see if any snakes were near. The dispensary was fairly clean when I arrived, but a crowd of people had gathered around it, eating and dropping banana peels, crusts of bread, and paper as they talked and frequently spat on the ground. The little children wore only shirts as they ate, played or relieved themselves whenever and wherever they had the urge. By dark the area, including inside the dispensary building, was littered with refuse and trash. Someone would need to clean it up before we saw patients in the morning.

The nurse in charge of the dispensary showed me what little he had in the way of equipment—a stethoscope, a blood pressure cuff, a flashlight, and a pan of disinfectant containing a hemostat, forceps, scissors, a syringe, and several needles. Penicillin was the only antibiotic on hand, and the other medicines were chloroquine, aspirin, and assorted vitamins. We supplied him with additional medicines.

When it grew too dark to see more patients, Nsaku told those remaining to come back in the morning. The dispensary building itself would be my quarters for the night, and I had come prepared with a kerosene lantern, a mosquito net, a portable cot, and a Primus stove. I put a can of beans and a can of corned beef into a pan to heat, and helped myself to a piece of bread that Winkie had baked for me. When the meat and beans were hot, I put on a pan of water for some tea, set my plate on the table I had used all day

When Bull Elephants Fight

for consultations, washed my hands for the umpteenth time, and ate my supper alone in the soft glow of the lantern. I would have preferred to eat with Nsaku and the others, but they advised against it, knowing that hand washing was rare among the rural women who would prepare their supper. Intestinal worms and amoebae were ubiquitous and Nsaku wanted me to remain healthy.

I tried to read by the flickering lantern but was too tired from the day's work and the heat. I wrote a few brief notes in my journal before blowing out the light. I crawled under my mosquito net and tucked it under the sheet to protect me from spiders, scorpions, and snakes. But the greatest benefit of the net was keeping the bat dung off me while I slept. I listened to the whine of mosquitoes and the whirring of bat wings until I fell asleep. In the night I was awakened by the sound of rattling paper and the scuffling of tiny feet as the rats searched for food among the trash dropped by patients during the day.

It was early afternoon the following day when we left Kimbatafinda, driving to Kilembika where our next dispensary was located. The drive along the dirt road was refreshing and the hot wind blowing through the windows dried the perspiration and cooled my face. Large columns of red dust rolled up into the air behind us. The steep hills and valleys, the streams shadowed by the forest, gave way to a broad plateau covered with elephant grass four feet tall. The sun was far down in the west when we arrived at the dispensary building, which had mud walls and a thatched roof.

We first went to greet the chief, an old, skinny man sitting on a chair in front of one of the mud houses in the village. He welcomed us. The nurse responsible for the dispensary said that he had a few patients for me to see immediately, but the real clinic would begin in the morning. The first three patients were schoolteachers who had no obvious disease, but I knew that etiquette required that they receive some medicine from the white doctor, so I gave them each some multivitamins, iron tablets, and worm medicine.

The next patient was a refugee child with measles, a highly lethal disease among the Bantu people. This child was also thin, dehydrated, and already in respiratory distress. Death from measles is usually due to tracheal bronchitis and could be helped by humidified oxygen and antibiotics. We only had antibiotics and vitamins to offer, so I helped him with what we had available.

60

I awoke at 5:30 in the morning to the sounds of women sweeping the dirt outside the dispensary with palm branches. At 7:30 the school children paraded around the area carrying the new flag of Congo. It had a green field with a yellow center, in which there was a black hand holding a torch with a red flame. The children had several drums and a half-dozen "police whistles" with which they kept time. Nsaku told me the parade was in my honor for coming to "make them healthy." Nsaku and the teachers screened the students and selected forty for me to see—I gave them vitamins and worm medicine.

By the time I finished, more than a hundred skinny, poorly clothed, dusty refugees had gathered to see me—an old man with knee and elbow joints three times as big as the limbs, a child with wispy, thin red hair and bald spots on his head, a dozen children with potbellies filled with ascaris worms, pregnant women with hugely swollen legs and white conjunctiva, old people with scarred, gnarled hands and crooked fingers. These people looked like the "off-scouring" of the world for which almost no one seemed to care.

During my consultations with patients I practiced the Kikongo phrases that I had learned. Where do you hurt? How long have you had this? Can you bend your knee? The patients often understood my Kikongo and answered in Kikongo, but I couldn't understand anything they said. The nurse translated for me. The villagers thought it was strange the white doctor could "talk but not hear" Kikongo.

At 7:00 the next morning, before I began seeing the remaining patients, Tata Bamfumu, the pastor, led the villagers and refugees in some songs, and then asked Nsaku to say a few words. Afterwards, Nsaku told me what he had said.

"I told them that the doctor had come to treat them because Tata Nzambie, their words for Father God, loved them and wanted them to have strength. To show how great his love was for them, Tata Nzambie told the doctor to leave his home far away in America and come to them today." It was very simple. Back in college I had known that I was to be a boundary crosser and a messenger, but didn't understand what the message was to be. Nsaku expressed it that day. God is compassionate and He wants us to love and help each other.

When Bull Elephants Fight

Nsaku explained to me later as we drove to the next village that the refugees, villagers, and even the chiefs didn't understand what the fighting, killing, and stealing was about. But the refugees did know that their villages had been burned, their women raped, and family members killed. They knew their stores of food had been stolen and they had been forced to flee from their villages or be killed. And they knew their children were hungry, afraid, and sick. They repeated a proverb that helped explain their plight: "When the bull elephants fight, the grass gets trampled." My attempts to help were gestures, not a solution. I was helping some of the grass to survive.

Our term in Congo at the Sona Bata Hospital ended in March 1962. The nurses gave Winkie a lovely wooden statue of a Congolese woman's head, carved by a local artist. Winkie has now passed that statue on to our daughter Joy.

Winkie was a more effective messenger of God's love to the Congolese than I. "Cheer up and laugh," she seemed to say to them. "You can learn English even if the doctor can't learn French. You can make the difference." And it was the nurses who spoke words of hope to the Congolese patients who couldn't understand a word that I said. They overlooked my faults and extended themselves to learn my language and to teach me their culture. My contribution was simply being there, *un acte de présence*.

Eight
The Legacy of Our Parents

"The child is the father of the man."
—William Wordsworth

We experienced a reverse culture shock when we returned to Kansas City.

There was nobody talking or laughing outside our window when we awoke. Nobody was walking up and down the street in front of our house. There were no household helpers, no laundryman, no cook, no yardman, no night watchman. We could drink the water right out of the tap and the electricity stayed on all night.

The day after we returned home we drove to Clay Center, Kansas, to visit Winkie's parents, and arrived after dark. Winkie's mother greeted us with bubbling enthusiasm, especially for her granddaughters. Her dad's greeting was restrained. He walked slowly from the den and sniffed a couple times as he stood behind his wife, gazing fondly at his daughter. It had been difficult for them to allow their daughter and grandchildren to go to Congo—they thought it was both dangerous and foolish. As Winkie hugged her mother, she glanced over her shoulder at her dad and said softly, "Hi, Dad, how have you been?"

When Bull Elephants Fight

Dad Stewart's ramrod-straight body remained stiff, reflecting his disciplined career in the army, and his tanned face wrinkled into a grin. "Hello, darlin', you're looking mighty well," he said as he gently put one arm around her shoulders. He then retired to the den and read the newspaper while he smoked his cigar. Mom Stewart and Winkie talked nonstop as they fed the girls and got them ready for their baths and bed.

I sat in the den, waiting for Dad Stewart to put his newspaper down, or to ask me about our trip. He continued to read and smoke, unaware of my growing discomfort. He had been an army dentist for thirty years and had taken his wife and children to various army posts in the Pacific before the Second World War, but that was different. He had been in the army and went where he was sent. He seldom mentioned the military life except for the cryptic sentence he was fond of repeating: "A man must do his duty."

I wanted to tell him a little about what we had done in Congo at the mission hospital, but I didn't know how to start. I cleared my throat, and said, "It was a good experience for us in Congo, but I'm glad to be back in America." Dad kept reading and made no response. "Nobody got seriously sick and our family seemed to grow closer." A long silence ensued, so I blundered on, "There were sometimes two other little American children for Grace and Joy to play with at Sona Bata." Dad Stewart coughed once, but kept reading in silence. We all retired to bed early that night.

Winkie was already downstairs when I woke up the next morning, so I quickly dressed and joined them. Dad Stewart was drinking a cup of coffee and reading the newspaper. "Hmmm," he said, "the paper says this fellow Tshombe in Congo wants to make his area, Katanga, a separate country from the rest of Congo. Did you know him?"

"No, I didn't know him, but I talked with a number of Americans who did know him." It was an opening and I grabbed the chance to tell him the little I knew. "Tshombe and his brothers are strong Methodists, and they are politically and economically involved with the copper mines of Katanga. Those mines support the economy of the rest of the country. Our government and the United Nations don't want Congo split up because they think Russia will begin moving in if the country fragments." I waited but he didn't say anything, so I continued. "I think Congo will eventually break into several separate countries no matter what anybody says or does. The distances are too great, the roads are too poor, and there are too many separate tribes and languages. The people have no sense of unity beyond tribal lines." I stopped. I felt as if I were giving a lecture, and that Dad Stewart was not interested in my comments.

Without looking up, Dad said, "It doesn't sound like a safe place to be. I hope Washington lets those people sort it out for themselves."

I thought he meant that he hoped Americans would let Congo sort out its problems for itself, and his family, including me, would stay in America, so I made no comment. He continued reading the paper. It was going to be an uncomfortable day for me.

That evening, as Mom Stewart helped Winkie bathe the girls, she asked Winkie if Tata Kilola had given our children their baths. Winkie answered with a little defensiveness in her voice, "No, Mother, I bathed them myself, and I remember those baths that Coco gave us. She scalded us in boiling water every time."

"Well, that was their custom of doing things where she grew up," Mom Stewart replied. "People don't change very much." Then she added, "My mother always said, 'Birds of a feather flock together.'" That expression had always meant racial prejudice to me. Winkie didn't respond.

We left after breakfast the next morning to return to Kansas City, and the children fell asleep in the car. Winkie seemed lost in her own thoughts, and I supposed she was trying to integrate her Congo experiences into her American life. I was lost in my own thoughts—anxiety about resuming my responsibilities at the medical center after six months in the African bush. Winkie readjusted quickly to homemaking and childcare, and caught up with her old friends, while I picked up at the hospital as a surgical resident.

It was several months before I was able to get away from the hospital for a long weekend and we flew to California to speak at a church and to visit my parents. Dad had retired several years ago from his position at the Veterans Administration as a counselor for severely disabled veterans, and was now the visitation pastor in the large Methodist church where I had been invited to speak. He found this work difficult because his memory was becoming unreliable. Mom looked as alert as ever, but the skin on her face sagged and she had dark circles under her eyes. Her black hair was streaked with gray that she had tried, unsuccessfully, to hide with hair coloring.

The next morning Dad, Mom, and I sat around the breakfast table having a second cup of coffee while Winkie entertained the girls outside, and Dad reminded me of an experience ten years ago when I had joined a black fraternity at college. He asked me why I had decided to do that and whether that experience had anything to do with the more recent decision I made to take my family to Congo.

"I don't really know, but here is what I think," I replied. "I joined the black fraternity because I believed racial integration was right, like you and the church had taught me, but my real connection with blacks had begun before I started school. I used to play with Mr. Cates's kids, and Mr. Green's kids from across the alley before we started school. They all went to the black schools while I went to the white schools and I was in college before I ever had black classmates."

Dad held up his hand. "Not so fast. Everybody grew up like that. It was the law."

My mind rolled backward to March 1953, when I was a second-semester sophomore in college. The memory was vivid. Dad waited in silence.

Otis Simmons, a black graduate student in vocal music, was walking down Louisiana Street with me, and as usual we were laughing and joking. We often talked about racial prejudice and discrimination, and I asked Otis why the black students on campus who were Methodists didn't want to join us in our Methodist Wesley Foundation meetings on Sunday evenings.

"Maybe it's just too painful for some blacks to try to fit into your Wesley Foundation, Roger," he answered. "It's just easier to stay with your own folks."

"You're a part of my folks," I replied quickly, "and I'm a part of your folks. We're both Christians, so why can't we go to the same church?"

"It's not a matter of Christian or not," he answered. "It's a social thing. I go to my black church. It happens to be Baptist instead of Methodist, but I go because I'm comfortable with the people. I like them. They like me. You would be welcome in my church, Roger, but I'm not sure your church would welcome me. You would be more comfortable, more at home, in your white church, just as I would in my black church."

We walked along in silence for a while before Otis stopped and confronted me.

"You tell me something, Roger. A lot of the brothers in our fraternity are Christians, and a lot of the members of the various white fraternities here on this campus are Christians. So why are there no blacks in any of the white fraternities, and no whites in our fraternity?"

"It's a social thing, just like you said, but we need to become comfortable being with each other, don't we?"

Otis took a couple of steps before he stopped again and turned toward me. His eyes gazed intently over the tops of his glasses and he spoke slowly and deliberately. "If you believe that, Roger, if you believe Christians ought to get comfortable with each other regardless of race, why don't you come join our fraternity and learn to be comfortable with us, instead of insisting that we join your group and learn to be comfortable in it with you?"

I was caught completely off guard. The thought of joining a black fraternity had never occurred to me. I mumbled something about not being interested in "social" fraternities, but Otis didn't look away. He waited and watched me. I had no answer to his question. Finally I said defensively, "I have to study a lot and I don't have time for many social activities," then I added ambiguously, "and I wouldn't really fit in."

Otis had a growing fire in his eyes as he stared at me. "What do you think? Do you think I don't have to study hard in my doctoral program? Do you think the members of Alpha in the fraternity house don't need more discipline in their studies? Do you think you understand black students just because you walk down the sidewalk with them, or that black students understand white students just because they see them? Do you think you won't fit in, or is it that you don't want to fit in?"

I couldn't think of anything to say.

"Maybe you aren't really interested in racial integration," Otis continued. "Integration has to go both ways. We really become a part of your life, and you really become a part of ours. If you do believe in integration, why don't you join our fraternity?"

The thought of joining a black fraternity had never before occurred to me. Otis said I would have to apply, and the brothers would have to investigate me. He said a couple of the brothers already knew me, and that he was sure that none of them wanted any "white-ass publicity seeker" messing around with their fraternity." I wasn't seeking any publicity, but his vehemence scared me.

With trepidation I asked, "Have you ever had any white guys in your fraternity?"

"Never. Not one in the whole United States. Not on any campus. We are a fraternity of black men helping each other get a higher education so that we can help other black men and women." When Otis said this, he smiled broadly and his eyes danced. "You'd have to move into the fraternity house for a year. I'll talk to you later." He waved as he turned into the walk leading to the porch of the Alpha house, and I walked on down to the stadium where the tennis team had their changing lockers. I was almost late for practice, and the weather was perfect, but I couldn't focus on my game that afternoon.

I talked to my Dad as soon as I got home the next weekend, and he cautioned me that I was in college to get an education and become a doctor, and that if I lost my scholarship he and Mom couldn't help with my expenses. He said he deeply regretted abandoning his plans to obtain a PhD and have a career as an educator. "It's not because it's a Negro fraternity," Dad said. "It's right to be involved in social issues and to match your words with actions, but don't be foolish. You can do a lot more good for people, including Negroes, by completing your education than by joining a Negro fraternity, especially if it costs you your education." Dad smiled. "Just out of curiosity, and because you are the fifth son that I have watched grow up, let me ask one more question. Are there any girls that you are particularly interested in these days?" I told him I was very serious about Winkie, and he asked, "Is she white or black?"

I jumped to the conclusion that he thought I was interested in integration because I had a black girlfriend. "She is white," I said. But Dad wasn't worried about having a black daughter-in-law; he was concerned about Winkie and her family.

"Does Winkie know that you might join a Negro fraternity?" he asked. "Would it bother her? Would it bother her mother?"

I knew it wouldn't bother Winkie, but I hadn't thought about her family. Winkie had several black girlfriends. But her mother might have a problem with her daughter being associated with me if I joined Alpha. Her parents were from the South.

Before I answered Dad's question, he stood up and gave me a hug. "Do what you believe is right, Roger. Your mother and I will stand by you."

I talked to Otis the next Monday and told him that I wanted to apply to join Alpha Phi Alpha. If the brothers voted to take me in as a pledge, I would move into the house in September of 1953. I had the same sense that it was the right thing to do. I had had that same sensation when I was four years old and thought God wanted me to be a missionary doctor. There was nothing really strange or religious about either of the experiences—it was just the right thing to do, so I should do it.

Almost a month after I made a formal application to join Alpha, I was called in for an interview with the fraternity brothers to determine if they would accept me as a pledge. They were polite, but they were also concerned. They wanted to know why, really why, I wanted to join their fraternity. Herb Cates was president of Alpha, and he and his family had lived across the alley from us when we were all kids. The interview was held in a semi-dark room, packed with the active Alpha brothers, some from out of town. I was directly in front of Herb Cates, and facing him. Everybody else was behind me. I had hoped that Otis would be there, but if he was, he never said a word. I did hear Charles Kynard's voice, and I thought I recognized the voice of Lavannes Squires, two of the blacks I knew casually.

Herb's first question to me was, "Are you planning to write a book about your experience as a white boy in a black fraternity?"

"No," I answered, "that possibility had never occurred to me."

"What do you expect to get out of joining Alpha?" asked a voice from the back of the room. I couldn't see who had asked it, but I looked in that direction.

"I want to know you as brothers. I thought I knew all about blacks because I grew up with some of you, but I lost track of you when we started to school. I've never really known any of you like a brother, and I've never understood why none of you were ever interested in being a part of our church fellowship here on campus."

There was a little laughter and some whispered comments. I grinned self-consciously, recognizing how stupid I sounded.

Herb asked, "You couldn't understand why your black friends didn't want to rush out to join your white church?" There was more laughter.

"Yeah, it's kind of dumb, isn't it? At first I thought that you didn't want integration, but I thought integration was you becoming a part of my life. When I talked to Otis, I could see that you wanted integration all right, but you wanted to keep your friends, your own values, and your own churches. So I thought, why don't I do the integrating with you? You know, why don't I become a part of your fraternity. I've got a lot to learn."

From the back of the room I heard the low comment, "You sho' do got a lot to learn."

"Will you teach me?" I asked. "That's why I want to join Alpha." I was serious. I did want them to teach me.

There was a chorus of comments that I could barely understand, and some that I couldn't. "That's heavy, man." "You sure you ain't putting us on?" "You tell us, Herb, you know him."

Herb spoke up again, "Mr. Youmans, do you understand that if you pledge this fraternity, you will be treated like any other pledge? No favors?"

"Yes, I understand."

"You will obey all commands of the brothers of this fraternity?"

"Yes. I will."

"Do you understand that like any other pledge, you will live in this chapter house for at least one year, paying your proportionate rent and doing assigned jobs?"

"Yes."

There were a few more questions before I was sent out of the house. The brothers would discuss my answers and then each brother would vote. Acceptance of me as a pledge would have to be unanimous.

Two hours later Otis told me that I would be a pledge in September, so in September 1953 I moved into the chapter house and began my pledge year. Nobody on campus paid any attention to where I lived.

Nine
A Less Traveled Road

"Two roads diverged in a yellow wood, and I—
I took the one less traveled by,
And that has made all the difference."
—Robert Frost, *"The Road Not Taken"*

Dad was silently waiting for me to continue, but my mind was still filled with the memories of college.

I was the president-elect of the Wesley Foundation that spring of 1953, and the following September I became president and welcomed the new students who came to our first meeting of the fall semester. None of my new pledge brothers were there. I met some interesting new people that evening, but not any blacks. The most interesting person I noticed was a new girl, Judy, whom I had known eight years ago through her brother. Judy was a freshman now, just over five feet tall, with long blonde hair and a figure that had certainly improved since I had last seen her. Her bright blue eyes were her most striking feature. She was stunning.

As we laughed and talked about old times when we were kids, I was glad Winkie and I had broken up during the previous summer. I asked Judy about her brother and she asked me about my family and where I was living on campus. I was a little embarrassed to tell her I lived in the Alpha fraternity house, but she insisted, so I told her.

"You joined a Negro fraternity?" she gasped. "Did you do that because you wanted to be a missionary?" She remembered my talking about being a missionary doctor when I was a kid. I told her I really wanted to understand why my black friends didn't want to join us here in Wesley Foundation, and I thought I could understand their reasoning better if I joined their fraternity instead of trying to get them to join our all-white Wesley Foundation.

"You always were a daredevil," she said. "Remember that time down by the creek on your grandfather's place when you and my brother almost got in a fight with those other three boys? You didn't care if they were all bigger than you, but I was scared. You told those boys that your grandfather was coming down with a pitchfork and they better get off his land before he saw them." She giggled. "Are any of your pledge brothers or fraternity brothers here?"

I looked around. Everybody there was white. "Not now. Would you like to meet some of them?"

"Could I? I mean that would be great."

"Better yet," I said, "the fraternity is having their first dance at the house in three weeks. Do you want to come? Be my date? Okay?"

"I'd be scared, Roger." But her eyes were shining with eagerness. "Would it be all right?"

"Sure. I'll take care of you," I said with bravado.

"I'd love to go with you, Roger," and the way she looked into my eyes made my heart melt.

A couple of days later a reporter from the Associated Press was waiting for me at the chapter house when I returned from class. He had heard that I had joined the Alpha Phi Alpha fraternity, and just wanted to know how it was going. We walked up to the Jayhawk Cafe and had a cup of coffee together. We talked for an hour or so and he took notes. My story wasn't very interesting. Nobody had really noticed or cared. I guess it sounded phony to him so he asked me about my relationship with Negro girls. I explained that I knew several, but had never dated any. He asked about the social events at the fraternity—dances and such.

"Do you bring a white girl as your date to these social events?" he asked.

"I haven't done so yet," I acknowledged. "But the guys in the fraternity wouldn't care if I did. I don't think they would care if I brought a girl who was black or white, Chinese or French."

We both laughed. "One of the fellows told me that there is going to be an annual fall dance here at the house in a few weeks," the reporter said. "The fellow said that everybody is already making big plans for it. Are you going to attend?"

"All the pledges are required to be there," I answered.

"Are you bringing a Negro girl?"

I was caught off guard. "No," I said. "I already have a date with a white girl for that dance. I've known the girl for years."

"An old girlfriend, I guess," he said. "Are you engaged to her?"

"No, it's the first real date that I've had with her, but I've known her for years. Her brother and I were close when we were kids."

"Have the kid sisters of any of your friends in the fraternity ever taken a shine to you?" he asked.

I knew he was fishing for something interesting to write about. "I've only been living here a few weeks. Herb's kid sister, Margie, is the only sister of any of the guys that I've ever met. She's a pre-med student, I think. She's in some of my classes."

He dropped the questions, and we walked back to the house. He took a few photographs of me, and then left. Three days later his article appeared in the *Kansas City Star* newspaper, and was picked up by the AP and the UP wire services and published widely across the United States. It was a balanced, factual report on my joining the black fraternity. It wasn't front page but it was a fairly long article, accompanied by a photograph of me sitting on the front porch of the Alpha house. The caption under the picture read as follows:

Joins Negro fraternity at KU – Roger Youmans, a junior in the College of Liberal Arts and Sciences at the University of Kansas, has joined the KU chapter of Alpha Phi Alpha, a national Negro social fraternity. Roger's home is Kansas City, Kan. At KU, Youmans was reported to be the first white boy to have ever joined a Negro national social fraternity. He is a Summerfield Scholar at the university and a varsity letterman in tennis.

Several of my friends and relatives cut out the article in the newspapers about my joining the fraternity and mailed it to me, but the first local reaction came several nights later while I was asleep in the Alpha house.

It was a moonless Friday night, and the exact story is not clear, but at about two in the morning a burning cross, the symbol of the Ku Klux Klan, was burned on the lawn of the Alpha Phi Alpha fraternity house on the University of Kansas campus in Lawrence.

Wilbur Crockett, my roommate, saw a flash of light through the window as he lay in his bed. He watched the light for a few seconds before he realized it was a fire. He woke Lavannes and they both looked out their window and saw a burning cross on the front lawn near a tree. I was still asleep. My two roommates went to the telephone and called the fire department and police. Then several other brothers woke up and saw the burning cross. They were hesitant to go outside. They had heard stories of the Klan killing Negroes as they attempted to flee burning houses in the past, and they knew the history of Quantrill's raid on Lawrence during the Civil War. They stayed inside and watched until the police arrived with their red lights flashing. Two policemen with flashlights searched through the darkness around the house while a third policeman sprayed the cross with a fire extinguisher. The fire truck, with siren and flashing lights, arrived a few minutes later. People across the street were now awake and a few curious spectators gathered. The trees had not caught on fire, so the fire truck left. The police talked with Lavannes and other brothers, and then made sure there was no property damage. In less than an hour the remainder of the cross had been removed from the front yard and placed out of sight behind the house. The neighbors went back to sleep. The police left and the street was silent and dark again.

The next morning Lavannes and Wilbur told me what had happened in the night, but I didn't believe them until they took me outside and showed me the remains of the burned cross. I had slept through the excitement and had not even heard the sirens. During my first class that morning I was given the message that the chancellor of the university, Dr. Franklin Murphy, wanted to see me in his office. When I arrived at his office, I was quickly ushered in to see him.

"Thank you for coming this morning, Roger," Dr. Murphy said as he walked around his desk and shook my hand. "I know you are busy and I appreciate this time to talk with you." He smiled in an effort to put me at ease. "They told me about the fire at the house where you stay."

"Thank you for your concern, sir, but it really wasn't much of a fire," I responded lamely.

"Well, I'm certainly glad that it was small, but the principle and the issue behind it may be much more important. I understand that you just pledged the Alpha Phi Alpha fraternity this fall. How has it worked out so far?"

"Pretty well. Nobody outside of the fraternity has paid much attention to my presence, except that one AP reporter. In the house, I'm just another pledge."

"It's unusual for a white student to join a Negro fraternity, Roger. You must have given that considerable thought before you decided to do it. Did you discuss it with your parents?"

"I did discuss it with my parents and my brothers and sister, too. I talked with some of the members of the fraternity, guys that I had known back in Kansas City as well as some that I had met here." I laughed a little, embarrassed. "My family wasn't very enthusiastic but said I should do what I thought was right."

"So you joined because you thought it was right?"

I nodded my head. "One day last spring when I was talking with Otis Simmons—he is an Alpha and also in the graduate school of music—I asked him why the blacks didn't want to integrate with us at church. He said, 'Why should we join your groups? Why don't you join our fraternity, if you think integration is important?'"

"So you decided to join the Alpha Phi Alpha fraternity to foster racial integration?" he asked.

"Yes."

"I think Mr. Simmons's point was well taken," Dr. Murphy said. "Were there any other reasons involved?"

"Yes, I guess another reason was that I want to be a missionary doctor, maybe in Africa. That's really why I'm studying a pre-med course here."

There was a long silence as the chancellor looked at me curiously. Eventually he smiled and said, "I guess that's a pretty good reason. Your academic record here has been very good. I want to wish you well in your career, and if I can be of any help, please let my office know." He smiled again and put his arm around my shoulders and walked me back into the reception area.

During the following week I received numerous letters enclosing copies of articles from other newspapers that focused on the burning cross and speculated on a possible connection with the Ku Klux Klan. Some of what I received was just hate mail. Some letters accused me of being a Negro; one expressed the opinion that among my ancestors, somebody "got hit with a tar brush." Other letters said I was stupid and evil. One letter described the ways I was going to suffer in hell for living with Negroes. A few letters offered encouragement, but most advised me to find another place to live. Some suggested that I talk to a Christian pastor who would show me in the Bible that God never intended for different species of animals to mingle or mate. I thought the letters were ridiculous.

I never knew if the burning cross was a real threat or just a prank. At the time I wasn't even aware that the Supreme Court of the United States was considering the problem of racial segregation in schools. Eight months later, in April 1954, Thurgood Marshall won the case of Brown vs. The Board of Education of Topeka, Kansas, overturning the Plessy-Ferguson decision of 1896 that had established the "separate but equal facilities" principle. Separate schools for black students and white students was judged to be unconstitutional, and racial justice took a giant step forward in the United States. Topeka is barely twenty miles from Lawrence.

Dad nodded and smiled. "Every step on one branch of a divided path takes you farther from other branches." I thought he understood me better than I understood myself.

Ten
A Bold Transition

"Wisdom is using knowledge
appropriately and generously."
—Anonymous

My college life continued with long hours of study and a heavy load of classes and laboratories. I continued meeting with the other Summerfield Scholars for dinner and intellectual discussions every month, and even though we were a small group, my fraternity was never mentioned. It was the same with my tennis teammates who were all white. I think they were embarrassed and I was eager not to stir up trouble. Friends in various classes with me were equally indifferent to where I lived. Except for two.

Judy called me on the phone and told me that she would not be able to go to the dance with me. She said she had to be back in Kansas City that weekend, but when I pressed for the real reason, she confessed that her mother told her not to be seen with me again. I was crushed by her breaking our date. Maybe it was just because she was a pretty girl rejecting me. Or maybe it was because she was an old friend from whom I had expected better.

I was still obligated to attend the Alpha dance and I needed a date. Winkie was one of the few people who had been genuinely supportive of my decision to pledge Alpha. I had ignored her since the school year had started because she had not answered any of my letters during the preceding summer. But now she was the only girl I knew whom I felt I could ask to be my date. I called and unintentionally mentioned that Judy had broken her date with me.

After only a moment's pause, and before I even asked her to go with me, Winkie said, "I'll go to the dance with you." I had no idea that her mother had told her not to be associated with me after the publicity about the fraternity. I also discovered that she already knew a lot of the black women whom my fraternity and pledge brothers dated.

I'm not a good dancer, but at the fraternity dances, it didn't matter. The dance floor was so densely packed with people that all anybody could do was to keep time to the music. Winkie encouraged my efforts, and she went to each of the fraternity dances with me. I was impressed by how easily and gracefully she mixed with my brothers and their dates. Interracial social activities and dances were rare in Kansas in the early fifties, and Winkie and I were the only white couple at any of the dances.

Sometimes I went to church with my pledge brothers and thoroughly enjoyed the drama of the black preacher's sermons, the joy of their Gospel singing, and their simple worship of a mighty God. But I still had difficulty getting my pledge brothers to go to the social or religious functions of my white Methodist church unless Winkie and some of her black girlfriends came. Then the guys would come, too.

I was learning the ease and the difficulties of bridging cultural and racial barriers in a prejudiced and discriminating world. I had a lot more to learn, but I was beginning to grasp the importance of doing little things that you knew were right. I was initiated as an active member of Alpha Phi Alpha at the end of the fall semester, and my friendship with my new brothers deepened. One would come to Africa and work with me twenty years later.

I addressed the Alpha Phi Alpha National Convention in Miami, Florida in December 1954, after spending several days in Prairie View, Texas, at the home of Ralph Jones, one of my fraternity brothers. This gave me a chance to get acquainted with his whole family, and they treated me as if I were one of their own. Ralph, his father, another fraternity brother, and I drove together across the South to the national convention. We ordered food from the back door of restaurants and ate in the car. We slept in the dormitories of black schools at night. In Miami, they found a room for me in the black neighborhood, but didn't allow me to go out on the street alone at night. Even in the daytime I was encouraged to have a fraternity brother with me. The delegates at the convention received my talk warmly and published it twice in the fraternity's official magazine, *The Sphinx*.

My pre-med studies had to be integrated with my social idealism and Christian convictions if I was to be admitted to medical school. My academic scholarship was only good for four years at Kansas University, and I wanted to be accepted into medical school after only three years of college so I could get my first year of medical school on the scholarship. Only a few students were accepted into medical school after only three years of college, and only if they had taken all of the pre-med courses required and had high grades and stable personalities. There were more than a thousand other qualified applicants for the KU medical school in the fall of 1953, all wanting to start in the class of 1954. Many of the applicants had advanced degrees, nearly all of them were older and more mature than I. Many were veterans of the Korean War and some were even veterans of World War II. The admission committee would accept only eighty applicants, and I needed to make a good impression on the committee.

Dr. Merrill Eaton, a psychiatrist on the admissions committee, interviewed me. He was a tall man with black hair, brown eyes, and a prominent nose, and he fit my stereotype of an Eastern European, Freudian psychiatrist. Although I had never met or even seen Dr. Eaton before the interview, I had heard stories about him and I was thoroughly intimidated before I ever entered his office.

I sat in the waiting room for fifteen minutes before Dr. Eaton's secretary told me I could enter his private office. I stopped for a moment inside the door to let my eyes adjust to the semi-darkness. The only light came from a lamp on his desk. Dr. Eaton was scraping the bowl of his pipe. He nodded toward a chair in front of his desk without looking up. When the pipe bowl was clean, he filled it with tobacco. He nodded in my direction again and I sat down.

He lit the pipe with a wooden match, leaned back in his chair, and blew smoke rings. The air was filled with the sweet smell of high-quality tobacco. I couldn't tell if he was looking at me while he smoked, or even if his eyes were open. Several minutes passed. When he finished, he tapped out the pipe and filled it again with tobacco. He lit the pipe, leaned back in his chair again, and blew more smoke rings. Finally he leaned forward in the lamplight and looked directly into my eyes.

"Are you always this calm, Mr. Youmans?" he asked.

"No, sir," I quickly admitted.

He seemed to watch my discomfort for several moments before he added, "When are you not calm?"

I was caught off guard by that question. I had expected some scientific question for me to discuss. I stammered a little as I answered, "When I…when I am doing something very important."

Immediately I regretted my answer. I hadn't meant that sitting in his office for an interview wasn't important, but only that watching him blow smoke rings was trivial. I didn't try to explain.

He gave me a twitching smile. Finally he asked, "So, Mr. Youmans, you want to be a missionary?"

I answered quickly, "Yes, sir."

"Tell me, how would you preach a sermon on this verse in the Bible: 'You shall not allow a witch to live'?"

I had never read or heard of that verse. I couldn't imagine how I could preach a sermon on it.

"I'm not familiar with that verse, sir. Where is it found, and what precedes it and what follows it?" I asked.

"It's in Exodus, in the middle of a long list of 'ye shall's' and 'ye shall not's.'"

I was stumped. "I guess I would have to convert her, because I'm sure not going to kill her."

Dr. Eaton smiled, and then asked me the kind of questions I had expected. Near the end of the interview he asked me about my parents, my siblings, and did I have a girl friend or was I married. That was all. I was surprised when the admission committee recommended my acceptance.

After my first year of medical school I married Winkie, and our first child, Grace, was born three years later, in 1958, just before my graduation. The Methodist Board of Missions recommended that I take a year of internship after medical school and four years of surgical training, plus some seminary study, followed by six months of missionary orientation, and then a year of tropical medicine and French in Belgium. That would take over seven more years!

I did enjoy medicine and surgery and I had already completed several seminary courses in church history, Bible, and theology, so I agreed to follow their recommendations. But in 1960 Congo got her independence from Belgium and the chaos there began. That was when I received the postcard from the Christian Medical Society asking for medical volunteers to go to Congo, when I had the vivid dreams of dying women and children too sick to brush away the flies. Our second daughter, Catherine Joy, was born in the spring of 1961. Winkie had taught school to get me through medical school, but now she was a full-time mother.

As the months passed, I was not able to shake the feeling that Congo was my calling. I eventually met with Dr. Allbritten, the chairman of the department of surgery, and asked if I could take a six-month leave of absence without pay, and when I returned, re-enter the surgery program at the same level as when I had left. I had never heard of such a plan being accepted anywhere in America, but at least his refusal would settle the issue of going to Congo.

"You want to drop out of this surgical program for six months so you can go to Africa, to Congo of all places?" Dr. Allbritten asked. "And you want me to hold a place for you to come back into the program in six months when you return?" He took a breath, and then asked, "Why in the world would you want to do that?"

"They need medical help in Congo now, and I can help," I answered.

"You would be a lot more help to them, or anybody else, if you finished your training here first." He sounded like my father.

"Yes, sir...but the need there is urgent now." I explained that their army had mutinied, and thousands of Congolese and Belgian civilians had been killed and many more had been wounded. All of the doctors in the country were foreigners, mostly Belgians, and now most of those foreign doctors had already fled from Congo. There were no Congolese doctors, so when the foreigners left, the people had no medical help. Even the few American missionary families who stayed needed medical help.

I hadn't really expected Dr. Allbritten to be sympathetic to my request, and I was astonished when he agreed. I thanked him and hurried to call Winkie and tell her. She was shocked.

"You're going to do what?" she asked.

When I tried to explain the miraculous fact that I had gotten permission from Dr. Allbritten to go to Congo for six months, she asked, "Why do you think Dr. Allbritten's permission is any more important than mine? Or anybody else's?" We talked a little while longer, and she concluded, "We'll talk about it when you get home. Your second child," she reminded me, "is not yet six months old."

Winkie was as idealistic and as religious as I was, and she had confidence in my judgment and was incredibly loving and loyal. We talked together, prayed together, and then talked some more. She kept asking how I knew this was God's will for us, and I had no answer, only that there was a need I could meet and the challenge excited my faith—and Dr. Allbritten had promised to hold my place in the surgery program. I just had a feeling, an assurance that this was God's will for us.

Our family was a high priority for both of us, and we agreed that whatever we did, we would do together. Winkie and the children would go with me. But money was a problem. In the end, we concluded that if I was really meant to go to Congo, the money would be provided for Winkie and the children to go along. This was an act of faith, but not exactly blind faith.

Winkie took the girls across town in our unreliable car to get yellow fever and smallpox vaccinations in addition to the typhoid and paratyphoid shots. Then she nursed them during the fevers that followed each immunization. She got photos of herself with the girls, and obtained passports and visas for them. She had the faith. I obtained a separate passport and visa, and received the same immunizations while I continued working eighty or ninety hours a week at the medical center. We did this even though we didn't have enough money for the family's tickets to Congo or for our subsistence once we got there.

In September our local church invited me to speak at one of our fellowship dinners. I told them about the chaos that had followed Congo's recent independence and the assassination of Patrice Lumumba, their first prime minister. I even told them about common diseases we would encounter.

To my surprise, the congregation had already taken up a collection for us. They presented me with a check for enough money to pay the airfare for Winkie and the girls to go to Congo and back with me, and with a little left over.

How did I know it was God's will for me to go to Congo? Objectively, I'd have to say it was circumstantial—the urgent humanitarian need for doctors in Congo, the unsolicited invitation from Operation Doctor to send me, the permission from the chairman of the surgery department, and the financial gift from our church that provided for my family to go with me. Looking back, I certainly wish I had learned French before I went, but that failure in my preparation forced me to depend on the Congolese nurses. And that had its rewards.

Eleven
Our Elephant

"Live dangerously and you live right."
—Johann Wolfgang von Goethe

Near the end of my third year as a resident in surgery I came home from the hospital about six in the evening, earlier than usual. Winkie was sitting by the kitchen table with our two daughters. Her eyes were red and her cheeks were streaked with tears. Her hair was a mess. The breakfast and lunch dishes were in the sink, and our two little girls sat across the table from her with half-eaten bowls of macaroni and cheese in front of them. They looked at me with a blank hopelessness.

I saw an envelope on the floor with part of a letter protruding from it and there was another letter on the table. I thought she had received some bad news.

"What happened?" I asked. Winkie was trembling as she looked up at me through red, pleading eyes.

"Who is the letter from?" Her lips quivered, but she couldn't speak.

I put my arm around her and asked, "May I read the letter?" She nodded.

When Bull Elephants Fight

The letter was from Dr. Eaton's office and it was dated two weeks earlier. He was the psychiatrist who had examined Winkie as part of her evaluation by the Board of Missions, and coincidentally had interviewed me for admission to medical school years ago. I wondered why I had not seen the letter earlier. One sentence stood out:

> ...*Please get in touch with our office for an appointment for a follow-up visit at your earliest convenience.*

Dr. Eaton had signed the letter.

I opened the other letter. It was from the World Division of the Board of Missions of the Methodist Church, with whom we were applying for an appointment as missionaries. They had accepted me several years ago, but Winkie had been slow in submitting the necessary letters, affidavits, and other documents.

> *I want to thank you for applying with your husband for a position as a missionary with our board. Your file is complete except for the psychiatric evaluation. Dr. Eaton indicates that some significant emotional problems need to be addressed and resolved. He requests that you make an appointment to see him at your earliest convenience. We will delay your application pending the resolution of this matter.*

The personnel secretary of the mission board had signed it.

"What did Dr. Eaton say when he saw you?" I asked.

"He didn't say anything was wrong, " she answered. Then she added, "I'm never going back to him again, no matter what anybody says." She stared at the table and began sobbing again. The children watched in silence.

I tried to think of some possible reason that might have made Dr. Eaton, a highly respected psychiatrist, question Winkie's ability to be a missionary. Was there some childhood trauma that I didn't know about? I thought there must have been a misunderstanding on Dr. Eaton's part. I reassured her of my confidence in her, and reminded her of the excellent recommendations that her fellow teachers and her principal had written. I held her in my arms, and then together we put the children to bed and cleaned up the kitchen.

The next morning Winkie seemed much better. It was Saturday—I could skip my rounds and go in at ten o'clock and nobody would mind. I was reluctant to leave Winkie alone, but she seemed to be okay. I tried to reach Dr. Eaton, but his office was closed for the weekend.

On Monday I went by Dr. Eaton's office at the medical center, but his receptionist said that I couldn't see him without an appointment. She penciled me in for Thursday, and asked me what I wanted to discuss with him. I explained briefly. That night I told Winkie what I had done.

"You can talk to him if you want to, Roger, but I am not going to see him or talk to him ever again."

The following day Dr. Eaton's secretary paged me at the hospital and said that Dr. Eaton had cancelled my appointment, stating that he could not discuss my wife's situation with me, but would be glad to see her if she wished to make an appointment. His report had been sent to the Secretary of Personnel of the Mission Board, and they were at liberty to share it with whomever they chose.

When I contacted the Board in New York, they wouldn't discuss the report, but they did make an appointment for Winkie to see another psychiatrist. The second psychiatrist examined her and carried out several psychometric tests, and then reported that she was emotionally stable and needed no further evaluation or treatment. The Board of Missions then approved us both, pending the completion of my surgical training. I was never able to learn what Dr. Eaton had allegedly found, and Winkie didn't care about whatever it was. I tried to put the incident out of my mind, and also tried to protect Winkie from as much stress as possible in the future. I focused on my work as the chief resident, running my own surgical ward with one of the professors of surgery as my consultant. I finished my residency with honors and passed the American Board exams.

Winkie and I were commissioned as Methodist missionaries as soon as I completed my residency, and we then began an eighteen-month period of missionary preparation, including six months of missionary orientation in Stony Point, New York, where we lived with seventy other missionary candidates and their seventy children. It was a madhouse of noise and confusion plus lectures, seminars, books to read, and papers to write.

In March 1965 we flew to Belgium with our three children, John having been born just before we began our orientation at Stony Point. I studied French for several months and then began the "superior course" in tropical medicine at the Princess Astrid School of Medicine in Antwerp, which was taught in French. Our second-floor flat in Brussels had a small private yard called a "garden," where we played with our children, trying to help them cope with the stress of attending a French-speaking school, but in fact, it was they who helped us cope by their childish enthusiasm. Winkie delivered our fourth child, Roger (we called him Rogé) in a French-speaking Belgian hospital on my birthday in 1965.

Thirty other students were in my tropical medicine class, and two of them were American doctors. We car-pooled from Brussels to Antwerp for classes, often studying together as we drove. I learned tropical medicine primarily from the textbooks in English that I had brought from America, but faithfully attended the lectures in French every morning. That was an extremely hard year for me, but I passed the tropical medicine exams in French and received the grade of *supérieur*. Our children thrived and Winkie held the family together.

Shortly before we left Belgium, Bishop Shungu, the first Congolese Methodist Bishop, visited with all of the American missionaries going to Congo under the Methodist church. In addition to another doctor and myself, there was a group of young Methodist men referred to as the "Congo Team." They would spend two years teaching in the secondary schools the Methodist church operated in central Congo. Because Bishop Shungu would be the church's authority over us, he met with us in Belgium to allow us to get acquainted and to brief us on the continuing crises in Congo.

The bishop told us that the United Nations soldiers had put down the Katanga secession and that peace had been re-established there. He reviewed the status of the civil war between the central government in Kinshasa and some rebels in the north who called themselves the Simbas, which in English meant the "lions." The

Simbas had killed one American Methodist missionary in Wembo Nyama, a village in the heart of Congo—the other four missionaries had been rescued. The bishop told us that during the past few months the army under General Mobutu had defeated the Simbas, and that Wembo Nyama and the entire Sankaru District was now considered safe. I wasn't concerned about those problems in central Congo, because I believed that our family would be hundreds of miles away from Wembo Nyama, living in Kimpese, not far from Kinshasa, the new name for Leopoldville.

Bishop Shungu encouraged us to cooperate with the Congolese pastors and leaders under whom we would work, and emphasized that we all needed to work together. He told us a Congo folktale to make his point.

> *A hunter lived in a village that was deep in the forest, a day's walk from the area where elephants were often seen in previous years. But this year none of the hunters in the village had been able to find and kill any elephants. The people were very hungry. The hunter walked in the forest far from the village, looking for any animals that would provide food. He was very happy when he came upon a forest elephant pulling branches off the tree and eating them.*

The bishop gestured with his arms and hands, imitating an elephant pulling down branches with his trunk and putting them in his mouth.

> *The hunter managed to kill the elephant after several days of struggle, but the hunter was so weak from exertion and hunger, and the elephant was so big he could not drag the elephant back to his village no matter how hard he tried. He knew that other animals would soon come and eat his elephant if he did not move it to the village quickly. He ran all the way back to his village. He was exhausted when he arrived, and anxiously called for help.*
>
> *"I have killed an elephant. Come help me drag my elephant home." But nobody in the village paid any attention to him. Then the hunter became wise, and changed his request for help by crying out to the villagers, "I have killed an elephant. Come help me drag*

our elephant to our village."

Immediately all of the men ran to join the hunter. They tied strong vines to the elephant and began to drag the elephant to their village. As the men pulled together they chanted, "Our elephant. Pull! Our elephant. Pull!"

I wasn't particularly interested in pulling anybody's elephant out of a forest, but I liked the tale. Winkie and I were ready and eager to return to Congo and work in the Kimpese hospital where I could practice medicine and surgery with medical colleagues. But that was not to be.

Part II

In the Heart of Congo

*"If you're not living on the edge,
you're taking up too much room."*
—African proverb

Twelve
Betrayed

"Cross the river before you abuse the crocodile."
—Fanti proverb

This time in Congo it would be different. I knew French, I knew tropical medicine, and I was fully trained and certified as a surgeon. I had been in Congo before and I knew the drill, or so I thought. It was already dark when we landed in Kinshasa in March 1967. The airport officials were far more competent as we passed through passport and health card checks, got our luggage, and quickly passed through customs. Joe Davis, the administrative assistant to Bishop Shungu, met us in front of the terminal building and drove us to the Union Mission House.

The continuing warfare was now a thousand miles away, in the forests of northeastern Congo where the Simbas had retreated in disarray, having been defeated by the Congolese army and mercenary soldiers. Kinshasa and lower Congo were considered secure. But the Mission House was full of missionaries and their families leaving the country, and they didn't talk as though things were settled in the bush.

Joe left us in the care of Tina, the hostess for the Mission House, with the words that Bishop Shungu wanted to talk to me when I got my family settled. "Come down to his room in about an hour," he said.

Tina asked if it would be okay with me if I shared a room with a Congolese pastor for the night, and Winkie and the children stayed together in another room. I agreed. Our children had a snack of milk and crackers in the dining room before going to bed. We expected to be in Kinshasa for only a few days before we moved down the Matadi Road to the large mission hospital at Kimpese.

Winkie smiled at me after we told the children a bedtime story. "This sure beats the Continental Hotel and the reception we got when we arrived in Kinshasa before." I heartily agreed. My anxieties had already begun to fade even before Joe appeared at the airport, and now I was regaining my optimism. As soon as the baby, Rogé, was asleep and the three other children were resting on their beds, I slipped out of the room to find where I was to sleep.

My roommate, a Congolese pastor, was already in bed reading when I put my suitcase in the room and then continued on my way to meet with the bishop.

Bishop Shungu greeted me warmly, choosing to speak in English as he had done in Belgium, and he left no doubt about who was in charge.

"Come in the room with me and we will talk about your family. You will stay here for the next several days. Okay?"

"Okay," I repeated with a chuckle, appreciating his American slang, and followed him into the small room. He closed the door behind us and we sat down.

The bishop spoke brusquely. "Dr. Youmans, your training and experience are exactly what we need. We have a brand-new hospital, fully equipped for you. Mr. Paul Koi speaks very good English, and he will be the nurse to help you run the hospital. I think you do not yet have a medical license here in Congo. Give your American license to Joe in my office tomorrow, and he will arrange your medical license and driving license for Congo. No problem."

He watched my face as though he expected a response. I felt uncomfortable, as though I had been put on the spot. I sensed that there was some significance to what he had said and what he had not said, but for a moment I wasn't sure just what it was. He hadn't mentioned the hospital in Kimpese, but was talking about a new hospital. I wondered why.

Having recognized his omission, I asked directly, "Where is this new hospital? Is it in Kimpese?" When he didn't answer, I continued, "The Mission Board in New York indicated that I could expect to work with other doctors in the large hospital there and I believe it is already functioning."

The bishop studied some papers on his desk. Then he looked up at me and slowly said, "The Simba rebels have been stopped and the Sankaru District, in fact, the whole of the Kasai Province, is now secured by the Congolese National Army."

I knew much of the Methodist work was in the Sankaru District of the Kasai Province, and that the Simbas had killed a Methodist missionary there, in Wembo Nyama where there was a new hospital. It then occurred to me that the bishop was going to send our family to Wembo Nyama instead of Kimpese, so I again asked directly, "Are you saying that I will not be sent to Kimpese, as I was led to believe?" He didn't answer or change his expression. Africans do not like to tell someone something that they don't want to hear.

He sidestepped my question. "The church has four hospitals in the Sankaru," the bishop said, "and none of them have doctors. There are forty rural dispensaries there without supervision. There are five hundred thousand Batetela people living in the Sankaru District. You and your family are needed at Wembo Nyama. As I said, the hospital there is brand-new and fully equipped, but has not yet been opened. You need to open it." He stopped and looked into my eyes as he waited for my response. Then he added, "We have only two doctors in Central Congo and we have one in Kimpese. I cannot send another surgeon to Kimpese."

I tried to remain calm, but I felt betrayed. We were promised. But I sensed that I was trapped and had no choices. I felt the sweat running down from my armpits as I protested.

"My wife and I were expecting to be at Kimpese where our children would have other children to play with. Our two oldest children will both need to be in school. My wife will have two little preschool boys to look after. She can't teach both girls and look after the two boys at the same time." I was trembling.

"That won't be a problem," he said. "We will get help for the children, and a cook and a laundry man, too. Your wife is a teacher, is she not? As for other children, Dr. Isley has three children. He will join you when he arrives. His wife is a nurse, but of course she will want to spend time with her children, just as your wife will. He is a specialist, isn't he?" Again he waited for me to respond.

"Dr. Isley is a pediatrician. He took his tropical medicine training in Belgium at the same time that I did. I'm a specialist in surgery, and I will need to have other specialists—an anesthesiologist, an internist, a pathologist, as well as a pediatrician, and others." My voice had risen in decibels and in pitch as I began to realize the inevitable.

We would have to go to Wembo Nyama as the bishop was saying, or we would have to go home. I couldn't abandon my commitment to be a missionary doctor, could I? I wasn't sure exactly where Wembo Nyama was, but I knew that it was somewhere near the center of Congo. All I had ever heard about transportation to that village was that it was by air or by boat. There weren't any roads from Kinshasa to the Sankaru District. How could we escape if there was trouble with the Simbas again?

After a silence, the bishop continued. "I cannot send you to Kimpese when the Batetela people have no doctor. As bishop, I must make the assignments for all the pastors and missionaries in the Conference. I need you and your family to go to Wembo Nyama."

That made the situation quite clear. I could easily understand his position, and I knew that in the last analysis we were under the direct authority of the bishop. We had undergone five months of "missionary orientation" in America, traveled all over the country raising our financial support, and then spent a year learning French and tropical medicine in Belgium. Could I now refuse this assignment and go back to America? Could Winkie accept going to Wembo Nyama? It seemed unthinkable that after all of this preparation, I would now refuse the assignment and take my family back to America.

"I'll have to talk to my wife about this. She is already asleep with the children. We must think of the safety of our children, too," I said awkwardly.

"I fly to Kananga tomorrow morning," the bishop said. "I will need to tell the cabinet there if you will work in Wembo Nyama. You and your family will be safe there."

I asked the bishop if I could let him know tomorrow, but he was leaving at five in the morning, and insisted that I give him a response tonight. I considered waking Winkie to discuss it with her, but I knew that she was as tired as I was and wouldn't be able to think straight. I thought she would trust my judgment, and I didn't think we really had a choice.

"I believe that we will go wherever you send us, Bishop. I think Winkie will understand that hundreds of thousands of people in the Sankaru District need us more than Kimpese does. I'll talk to her about it in the morning."

The bishop smiled. "I prayed that you would see the needs of my people. I noticed the car that you shipped down from Belgium. It is not strong. There is a truck at Wembo Nyama and I will get a Landrover for your family. You and your family will be safe and happy at the Wembo Nyama Hospital. It is good to talk with you."

I shook the bishop's hand and left. As I walked down the corridor to my room, I noticed that the room where Winkie and the children were sleeping was dark and quiet. My roommate was already asleep when I returned, so I got into my bed quietly. But I couldn't sleep because I knew Winkie would be very disappointed, maybe angry, that we weren't going to Kimpese. I was afraid that our children wouldn't tolerate the isolation and poor sanitation in a remote village like Wembo Nyama.

When I did fall asleep that night, I dreamed that Winkie went back to America and that I stayed at Wembo Nyama alone, working where everybody spoke Otetela and my previous struggles with French were wasted. The dream shifted and Winkie became hysterical and had a mental breakdown when I told her we were going to Wembo Nyama. I woke up sweating and kicked off the sheet. What if I got malaria, I wondered, or if I died and Winkie found herself alone in Wembo Nyama with four little children? I agonized over the half-million war-weary, malnourished, sick people without any medical help, of Congolese widows with babies and children but no food. And nobody cared enough to help. Guilt and compassion mingled in my mind with concern for my own family and I felt overwhelmed. I was afraid to plunge into the very heart of

Congo where thousands of Congolese, and even an American missionary, had been killed in the last few years.

Dawn came and I was still not able to think clearly. I needed a cup of coffee.

Tina was already busy in the kitchen, but the only coffee she had was left over from the night before. I drank it anyway. It was strong. I thought about the bishop—he was a Batetela from a village near Wembo Nyama. He had a responsibility for all of these people and he knew hundreds of them by name, maybe even thousands. Tribal politics drove national politics in Congo and it probably drove church politics as well. I rejected that thought as cynical. Where was my compassion when I needed it? The bishop had no real choice but to send us to Wembo Nyama. I needed the courage to just go there.

Winkie looked much more rested when I saw her before breakfast, though traces of fatigue and anxiety still marked her face. I thought it might be better to wait a few days to tell her about the change in our plans, but if she asked me questions, I'd have to tell her. It would be disastrous if I tried to deceive her. After breakfast, I asked Grace to stay with Joy and John, and to watch Rogé who was asleep, while Winkie and I walked around the Union Mission House to the small yard in back.

The Mission House was a rambling, single-story building with screened-in porches on one side and on the back. Several large eucalyptus trees provided shade. A bougainvillea and hibiscus were in full bloom. We watched a line of ants in the dust. We saw little lizards lying on the wall in the warm sunshine. The buzzing of insects was constant, and the sound of traffic on the road in front of the house made conversation difficult.

"It's a beautiful morning," I said halfheartedly.

We walked on in silence for a time, and then she asked, "Did you talk to the bishop last night?"

"Yes, I talked to Bishop Shungu for a few minutes last night."

"What did the bishop say?" she asked hopefully.

I talked about the tribal and church/hospital relationship for a moment, and then I said, "The bishop is sending us to Wembo Nyama instead of Kimpese."

She stared at me in stunned disbelief. "He said *what?*" The hopeful contentment that I had seen in her eyes at breakfast was gone, replaced by fear that seemed about to explode into anger. "Did you tell him that the Mission Board in New York told us we were going to Kimpese? Did you tell him we had worked in Kimpese, and that we had already learned some Kikongo?" I nodded.

She sucked in a quick breath and continued. "Are there any schools in Wembo Nyama for Grace and Joy? Our car won't survive a year in the bush. How will we be able to care for the baby and the children out there? What if we get sick? Or what if you get sick? Isn't that where Burleigh Law was killed?" There were tears in her eyes and her voice trembled. "You didn't agree to go there, did you, Roger?"

I tried to put my arm around her, but she pulled away. Her fear faded into despair, and her eyes grew dull in spite of the tears. She knew I had agreed.

"We'll manage," I said. But I didn't know how. I had pushed her too far. My voice came out harsh and defensive. "Other missionaries have done it, and so can we. The bishop is going to provide us with people to help around the house, like we had at Sona Bata. He will trade our Volkswagen for a Landrover for the bad roads."

"How could you agree to this, Roger? Without even talking to me about it?"

She had trusted me, and I had betrayed her. If I had known what lay ahead in the next few days, I don't think I would have taken my family to Wembo Nyama. But at that moment I could not refuse the bishop and my sense of duty. If I went back to America with my family, we would be missionary failures.

We stood in the yard behind the Union Mission House with the morning sun already getting hot. Winkie was trying to control her tears and sobs of anger and helplessness, and I was silent. There wasn't anything more to say. Our plans to live and work with other American medical missionaries at Kimpese were gone.

I heard a cough and turned to see Joe Davis standing a respectful distance from us, aware that he might be intruding at a difficult time. Two Congolese men were with him. I recognized the shorter man from last night as a driver for the Methodist church, and I assumed the other young man was a male nurse from the Lambuth

When Bull Elephants Fight

Memorial Hospital at Wembo Nyama. They were to help us get our permanent visas and licenses. Their broad smiles and shining eyes expressed their anticipation and joy that a doctor had come to open the hospital at Wembo Nyama. It was a striking contrast to our attitude. They looked at the future with hope.

Thirteen
Congo Crocodiles

*"Do what you can with what you have
where you are."*

—John Wesley

Andre Tunda stepped forward to shake our hands and tell us that he was a nurse from the hospital who would help us deal with the red tape involved in getting our proper documentation. He also told us he was a nephew of Bishop Shungu. After assuring us that Andre would take care of us, Joe returned to his office in the Mission House. Andre waited until we were ready, and then accompanied us to the various government offices. The process took longer than expected, but by the third day we had all of our documents. We picked up a salary advance from the mission treasurer and bought a few groceries, mainly for the baby. Most of our stock of food would be purchased in Kananga, the capital of the Kasai Province, over five hundred miles east of Kinshasa. (Kananga is not to be confused with Katanga, later renamed Shaba, which is a province in the southeast corner of Congo, with Lubumbashi as its capital.)

We had a free day before Wes Eiseman, the American pilot for

103

the Methodist church, would fly us to Kananga in the Cessna 180, so we borrowed a car and drove to Sona Bata to see our friends there. When Kimpiatu, Nsiala, and Nsaku heard that we would be working in the Kasai Province, and specifically in the Sankaru District among the Batetela tribe, they shook their heads and clucked their tongues as a warning for us not to expect much from such primitive people. But none of them had ever actually been to the Sankaru District. They made the Sankaru sound as if it were the primitive and dangerous heart of Congo, and I thought of Joseph Conrad's classic book, *The Heart of Darkness*.

We had only been in Congo five days when Wes Eiseman loaded our family into the small plane and took us to Kananga. Winkie was resigned to our assignment and seemed willing to make the best of it. We both had an enormous amount to learn about its history, and about the Batetela people and their language.

Kananga was formerly known as Luluaburg and had been a big city of about three hundred thousand people before the independence of Congo, but rebellion and tribal warfare had reduced the number of people living there to little more than half of what it had been. The city looked peaceful as we saw it from the air, built on a plateau with railroad tracks and dirt roads emerging from it and disappearing into the forest. The unpaved streets were laid out in a grid amid buildings with corrugated metal roofs. Wes told me the construction site, which was about ten or fifteen miles northwest of the city, was to be the new Presbyterian hospital.

Several Congolese from the Methodist church met us at the Kananga airport and drove us to the guesthouse, where we would stay for several days to learn a few phrases in our new language and to talk with missionaries and Congolese leaders who would be our lifeline when we got to Wembo Nyama. Here in Kananga we began to learn specifics about the tribal warfare engulfing the region that after five years was now quiet.

Rev. Alex Reid was an experienced missionary among the Batetela tribe and had already gone up to Wembo Nyama to make arrangements for our family's arrival, and to oversee the preparations for the official opening of the new hospital. Winkie quickly became close friends with Hazel, Alex Reid's wife, and with June, the wife of our pilot, Wes Eiseman. Both of them helped

Winkie with the children, offered advice on shopping in Kananga, and shared tips on how to survive in Wembo Nyama. Hazel would be in Wembo with us for the first year, and June would stay at least several years in Kananga and check in with the various Methodist mission stations in the Sankaru District regularly by radio. Every week Wes would deliver our mail to Wembo on his way to Lodja, and would bring bread and meat to us if Winkie ordered it and June bought it for us. Wes and June had a daughter about a year older than our daughter Grace, and a son who was about Joy's age. We were relieved that our girls could make friends with other children here in Kananga, but we were both apprehensive about living two hundred miles deeper in the forest at Wembo.

We met so many people in Kananga that I couldn't remember their names, or what their function was in the church, but I focused on several. Rev. and Mrs. Lovell would stay six months in Wembo before going to Kindu on the far side of the Lomami River, and Rev. and Mrs. Reid would stay a year before they retired and returned to America. Dr. and Mrs. Hughlett lived in Kananga and ran the medical depot from which I would order medicine and supplies. Dr. Hughlett and Rev. Lovell were two of the five missionaries who had been held hostage by the Simbas in Wembo Nyama for a year back in 1963-64.

Winkie and I learned to use the single side-band radio by which the major stations of the church maintained communication with each other. I was most interested in the location of the three other Methodist hospitals that had no doctors, and the names of the district superintendents and nurses in charge of each hospital. Although Rev. Reid would operate the radio schedule for our station most of the time, we all needed to know the system. We were also trying to learn a few phrases in Otetela so we could greet people. And most important of all, I was trying to help and encourage Winkie in making preparations for the children. The older missionaries and the Congolese kept telling us not to worry, that they would help us and that everything would be fine. They were optimistic and confident in our ability to open and run the hospitals, and in their ability to help us do so.

Four of the young, single American men who had come to Congo as teachers with the Congo Team were already teaching in the Wembo secondary school and would be stationed there for the next year and a half. There were four hundred Congolese students in that secondary school and eight hundred more students in the primary school on the Wembo Nyama station. There were another two thousand students in the villages immediately adjacent to Wembo. This was a large and complex mission program, and the logistical support for all of it would depend on Wes Eiseman and his airplane. Dr. Isely and his wife would arrive in a month or two and work in the hospital with me. Being the only doctors for hundreds of thousands of people seemed to me to be impossible, and I feared that Ray and I would both sink in the ocean of sick patients from the hundreds of villages in the Sankaru District. I was overwhelmed by the prospects, and I had not yet even seen the hospital.

My personal responsibilities in Wembo would be to run the 135-bed hospital and the 20-bed obstetrical ward. I was to supervise, loosely they said, the 50-bed, open tuberculosis camp. I was to do what I could for the three other Methodist hospitals for which I was responsible in the Sankaru District—Minga, Tunda, and Katiko Kombe. Finally, it was mentioned that there were thirty-nine rural dispensaries dependent on the Wembo Hospital for medicines and salaries. There was a two-year auxiliary nurses' training school at Wembo Nyama for which I was responsible in name, but I was assured that the Congolese nurses would provide all the teaching that the twenty-four students needed. The medical opportunities and responsibilities were enormous, maybe impossible. Winkie was making a valiant effort to prepare for these new realities of our missionary life, but she found Kananga so depressing that she could hardly even think about our move to Wembo Nyama. God help us, we were clearly in over our heads.

During that week of orientation in Kananga I learned more about recent events in the Sankaru and in Congo. Patrice Lumumba, the first prime minister of Congo, was a member of the Batetela tribe and was born and raised in a village near Wembo Nyama. He had been chosen by the people of the area to be their representative to the new Congo parliament. The parliament had chosen him to be the prime minister and head of the government of all of Congo. During the first few months of Congo's independence Lumumba took a strong position against Belgium and white foreigners in general. The American government saw him as radical and dangerous. Most of the members of the Congo Parliament, on the other hand, thought him a heroic spokesman for the people of Congo. Lumumba appealed to Russia for support against the continuing Belgian influence and, in so doing, alienated himself from the European and American governments. Congo's president, Joseph Kasavubu of the Bakongo tribe, and Moise Tshombe, the governor of the Katanga Province and a leader of the Lunda tribe, believed that Lumumba was a traitor to the interests of Congo. General Joseph Mobutu of the Ngbandi tribe and the commander of the ANC (Congo National Army) arrested Lumumba and delivered him to Tshombe in the Katanga Province where he was killed. Tshombe was believed to have been responsible for Lumumba's murder, but Kasavubu and Mobutu were believed to have conspired with Tshombe. The Batetela people were angry with their fellow countrymen who had murdered their hero, Lumumba.

After our family had left Congo in 1962, another rebellion began in the northeast in the name of Lumumba (already dead for several months) and Mulele. The Mulelist rebels (Simbas) overran two thirds of the entire Congo, including Wembo Nyama, where they took five American missionaries there as hostages. General Olenga was a leader of the Simbas and was a member of the Batetela tribe. The Batetela tribe and the people around Wembo had generally been sympathetic to the Simba rebellion until 1964, when a Simba warrior killed the American missionary Burleigh Law, who was much loved by the people at Wembo Nyama. Later in 1964 Belgian paratroopers dropped on Stanleyville in northeastern Congo and freed many of the European and American hostages, but Dr. Paul Carlson, another American missionary doctor, was killed there. Kasavubu asked his former enemy, Tshombe, to raise a mercenary army to help the ANC stop Mulele's Simbas. Tshombe did, and their bullets killed many Simbas without turning into water. They drove the Simbas of Mulele deep into the remote forests of northeastern Congo.

Bishop Shungu was the bishop for all of the Methodist churches and all of the Methodist missionaries in Congo, including those among the Batetela tribe (of the late Lumumba) and those among the Lunda tribe (of Tshombe). A large number of both tribes were

When Bull Elephants Fight

Methodist. Bishop Shungu and the Methodist church were thus straddling two large tribes with deep animosities toward each other. This was a recipe for trouble.

In the midst of such confusion and tribal enmity I thought that the folktale Bishop Shungu had told us in Belgium about "my elephant" did not apply to me. I didn't want to "grab a vine and pull an elephant" back to any village. I was a surgeon who would help as many people as I could while taking care of my family. I did not want to get involved in Congo's political or tribal mess. As far as I was concerned, let the bull elephants fight—I would try to stay out of their way—and do what I could to save some of the grass.

Fourteen
Uwandji Wechi Koi

"You can't be nobody but who you are.... That shadow wasn't nothing but you growing into yourself. You either got to grow into it or cut it down to fit you. But that's all you got to make life with. That's all you got to measure yourself against that world out there."
—August Wilson

Wes pointed and said, "That dark spot on the horizon, just above the nose of the plane, that's Wembo Nyama." I couldn't see any dark spot.

We had been flying north-northeast over dense rain forest for more than an hour and a half. I had started to worry that we had missed Wembo Nyama. The monotonous terrain over which we had been flying looked like vast fields of broccoli, broken occasionally by small clearings with a few grass-roofed huts. Brown rivers twisted like serpents through the green foliage below us. What would become of us if we ran out of gas before we got to the airstrip? Even if we survived the crash we wouldn't survive the night in the rain forest below. Only the calm confidence of our pilot reassured me.

When Bull Elephants Fight

But in a few minutes I got a good look at Wembo Nyama from the air as we circled the village and the mission compound. The new hospital had four metal-roofed buildings arranged in a rectangular shape, and several rows of grass-roofed houses. The mission compound looked quite large for being so far out in the bush. As we descended, Wes pointed out the various buildings. The large grass-roofed building we saw was the maternity, the only part of the original hospital still standing. Nearby were a large brick church, a primary- and a secondary-school building, and two rows of small houses with grass roofs for the workmen and the primary-school teachers. There were half a dozen brick houses for missionaries and church officials. One of them had been burned; only the chimney and some of the crumbling walls remained.

"The doctor here before independence lived in that burned-out house and was moved to Kimpese," Wes explained. "He tried to maintain discipline in the old hospital, and in 1960 some of the people burned his house down." Many Congolese, and I supposed more of the Batetela than any other tribe, believed what Lumumba had said the day Congo received her independence from Belgium: "We don't need foreigners anymore—we're free to do what we want now." After all, Lumumba was a Batetela.

Wes landed and taxied to the far end of the airstrip where a crowd of Congolese was gathered near several vehicles. As soon as Wes shut down the engine and opened his door, the cabin was filled with a cacophony of beating drums pierced by screams and whistles that hurt my ears as I climbed out through the door. The shouts from dancing men and women rose to a fever pitch as the crowd danced and yelled and milled around us. Red dust rose up in a drifting cloud and soon we were all engulfed by the choking haze. Grace and Joy grabbed my pants' pockets and held on to avoid being swallowed by the noisy crowd, or by the men pulling the suitcases from the baggage compartment of the plane. I helped Winkie out. She clutched Rogé in one arm and reached toward me with the other. Grace and Joy let go of my pants' pockets and grabbed onto Winkie's skirt as she moved through the crowd, looking for Hazel Reid. John was the last one to emerge from the plane, his eyes wide with fear and his small body trembling. I lifted him out and held him in my arms and scanned the crowd, looking for Winkie. When I spotted her, I quickly moved toward her, and the crowd moved with me.

Dozens of bare-breasted Congolese women yelled, threw dust into the air, and rolled on the ground. Others sang or chanted to the rhythm of the drums. The tumult was pierced again and again by the high-pitched warbling cries typical of the African women on occasions of frenetic celebrations. It was bedlam.

Winkie's anxiety showed in her face when she looked back to see where I was, before she pushed on toward Hazel. Grace and Joy held onto Winkie's skirt as though for dear life. The Congolese women and children laughed and jabbered in amazement at the color and texture of our children's blonde hair and white skin, and continually tried to touch them.

I resisted the hands that pulled me toward a group of men until I realized the hands were those of Rev. Reid. I was guided to a sedan chair tied onto long poles on either side. Winkie, carrying Rogé on her hip, was pushed into a similar chair and John and Joy climbed in with her. She sent Grace to me, and I pulled her beside me. Hazel now stood next to Winkie, smiling as though to reassure her. Then four men picked up the four ends of the poles tied to each chair and lifted the poles shoulder-high, and began to trot the mile distance down the dirt road to the mission hospital. The crowd moved along in front, then beside, and finally behind us, shouting, laughing, and singing.

We were put down on the elevated cement porch of one of the hospital's pavilions that formed part of the rectangle of hospital buildings. There were hundreds of people waiting in and around that rectangle, clapping, singing, and dancing—and always under all of the noise were the drums beating out a throbbing rhythm.

The crowd and the drums fell silent when Bishop Shungu began to speak to the people in Otetela. Then Alex Reid gave a short speech, also in Otetela. I couldn't understand what was said but Hazel provided simultaneous translations for us. "Here is the doctor who has come with his family to open the hospital and care for our sick people," she whispered to us. "The suffering of the last two years is over. The Congo Team of American teachers is here and they will teach our young people. The pastors' school will be reopened and revival will be proclaimed. The Simba rebels killed many teachers, pastors, and believers. They said those who had been taught by white people were contaminated. But God triumphed. The pastors, teachers, and believers hid in the forest and survived. They slept on the ground and lived with the rain. They were hungry and many of them became sick. Some died of exposure and starvation in the forest, and many, many babies died. But all of that is past now." Hazel looked at me and concluded her translation, "God has smiled on His people. We thank God and praise Him for this deliverance."

We stood there on the porch of the hospital to receive homage from the throng of poverty-stricken, emaciated, sick people while the bishop and Rev. Reid spoke. I can still see and hear it all even now when I close my eyes. The people. The drums. The shouts. I can still feel the heat, the dust, and my uncertainty in the midst of their enthusiastic welcome.

The chief of Wembo Nyama spoke next, promising that he and the Batetela people would protect us. We were given Otetela names, as though we had now become members of the Batetela tribe. I was named "Uwandji Wechi Koi," the "chief doctor, with the strength and cunning of a leopard." An exalted name, I was told. Winkie was given the name of "Uya Koi," the "belt that holds up the leopard's pants."

Then the chiefs from twenty villages surrounding Wembo Nyama came forward and stood before me. They were a pathetic group. Their ebony faces with their tribal scars were further marked with age and years of pain and suffering. These chiefs looked weary as they trudged forward and stood in a row on the ground before me, while I stood on the porch. They didn't look regal like one would expect chiefs to look. They were skinny, old, barefoot men in ragged clothes and with hunched shoulders and tired faces. One chief wore the remnants of a suit coat that was now little more than a long black sleeve on one arm connected by the lining to a sleeve on the other arm. They had been threatened and abused by the rebels for more than a year, and they now stood before me to pledge their lives in protection of my family and me. I felt honored and embarrassed by their deference to me, and their homage.

One by one, each chief shuffled forward to present me with a gift, a token of his commitment to our welfare. The burden of the chiefs' gratitude seemed too heavy for me to bear—I did not want to be here in Wembo Nyama. But I received each gift with both hands, as a Batetela would, and thanked each chief in Otetela—*"Lusaka efula, Uwandji. Lusaka efula"*—and blinked back tears. I feared that by receiving the gift, I was committing myself, and probably my family, to them.

One chief gave me an egg as he bowed his head and bent his knees before me.

Another gave me a half-cup of rice with the same gestures of gratitude and obeisance.

A third chief offered me a scrawny chicken with its feet tied together and its wings flapping. I thanked the chief, and quickly handed the struggling chicken to Winkie, who handed it to Hazel. One after another, the chiefs came before me, a stranger, and claimed me as their *wechi*, their doctor.

My anxiety deepened. Unwanted adulation is a terrible experience, especially when it is also unmerited. I felt as though I was now under their power and influence. Their deference and desperate hopes seemed to draw me into an uncertain web of alliances.

Bishop Shungu spoke again in Otetela, and then he prayed. Finally it was over and the drums and dancing began again. I looked at Winkie. Her hair was limp and yellow-orange with dust; her eyes were dark and sunken, filled with resignation and fatigue. A crowd of children and curious parents trailed behind us as Hazel guided us to the house where we would live.

Our new home was a two-story, burned-brick house with cement floors. We learned that the Simba rebels had used the original doors as firewood and new wooden doors had been installed the day before we arrived. The flooring of the second story had also been used for firewood and I could see the stairway leading up to the joists, and above them, the rafters and the metal roof. There were wooden "barn door" windows upstairs, one at each end of the house. We would have mosquitoes and bats at night, and the metal roof would radiate heat down on us during the day.

The kitchen had a large wood-burning cooking stove, and a non-functioning kerosene refrigerator. There were three bedrooms and an indoor bathroom. There was a double bed in one room and two single beds in each of the other bedrooms. If we could put grass mats across the ceiling joists later, it would be cooler during the day, and keep the bat dung from falling on us as we slept. The house wasn't as nice as the one we had lived in at Sona Bata, but it would be adequate.

When our missionary hosts and other guests left so we could rest, Winkie sat on her suitcase and fed the baby while I got the cookies she had brought for the children. They ate them and drank a glass of cool, bottled water, and fell asleep almost immediately. Winkie looked at me with a glazed expression of hopelessness and began to cry. We were trapped in the middle of Congo. I knew Winkie felt deceived by the mission board in New York and by the bishop, and I had been complicit in the whole affair. I knew she felt betrayed by me—the one person she loved and trusted—and I had brought her here to stay in this half-finished house in the middle of the forest. We lay down but couldn't sleep. Mercifully, our children slept for an hour, and awoke refreshed. They played quietly until the sun went down. Winkie and I took solace in their contentment. They didn't know what was going on, and for now, they didn't care.

Dinner at the Lovells was a simple affair, but we barely ate. We were too overwhelmed by the day's events and the sultry heat. Conversation lagged. We soon excused ourselves and put the kids to bed.

Winkie sat on the edge of the bed, head bowed, and began to cry again. I held her in my arms and told her I loved her. Then we fell asleep, and dreamed nightmares that could not be recalled in daylight.

I awoke to the sound of women singing as they swept the path in front of our house. I opened my eyes and looked up at the bare rafters and joists above my head. Winkie was awake, looking up at the metal roof and listening to the singing. A slow smile crept across her face. "I guess we are back in Congo now," she said. Then we heard Rogé crying. It was 6:30 in the morning and it was time to get up and face the day.

We dressed and I greeted the men who were going to help around the house. The cook and domestic helper was named François. He was tall and handsome, but he had a glint in his eye that suggested deviousness to me. He started the fire in the wood stove and put a kettle of water on for tea, and a large pot of water for baths or laundry, or both, without having to be told. Papa Ngongo could not speak French, but he smiled and laughed easily and had a warm and friendly face that inspired our immediate trust. He put water in a washtub and gestured to Winkie about dirty clothes needing to be washed. Rev. Lovell stopped by and invited us to breakfast next door at 7:30.

Papa Paul Koi, the nurse director of the hospital, came by the Lovells' as we were finishing breakfast. He was about five feet eight inches tall with milk-chocolate-colored skin. His brown eyes were bright and intelligent, with smile lines at the corners of his eyes. A warm smile revealing white, even teeth lit up his face. I liked him immediately.

Paul asked when I would come to the hospital and I suggested nine o'clock because I wanted a little time with my family, but Rev. Lovell told him ten. Then Rev. Lovell looked at me and added in English, "If you try to do too much, you'll burn out and go home. We need you here. So rest."

Winkie and the kids were nodding their heads in agreement, and they laughed. I had missed their spontaneous laughter for too long, and that morning was like a healing balm for me. We returned to our house to organize it, and ourselves. François became Winkie's "foreman." He was the only one of our four helpers who understood or spoke French. He would have to translate her instructions to the others and also translate their questions back to her. We unpacked and played with the children until mid-morning, and then I went to the hospital to meet the nurses and patients.

The hospital was new and better designed and built than the one at Sona Bata. Built to be a medical center for hundreds of thousands of people and to accommodate five doctors, it had five offices and five examining rooms. There was a separate room for X-ray machines, with a large Picker machine and two small, portable, army field X-ray units, none of which worked. There were developing tanks, lead-lined gloves, and a portable leaded glass shield. A very nice setup, if only the machines had been functional.

The surgery suite included two operating rooms, each with an anesthetic machine, surgical light, operating table, and Mayo stands. I met Victor Olenga, the male nurse who supervised that area. His eyes and manners were intense, but polite, and he was lean and exceptionally tall. He shook my hand and answered my questions, but lacked the warmth of Papa Paul Koi. The autoclave worked, but the hospital generator did not. We would have to use the station generator when we needed lights in the operating rooms. He showed me a wooden chest containing surgical instruments that he kept locked. He said the surgical lights worked when the generator was on.

Two of the medical-surgical pavilions contained forty beds each; unfortunately, ten beds had been stolen from the third and it only had thirty beds. The hospital pavilions were already half-filled with patients waiting to see me. The cooking and sleeping arrangements were like those at Sona Bata. There was an area outside for the families to prepare meals for their patient, and at night the family slept on the floor, under and between the beds. Even though I had worked before in an African hospital that lacked food, laundry, and bedside care, I had a fresh jolt of culture shock. This was not a clean, modern hospital in a medical center where "state-of-the-art" surgery was routine. The maternity ward had twenty beds and fifteen bassinets. There were two delivery tables and three labor beds.

I would be the only doctor in the Sankaru District until Dr. Isely arrived, so I had nobody with whom to discuss medical problems until later, and even then it turned out to be less than satisfactory. Not one of the Congolese nurses had ever given a general anesthesia. There was no technician to look after the X-ray machines. There were enormous problems to be resolved. Paul Koi informed me that a few miles away there was a branch of this hospital for open-tuberculosis patients. There had once been fifty patients there, but when the Simba rebels passed through, twenty-five of the patients ran into the forest to hide, and never came back. The twenty-five patients who were still there had not received treatment for over two years. That was bad enough, but the fact that 25 patients with open tuberculosis were running around exposing other people to the disease was even worse. I hoped Ray would care for the general medical patients in addition to his real specialty, pediatrics. That would leave only the surgery patients, obstetrical patients, and gynecological patients for me plus the hospital administration that I would share with Paul Koi. I really couldn't imagine how I would learn Otetela unless there were more doctors coming to help.

Before I went home for lunch, Paul Koi asked me to see several of the sickest patients. The first patient was suspected of having sleeping sickness, a disease caused by a parasite, a trypanasome, which invades the central nervous system of the patient who then becomes progressively more somnolent for several months before dying. The tsetse flies that carried the parasite from sick patients to healthy people were common in the forests around Wembo Nyama. I had never seen a case of sleeping sickness, but I had studied the disease in Belgium. The treatment carried a high risk of serious complications and only a limited prospect for a cure. Paul said that a missionary wife at Wembo Nyama had gotten sleeping sickness, had received treatment outside of Congo, and eventually got well. The logical management for us was to draw some blood and spinal fluid and look for the trypanasomes, and if present, try to persuade the hospital in Kananga to accept the patient. I didn't yet realize the limitations of the other hospitals in Congo, whether operated by the government or by a mission.

The next patient had coughed up blood and needed to be treated as an open case of tuberculosis until we could get the laboratory studies to confirm the diagnosis or to reveal another cause for his symptoms. The third patient had fallen from a palm tree three weeks ago, and broken his left leg. He had arrived last night with a high fever. There was motion at the fracture site and pus draining from the skin wound. These three patients could easily occupy half of my time for the next week. And they might die no matter what I did. And there were fifty more patients in the hospital waiting to be seen. I was sure there would be even more tomorrow.

I went home for lunch, depressed by the needs of the patients, my lack of experience with some of the conditions, and the limited personnel and resources that were available. Winkie and the children met me at the door and showed me the flowers they had picked and arranged into bouquets. There were flowers on the dining-room table and in each bedroom.

When Bull Elephants Fight

François had prepared rice that he had borrowed from the Lovells, and a sauce to go over it, made with corned beef that we had brought with us. Some canned peas balanced out our lunch. The food was good, but I couldn't stop thinking about the patients in the hospital. I was overwhelmed, and still tired from the stress of the day before. Michelle Lumbu was a lab tech and ran our laboratory, but with only a microscope and a centrifuge, he was severely limited.

In the end I sent word to Paul Koi that I would not return to the hospital after lunch. I spent the remainder of that day with my family, and talked briefly with the Reids and the Lovells about my frustration. I had been given more responsibilities than I could handle, and for the time being there was nobody else who could help. I had been deeply touched by the enthusiastic reception the chiefs and the people had given us yesterday, but they expected too much. Taking care of my family was still my first priority. Gene Lovell told me not to worry, assuring me anything I did would be far better than any medical care that these Batetela people had ever had before. He urged me to get some sleep, play with my kids, and try the hospital again tomorrow. Try was about all I could do.

Fifteen
Coping in a Bush Hospital

"There is more good in the worst of us,
and more bad in the best of us,
That it behooves the rest of us
to say nothing about any of us."
　　　　　　　　　—German proverb

It was a new beginning for the Wembo Nyama station and hospital, not because of me, but because the Congolese army had driven out the Simba warriors. In preparation for our arrival, carpenters had worked hard under the direction of Bishop Shungu and Rev. Reid to restore the buildings and restart the schools, but limited time and money required many improvisations. Paul Koi, the male nurse in charge of the hospital when I arrived, had emerged as a leader in protecting the station property and missionaries during the occupation by the Simba warriors, and was now the official hospital administrator.

My arrival at Wembo Nyama was a new beginning for me also. I was far more mature and confident than I had been at Sona Bata, and with more administrative and surgical skills than five years earlier. The bishop and Rev. Reid had expressed their confidence in me, as yet an unproven leader, and the people had welcomed me with hopeful enthusiasm.

I believed I knew how a bush hospital should run, and I understood that my responsibility here was to lead and to help Paul Koi and the other nurses provide good medical care to all the patients who came to us. If possible, I was also to help the nurses who were still at the other three Methodist hospitals without doctors. I would have to modify my American medical-center standards and improvise solutions to the seemingly insoluble problems I encountered. Improvisation had always been my strength. But I needed the endorsement of leaders whom the people trusted—the older missionaries, Paul Koi, and the bishop—and it would take time and successful treatment of patients to obtain continuing support.

The Wembo Nyama Hospital was at the end of a long supply line, and much of what had originally been here had been stolen or destroyed by the Simbas. It would be a long time before the needed supplies, medications, and equipment could be ordered and paid for, and an even longer time before the ordered items could arrive here in Wembo.

I narrowed my focus to do what was necessary to open this new hospital built on the site of an older and more primitive one, and to set the standards of care. I would begin with what I was most confident I could do—surgical procedures—and do what I could to get what I would need to start. Victor Olenga was the nurse in charge of the operating room and I thought he would cooperate with me to minimize surgical infections and increase efficiency. This meant preparing the proper instruments and linens in various packs for different operations, then autoclaving the packs to sterilize them. Care had to be taken to label and date the packs and to keep the sterile packs separate from the ones not yet sterilized. I also expected Victor to assist me in the operating room when I performed surgical procedures so I could evaluate what he knew and what he was capable of doing. I had far more difficulty getting Victor's cooperation than I had expected.

Victor had performed some surgical operations during the recent political situation when the rebel Simbas had occupied

Wembo Nyama, but Victor had never received any surgical training—and his surgical results had not been good. Lacking Paul Koi's optimism and enthusiasm, he was not well regarded by his fellow nurses. Nevertheless, he was willing to do what I asked him to do, and I was reluctant to do anything that would make him my enemy. Dr. Hughlett had warned me that Victor could be a troublemaker and implied that he had been one of the nurses involved in the burning of the previous doctor's house. The charred remains of that house reminded me daily that not everybody in Wembo Nyama had always appreciated foreign doctors.

Antoinette was the young assistant nurse assigned to help me in the outpatient clinics each day. She would translate the patients' complaints to me in French, and then translate my questions and instructions to the patients in Otetela. She not only told me what patients said, but she also told me what the patients meant by what they said. Their responses in Otetela were in terms of their animistic worldview, which included malicious spirits that inhabited plants, animals, and sometimes humans. She seemed to understand both the Batetela culture in which she lived and the scientific culture in which I lived. She respected the patients and me, and seemed to understand what my questions to the patients were intended to reveal. She dealt easily with language and cultural differences. When she later was sent away, I would learn how much I had depended on her.

Winkie took care of the house, taught Grace and Joy in a one-room schoolhouse, and took care of John and Rogé, both under two years. Her strength was in interpersonal relations, which she could establish and maintain in nearly any situation. Her anger—at the bishop for sending us to Wembo Nyama instead of Kimpese, and at me for my complicity with the bishop—quickly mellowed. She accepted her situation and decided to make the best of it. She empathized with the extreme poverty of the Batetela people and particularly sympathized with the underfed children and the over-worked women, with whom she had contact. She cooperated with the other missionaries, asked them questions, and learned from them.

When groups of visitors from churches in America came to Wembo Nyama as part of a mission tour, Winkie welcomed them, and fed half of them while Hazel Reid entertained and fed the other half. Alex Reid and Gene Lovell conducted the tours for our visitors. I often greeted the visitors in the hospital, but they were more interested in Winkie, an American mother raising her children in the bush, than they were in the hospital. Winkie charmed them with her simple and direct honesty. She thrived in her new situation. If we had fresh meat, she served it to them. If we didn't have fresh meat, she offered them one of our precious canned hams. If there were no cans of ham available, she fixed them vegetable omelets. I was amazed and proud of her resilience and flexibility, and especially of her spirit of optimism and her devotion to her family. She quickly became a "missionary mama" with a generous heart and an enthusiastic spirit.

Her language skills far surpassed mine. Her fluency in French enabled her to give instructions to François, and through him to our other household helpers. She made friends with the women who came by to sell things every morning and laughed and joked with them good-naturedly. François helped her with the Otetela words she didn't know, and she soon bartered directly with the Batetela women every morning with words and phrases of Otetela. The women always added an extra egg or banana to whatever Winkie bought, and Winkie added a *matabish,* a gratuity, to what she paid. She quickly learned enough Otetela to talk with our other household helpers in their own language. They loved it. My linguistic progress at the hospital was slow by comparison.

Most of my time, especially during the first few months, was spent in the clinics and the operating room. I knew surgery and I could handle French acceptably well, but I was frustrated by the inefficiency of our hospital. I really wanted an American nurse, or even a foreign-trained Congolese nurse to teach the other nurses what I expected from them. During most of my time in Wembo Nyama, the Congolese nurses and I struggled to communicate and to keep our frustrations at bay. Antoinette and Paul Koi had to help me with this.

The nurses and patients had great respect for Paul Koi because he had kept the old hospital functioning during the occupation of Wembo Nyama by the rebels. He was patient with the villagers who were superstitious and afraid, and he encouraged the employees who were trying to adapt to my demands for harder and more efficient work. Paul even had patience with my compulsive work ethic, which I often tried to instill in the nurses.

After having been in Wembo Nyama for only a few weeks, Joe Davis contacted me about his wife's illness. Dot Davis was in Kananga with her husband, but her doctors back in America suspected she might have a malignancy. The American doctors wanted Dot to have a biopsy of the lymph nodes in the scalene fat-pad that lies behind the collarbone. Joe asked if I could do such a biopsy in the Wembo Nyama Hospital, or if she should return to America for the procedure. I had often done such biopsies and was sure that I could do one under local anesthesia at Wembo. I was honored, and perhaps a little flattered, that Joe asked me, the youngest and newest of the four Methodist doctors currently in other hospitals in Congo. While the biopsy procedure is relatively simple there are several complications that can occur, particularly injury to the phrenic nerve or a pneumothorax from puncturing the apex of the lung.

Dot flew up to Wembo and I did the surgery without difficulty. She and Joe expressed such confidence in me that the Congolese who had known them for decades became more confident in me and in my abilities and judgments. To the Congolese in the Sankaru District, I was growing into the Batetela name given me when I first arrived, Uwandji Wechi Koi, a chief and a healer who was as clever as a leopard.

But there was a lot of grunt work to be done in the hospital to obtain higher standards of care, and I became somewhat of an autocrat. This was particularly true in the operating room, although Victor and his assistants were slow to adapt to better ways of doing things. Victor resented the discipline of aseptic technique, and was indifferent to the pain suffered by patients during procedures done under local anesthetic. He was also touchy and easily offended.

The hospital had several unopened crates of brand-new surgical instruments that I sorted with Victor, telling him the names of each instrument and writing the names down in French so he could remember. Sometimes I asked Paul Koi to join me in order to make sure that Victor understood what I wanted him to do. I made lists of the instruments I would need for a half-dozen of the most common surgical procedures, and how I wanted them wrapped, sterilized, and labeled. Eventually the instruments for less common procedures like skin grafts, intestinal surgery, thyroidectomies, and so forth, were also wrapped, sterilized, and labeled. I didn't like spending so much time doing what the surgical nurses had always done for me in America, but there was no alternative. I encouraged and praised Victor at every opportunity, but he remained aloof.

When I wasn't in the operating room with Victor, I limited the procedures he was allowed to do to draining superficial abscesses and suturing recent superficial lacerations, both of which he could do satisfactorily. He reluctantly accepted the need to use sterile instruments at all times and to wash lacerations carefully before he sutured them.

Organizing the pharmacy was a little easier than trying to organize the operating rooms, because we had only a few dozen medicines that were usable, and even those existed in small quantities. Some mission-minded people in America had collected sample packets of medicine from doctors, and then put the individual samples into large boxes, and sent them over to our hospital. Each packet of these proprietary medicines contained only a few tablets, and each packet had to be opened and the contents added to the contents of other packets of the same medicine in order to have enough tablets to provide one patient with a complete course of treatment. The labels were all in English, and Victor and his assistants couldn't read them, so I spent hours sorting them myself.

The Methodist church did have a "medical depot" in Kananga that Dr. Hughlett supervised and from which I could order what I wanted. But the depot often didn't have what I wanted, and never had enough of what I ordered. Several times I sent carefully selected lists of what I wanted to the medical depot, only to have Wes Eiseman bring me a shoebox full of sample medicines a week or two later with a note of apology and explanation.

Dear Roger,

I know that you asked for a lot more than I am sending and I will try to get some of the other items. In the meantime, be as frugal as you can. We can't afford most of the modern drugs and we take what we can get.

God bless you.

Even as we struggled for supplies and medicine, an increasing stream of patients poured in on us daily. We used what we had and the patients got well. We improvised in the operating room and got good results and very few complications. The few male nurses who were running the other three Methodist mission hospitals in the Sankaru District and for whom I was officially responsible had almost no medicine and very few patients. These nurses came to me and pleaded for me to visit their hospitals, even if it was only for a day or two.

"You are our doctor too," they said. "We have nothing. Share some medicine and supplies with us. Come see our patients, too. If you would only come to our hospital and do surgery, many patients will come and we will be able to take care of them."

They were right about having nothing. They were wrong about being able to take care of their patients. The hospitals at Minga, Tunda, and Katiko Kombe were all within fifty miles of Wembo Nyama, but in different directions. I was even responsible for the additional thirty-nine rural dispensaries that the Methodist church had throughout the Sankaru District. It wasn't possible for one doctor to adequately cover so much distance, so many hospitals, or so many people. Ten doctors would not have been enough. But I was young, and tried to handle whatever problems I encountered.

Dr. Ray Isley and his family arrived and settled into a house near ours. Ray began caring for the pediatric and the internal medicine patients. But it was more difficult for Ray to care for these patients without a good supporting clinical laboratory than it was for me to do "bush surgery" without such support. Michelle Lumbu did his best in the lab, but without equipment or supplies our clinical laboratory support here wasn't even as good as what was provided in Sona Bata. Ray needed a good laboratory and technicians for electrolytes, bacterial cultures, electrocardiograms, and X-rays. We did manage to get one army field X-ray unit working by the second month, but we didn't have developer or fixative solutions, so the use of the equipment was limited to fluoroscopy.

A detailed medical or pediatric history also required fluency in the Otetela language and a deep understanding of the culture. As a pediatrician Ray was frustrated and spent time trying to learn Otetela. Ray and Ruth spent more and more time away from the hospital trying to learn the language and culture of the people. I saw them less and less frequently. I did not even notice when they left.

New patients came to the hospital faster than I could operate on them and send them home. Most of the inguinal hernias were easy to repair. But if a hernia was not repaired, it prevented the person from doing heavy labor, and heavy labor was the only kind of work most Congolese could find to do. Some of the hernias were more difficult to repair because they were as big as volleyballs. Other hernias were complicated because they were incarcerated or strangulated and some required resection of portions of the intestines. Usually we obtained very good results with our surgical operations, and our hospital developed a good reputation among the Batetela people.

Medical and pediatric problems were difficult for me, even more difficult than they had been for Ray, because I lacked his specialized training in pediatrics. Antoinette's assistance was essential for me to make even provisional diagnoses. Patients would tell her that something buzzed inside their head like an insect, or that worms were crawling around under their skin, or they couldn't eat any food, and she would discuss with the patient, in Otetela, each of the complaints before translating their symptoms to me. She would tell me in French that the patient says she "has a headache" or "itching," or "has lost her appetite." Such specific symptoms were often incomplete and sometimes inaccurate, but when combined with a physical examination, they were quite helpful in understanding what was wrong with a patient. By her assistance in the clinic Antoinette gave me a deeper understanding of the culture in which

126

I was immersed. She could intelligently discuss matters related to the church as well as to the hospital and the villages. I gained new insights and understanding about the Batetela from our conversations, but many mysteries of the Batetela people remained.

Sixteen
Medical and Cultural Judgements

"I believe in getting into hot water.
I think it keeps you clean."
—C. K. Chesterson

Anesthesia was a huge concern for me. Aside from the fact that none of our nurses had received training in administering ether or other anesthetic agents, we didn't have any oxygen. I used spinal anesthesia for most major abdominal operations, and Xylocaine local anesthesia for most hernias and other operations. I reduced fractures with local injections of procaine and intravenous Valium. I also used morphine but we only had a small amount available. Patience, gentleness, and on rare occasions, brute strength were necessary to get the fractured bone fragments realigned properly. Head and neck surgery was always done under local anesthesia and sedation. The patient's cooperation was essential when surgery was done with the patient awake.

When Bull Elephants Fight

A middle-aged village woman was brought to my clinic at the hospital in July 1966, because she couldn't breathe lying down. She had slept sitting up in a chair for months. Examination revealed that she had a thyroid goiter the size of a grapefruit, and her rapid pulse suggested hyperthyroidism. I treated her with a solution of iodine daily and mild sedation to relieve her anxiety about the hyperthyroidism, but she needed to have a partial resection of her thyroid gland to reduce the pressure on her trachea. I scheduled her for the following month and planned to use local anesthesia; however, my biggest concern was to avoid blood loss, because we didn't yet have a suction machine to keep the operative field clear and we didn't have any way to give her a blood transfusion. She and her family understood the risks and wanted me to proceed.

During the procedure her husband and two sons stayed in the operating room to reassure the patient, and Antoinette was there to translate for me. The patient was placed on the table in a semi-sitting position so she could breathe on her own during the operation. Victor, who had never seen a thyroidectomy before, was my assistant. I had not proceeded far in the operation before a vein behind the thyroid tore and the operative field was flooded with blood. I applied a little pressure on that lobe of the thyroid and the bleeding stopped. I cleaned away the blood and waited a minute for the torn vein to clot. When I removed the pressure on the thyroid lobe, dark blood quickly filled the operative field again and spilled onto the drapes and floor. Her husband and sons gasped at the sight, and the patient became frightened. She tried to climb off the operating table.

Victor and I held the patient's shoulders down and I reapplied pressure on the lobe of the thyroid. At the same time I tried to reassure the patient and the family that everything was still okay. Antoinette and the patient's sons lifted the patient's legs back onto the table and held them there while Antoinette translated what I had said in French. I kept light pressure on the thyroid for several more minutes until the confusion subsided and the patient leaned back against the table and relaxed. During those few minutes of chaos, I had doubts about continuing because I knew we lacked a secure airway, and there was no margin for error in her case.

I cleaned the blood out of the incision again while Antoinette talked to the patient and family in Otetela. She then said in French to me, "The family wants you to continue, Doctor."

I rearranged the operating lights so I could see a little better, and slowly released the pressure on the thyroid. The vein had clotted. I carefully looked behind the lobe of the thyroid as I slowly lifted it. I saw the vein and clamped it. The crisis was over.

I continued the dissection and the patient fell asleep before I finished. I left a small rubber drain in the incision so I would know if any bleeding occurred after I closed the skin. The patient awoke when Antoinette spoke to her, and smiled at her family.

Her recovery was unremarkable. She was now breathing easily. She began eating the following morning, and the day after I removed the small rubber drain she returned home.

Her husband, I later learned, was a Methodist preacher, and he told his congregation and his friends that both her operation and her recovery were miraculous. Neither Antoinette nor I had been told prior to the operation that the family had taken the patient to a larger hospital where several doctors and an anesthetist had started to operate on her thyroid, but the patient had not been able to breathe, and the operation had been abandoned before an incision could be made. The patient was well known among the Batetela tribe and the glowing reports the family gave to everyone they knew brought many more patients to us. I was pleased that the patient had done so well and was happy that our hospital was popular, but more patients meant more work. The harder I worked seeing patients and operating, the more new patients came to our hospital, and the farther we fell behind in our schedule.

Most of the patients were not candidates for curative surgical operations, but suffered from common tropical diseases like malaria, intestinal worms, and malnutrition. Many young women who were not pregnant came to be treated for sterility. The ones who were pregnant came for obstetrical care and sometimes needed caesarean sections. Many older people suffered from arthritis due to their lifestyle of heavy work. The men complained of hernias and urinary tract infections. Some patients came from deeper in the forest and had elephantiasis of their legs due to microfilaria, and other patients who lived close to fast-flowing rivers came with river blindness. These last two conditions defied effective treatment, but the patients received vitamins, aspirin, and encouragement. There were many medical problems like malaria, pneumonia, and ear infections, but it was the number of patients that came each day that was overwhelming. Paul and the other nurses screened most of the patients before they came to me, and they diagnosed and treated the common illnesses themselves. Some patients came for social or political reasons, and Antoinette and Paul made sure I saw the ones I really needed to see. These patients included chiefs and government administrators who were not really very sick. Occasionally the officials had bizarre requests, and Antoinette would alert Paul Koi of my need for help before I even knew I needed it.

Such was the case one morning when Antoinette intercepted an official who had arrived by car, and sent him to Paul Koi. The official, a judge from an area some forty miles away, had a dead man in the trunk of his car. The judge thought the man had been poisoned by an enemy and wanted me, the only doctor in the district, to do an autopsy. Paul came to me with the judge and explained the situation. I declined. The judge insisted, so Paul took me aside and asked why I refused to perform the autopsy. I explained that I wasn't a pathologist with proper expertise in autopsies, and besides, a man who had been dead for three days in the tropical heat would be so decomposed internally that my exam wouldn't be able to determine whether or not the man had been poisoned.

Because Paul insisted, the body was carried to a shed behind the hospital where I performed a limited autopsy. The stench of rotten flesh almost overwhelmed me. I saw no evidence of intestinal or gastric perforation, but I excised some tissue to send to the laboratory in Kinshasa. It was pointless. The tissues were decomposed, but I wanted the judge to know we had done what we could. I closed the incision, and we wrapped the body in the same foul-smelling sheet he had arrived in. I put the biopsies I had taken into a small bottle of formalin to be sent to the university lab in Kinshasa. I asked Paul to write a report for the judge stating that the autopsy was inconclusive but that biopsies had been sent to

Kinshasa. I signed the letter and gave it to the judge, who was very pleased and appreciative. The body was placed back in the car and the judge left. Paul and Antoinette knew who the judge was, and were relieved that I could not prove the dead man had been poisoned or murdered. They were even more relieved than I was to see the judge leave. A month later the pathology report came back from Kinshasa stating only that the specimen submitted was not identifiable. I never saw the judge again. It took a week to get the odor of rotten flesh out from my hair and skin.

Antoinette regularly helped me in the women's clinic. Many of the patients were about eighteen to twenty years old and had not yet had a baby. The Batetela women considered the absence of a baby by the time they reached age twenty to be a "sterility problem." I usually gave the women some brightly colored vitamins and Antoinette gave them precise directions on how to take them each evening. Most of the patients became pregnant within a few months, and thought the pills were wonderful. This deception wasn't intended to reinforce their good opinion of our hospital or of me, but to relieve their anxiety. Women without children had a difficult time among the Congolese, because children demonstrate to others in the community the virility of a man and the fulfillment of the very purpose of a woman. If placebos helped the Batetela couples to have children, I was glad to give them placebos. A woman without children is often doomed to prostitution and a short life.

The Batetela people were even more superstitious than the Bakongo people whom I had treated in 1961, and did not regard cause and effect in the same mechanical, physical, or psychological way that I was trained to do. Spiritual powers were everyday realities to them, and these powers were capable of afflicting people with a variety of diseases. They believed the cause of something does not need to precede that which it causes. I wish that I could have understood their language and worldview more adequately. I was like the Batetela in that I learned empirically about the world through my daily experiences, but I did have an advantage in having had books, teachers, and colleagues to teach me. In the long run I would have been less frustrated and more effective as a physician if I had learned their language and culture before trying to treat their illnesses, but I didn't have a long run.

I kept my medical evaluations of patients and their treatments as simple as possible. Later, when more personnel, better laboratory facilities, and a wider spectrum of effective drugs became available, I hoped to address the more complicated and subtle health problems of the Batetela. Right now the steady stream of patients in the clinic and the administrative headaches caused by inadequate supplies and medications consumed my time and attention. I usually couldn't even get morphine or Demerol for post-operative pain relief. I wanted a modern pharmacy and a hospital central supply out here in the bush, but I had to use what I could get. My frustrations grew, week by week.

At supper one evening about six months after our arrival at Wembo Nyama, I heard an unusual noise in the kitchen—like rain on a metal roof. I didn't know what it was—it wasn't raining outside. Grace saw our cook, François, filling a small sack with rice from our family's twenty-kilo reserve sack in the kitchen. When I went to the kitchen to see what François was doing, he froze with a partially filled tin cup of rice in one hand, a partially filled sack of rice in the other, and his eyes wide with surprise.

"What are you doing?" I asked suspiciously in French.

His mouth opened, but he didn't say anything. He dropped the cup on the floor, straightened up, and tried to hide the small sack of rice behind his back.

"That's the rice for our family," I said sternly. "Are you stealing our rice to take home? Why didn't you ask instead of stealing it?" My voice had grown progressively louder.

He still could not say anything. Then I saw a second small bag of rice on the floor that he was trying to hide behind his foot.

I asked him again if he was taking our rice home without

permission, and he slowly nodded his head.

"You are a thief! You're fired!" I said. "Take the bags of rice that you have filled, and go home. I don't want a thief in this house. I can no longer trust you. Go, and don't come back."

He took the two smaller sacks of rice and slowly walked out the back door. I noticed that he was barefoot. He had no shoes.

I was angry that someone we had trusted was stealing from us, yet embarrassed that I had lost my temper. He had a family to feed. And the price of rice was high. I went back into the dining room and sat down with my family, but my appetite was gone.

Winkie asked me what was wrong, and I told her that François was stealing our rice to take home. I asked her if she had told him to do that.

"No, but I do suppose that his family is hungry."

I told her I would have gladly given him rice if he had asked, but he hadn't, and I had fired him. I explained that I would take François's salary to Paul Koi at the hospital in the morning and ask him to find us a new cook.

Winkie was silent for several moments, and both Grace and Joy were staring at me. "I can do the cooking myself," Winkie finally said. "In fact, I would rather do my own cooking and not have somebody else in the house all the time."

I learned the next day from Paul that the relatives of François were angry that he had lost his job without the legally required one-month notice. They were discussing legal action against the hospital. Paul had pacified them by continuing François's employment with the hospital at the same salary for another month, but not at our house. He would work in the hospital and Winkie would do her own cooking.

What was I really doing here in Wembo Nyama? Was I really helping these people by working so hard that I became irritable and reacted in anger? For the next few days I couldn't get François out of my mind.

Seventeen
Talking Drums and Secret Magic

*"Every society is really governed by hidden laws, by
unspoken assumptions on the part of the people, and
ours is no exception."*
—James Baldwin

Winkie and I wanted our two school-aged daughters to have
an American education. She used the Calvert system for third-
graders with Grace and for first-graders with Joy. Winkie taught
them in a one-room schoolhouse that had been built for the
missionary kids on the station, but she needed somebody to look
after John and Rogé, who were two and six months old, while she
taught the girls. One of the boys in our assistant nurses' school was
from the Esonga Mena tribe about seventy miles north of Wembo,
and had a sister who wanted work to earn money for their family,
so the bishop asked her to be our babysitter. The Esonga Mena tribe
had all been cannibals until quite recently when some of them,
including the nursing student's family, had converted to
Christianity. The language of the Esonga Mena is sufficiently

different from Otetela that her brother was the only one on the station who could communicate with her. This was only part of the problem.

Our potential babysitter had never had any contact with foreign children before and had no idea what she should do to help. We could not communicate with her at all unless her brother was present, and he was in class during the day. The girl had no previous exposure to foreigners and did not know how we lived. Her foul-smelling breath and body odor was due to her poor personal hygiene. When she ate, she stuffed food into her mouth so fast that some of it always fell on the floor and she would casually pick it up and put it back into her mouth. The skin of her face, hands, arms, and legs had numerous scabs and sores caked with dirt. She had scars from tribal markings on her face and her visible teeth had all been filed to a point. The appearance of her face when she smiled was frightening. John and Rogé cried when she was in the room and would not go near her, and she didn't seem to want to be near them, either. Our pastor wanted us to give the girl a chance, but after just one morning we knew she would not be acceptable help for our kids and we let her go back to her village. Winkie reduced her school schedule with Grace and Joy to three mornings each week and I worked at home for two hours in the morning to care for the boys twice a week so Winkie could have a few hours of uninterrupted time to teach the girls.

Papa Ngongo did the washing, including diapers for both boys, several times a week, and dried the laundry by laying it out on the grass in the sun. Even diapers smell sweet and fresh when they are clean and dry. If it was raining, Papa Ngongo and Winkie took the laundry up the stairs to the attic where the clothes would dry in the fresh air blowing in from the large windows at each end of the attic. A few boards on the joists sufficed to enable Winkie and Papa Ngongo to hang diapers from one end of the attic to the other.

Our children were generally healthy, but occasionally they had diarrhea. If it persisted, we gave them water mixed with sugar and a little salt and baking soda. If they had a fever with the diarrhea, I gave them an antibiotic, usually tetracycline. Later research showed that tetracycline in children interfered with normal enamel formation on the teeth. As a result, Grace has had problems with her teeth all of her life.

Winkie prepared meals on a wood stove and bartered in Otetela for fresh food every day. She tried to get our children to drink powdered milk and eat pancakes topped with sugar water with artificial maple flavoring. She was lonely and longed for other young Americans to talk with about the challenges of her daily life. We both did what had to be done day by day, and sometimes we wondered if we were like Don Quixote, fighting spiritual windmills in this far-off and neglected place. But when the occasional American visitor did come to Wembo, even if only for a few hours, we celebrated, took courage, and were grateful.

The hospital at Tunda was one of the three Methodist hospitals in the Sankaru District that didn't have a doctor and was the only one that didn't have a single side-band radio either. I didn't know how to notify them about scheduling a visit there. Paul told me that Tunda was on the far side of the Lomami River, and that our only means of communication was by the "talking drums." When I decided on the date for my first trip to the Tunda Hospital I told Papa Koi, who then asked the *madimba* to drum them the message of when I would arrive. I couldn't understand what a talking drum was or how it could carry such a message.

Rev. Reid had told me a true story about a church group from America that visited the Wembo Nyama station before radios were common here. The group drove to several villages, but wanted to walk on a path to a more remote village as part of their tour. When they arrived at the distant village, one of the American women wanted to take a photograph but had left her camera in the car. Dr. Reid asked the *madimba* in the village to drum a message to the driver, who was waiting back at the car, to get the camera from the glove compartment of the car and bring it to the village. The *madimba* began beating various areas of the wooden drum, producing eight different pitches in a rhythmic way. In less than fifteen minutes the driver trotted up the path with the camera.

Rev. Reid explained that a person had to know the Otetela

language, the music, and the oral tales of the Batetela people before they could use the talking drums for communication. The *madimba* knew the tunes that went with hundreds of rhymes that the Batetela people sang and danced to as children. When the *madimba* played one of the tunes, all the Batetela people knew the words that went with it. The sequence of the words to the various tunes carried the message. I still found it hard to believe that the children's songs would have any words like "camera" or "glove compartment of the car," but the evidence couldn't be denied. The driver understood enough to bring the camera. Even the Batetela people thought there was some kind of magic in the drums, and only a *madimba* could play them.

It only took the *madimba* at Wembo Nyama fifteen minutes to tell the nurse at Tunda when we would arrive, but it took more than six hours for Samuel to drive the truck carrying medicine and supplies, an assistant nurse, and me to Tunda. We had to wait at the Lomami River for the ferryman to bring his barge across the river to us. But the beauty of the forest and the novelty of riding across the huge river on a raft hooked to a cable made the trip memorable. Most of the trip was an easy drive along the two dirt tracts through the forest, but some parts of the roads were extremely sandy, and we almost got stuck in the sand twice.

We arrived at Tunda just before dark. The only two patients in the hospital when I arrived were a new mother and her baby. The mother had had her baby the night before our arrival. The nurse had received the talking drum's message that the doctor was coming, but he didn't believe it, and the village people didn't believe it either. There hadn't been a doctor at that hospital for many years.

The two-story brick hospital building at Tunda had been built to hold a hundred patients, but except for the mother and baby there were no patients—just empty beds without any mattresses. I prepared my bread and beans for supper and slept alone on the bedsprings with one sheet under me and one over me, but I didn't have a mosquito net like I had used in the dispensaries around Sona Bata five years earlier. Here I used insect repellent to protect me from the mosquitoes. The doctor's house next to the hospital would be available to me the next time I came.

About twenty-five patients showed up the next morning. I

drained one abscess and cleaned up two tropical ulcers. There were two patients with hernias and I promised to repair them surgically when I returned later. The rest of the patients were suffering from malaria, diarrhea, and arthritis. The nurse seemed capable, and repeatedly assured me that there would be over a hundred patients waiting for me the next time I came. He was greatly encouraged and thanked me many times for coming and bringing him some medicines. When he asked when I would come back, I told him I would send a message by the *madimba*.

Every month when the moon was full we could hear the drums all day and most of the night. In the daytime it was the talking drums transmitting messages between villages. In the evenings and long after midnight the drums were for dancing. Children, young men and women, parents, and old people all joined in the festivities—singing the simple melodies that told the stories and fables of their childhood.

I was fascinated by the talking drums and asked Papa Paul Koi where I could buy one. He laughed, and said, "Only *madimba* has drum. Only he can make drum talk."

"Okay," I answered, "but I want to take such a drum back to America. I can at least beat on the drum."

"No, *madimba* would never give you drum," he said sharply. "Only *madimba* has drum."

When he saw the disappointment in my face, he added, "Ask Samuel, your driver. He knows *madimba*. Maybe he can help you get one, but *madimba* must see your face," meaning that I would have to personally visit with the *madimba* and win his confidence.

Later I asked Samuel if he would help me get a talking drum. He was intelligent though not well educated in European culture, but he knew a lot about the Batetela culture and tried to teach me whenever I gave him a chance.

Samuel grinned, his brown eyes laughing and his white gleaming. *"Eluh, Uwandji?"* I interpreted the quizzical expression on his face to mean "Are you a *madimba*, master of the soul of a talking drum?"

"I can't play a talking drum," I answered. "But I want to take one back to America some day and show them how clever you Batetela people are. You can talk without words."

"Maybe we go village where *madimba* live," he said after thinking about it for a while. "He not want give you drum. You white." He paused a long time, and then added, "But you *Uwandji*. I talk for you." He knew more pidgin English than French because of his contact with American missionaries as a boy.

Several days later, Samuel told me that we must go to the village of the *madimba*. "It not far by truck," he said. I had never heard of that village before, but I wanted to go as soon as possible, maybe the coming Saturday. Samuel grinned and said, "Okay."

The next Saturday morning Samuel drove our entire family to the village. As we followed the tire tracks on a little-used road, I asked Samuel about the Simba rebels that Mulele had led in battle a few years ago.

"How is it possible that the Congo army, with guns and trucks, and many, many soldiers, could not defeat the Simbas three years ago?" I asked. "The Simbas used spears, but the Congo army had to have mercenary soldiers before they could defeat the Simbas."

Samuel continued to drive, presumably trying to think of how he could explain this phenomenon to a white foreigner. Finally he glanced at me and said, "You know many my people, Simba warrior Mulele, Olenga, Lumumba?" I knew that Simba was the name for the tribesmen in northeast Congo, and that most of the other men that he named were involved in some way with the Simbas. I grunted affirmatively.

Samuel continued, "You know elephant?" and he swept his right hand down from his nose like an elephant's trunk. I grunted again.

"Big. Big-big," Samuel said, repeating the word twice in rapid succession. "You know pygmy? Small-small. He kill elephant. Spear. No gun." He glanced at me again to see if I understood his explanation.

I didn't. "How does a very small pygmy with a spear kill a very big elephant?" I wanted to know.

"Magic," he replied. "*Secret magic.* Elephant big, but pygmy know secret magic. He kill big elephant." He stopped as though he had completed his explanation.

"What is the 'secret magic' that the clever pygmy knows?" I asked.

He ignored my question but pointed his chin toward the widening path ahead of the truck. "Village of *madimba*," he said. Six mud huts with grass roofs were in a clearing ahead of us, and Samuel said, "I tell you secret magic of pygmy after you get talking drum."

There were about twenty adults, mostly men, standing around the huts. Several women with big bellies came out of one hut. At least a dozen children stood behind the adults, peeking out at us with large brown eyes. I then noticed that all six of the women who had been standing with the men had babies on their backs. The *madimba*, a skinny, older man was sitting on a rickety chair in front of a dilapidated hut.

Samuel introduced me to the *madimba* and we both bowed slightly and grasped both of each other's hands. *"Moyo, Uwandji. Welu wulu?"* I asked politely, snapping my fingers as our hands slid apart. He snapped his fingers at the same time I did.

"Eluh. Uwandji. Dimi la wulu," he replied. This translates as, "Yes, chief. I have strength."

Samuel told the *madimba* I was the doctor, *Uwandji Wechi Koi*, at the new hospital in Wembo Nyama. The *madimba* had heard of me. They palavered together loudly and with animated gestures for another five minutes, and then the *madimba* turned and entered his hut.

"He give you drum," Samuel said to me triumphantly, "you give him two thousand francs."

The Congolese children had been inching closer to our daughters, trying to touch them and to feel their blonde hair, giggling and shuffling their feet in the dust. Winkie indulged them, but kept the baby in her arms and allowed John to hide behind her skirt.

"Moy'anyu," Winkie said, smiling at the children. She nudged Grace and Joy forward. The girls smiled and the other children giggled, and they began shaking hands with each other.

The *madimba* returned with a wooden drum in his hands. It was about three feet high, two feet wide, and five inches thick. It had been made of a single piece of wood that had been chiseled hollow on the inside, leaving the walls of the wood from two to ten millimeters thick. He demonstrated that striking the sides of the drum in six different places produced six distinct tones. The drum was smaller than the talking drums I had seen before with eight tones.

The *madimba* struck a rapid succession of tones from the drum, causing everybody to burst out laughing. The madimba grinned broadly. Samuel was also laughing.

"What did he say with the drum?" I asked Samuel.

"He say, 'White chief pay big money for drum.'"

I laughed. I could hardly believe any Batetela song or chant would include that message, but obviously the people had understood it. I gave the money to the chief with both hands.

We shook again, both of us smiling. "*Lusaka. Uwandji. Lusaka efula,*" I said. Then we headed back to the truck, waving to the villagers.

As we drove back to Wembo Nyama, I asked Samuel to finish telling me what the "secret magic" was that allowed pygmies to kill elephants with a spear.

"The secret magic is what pygmy know," and Samuel tapped the side of his own head several times. "Pygmy know forest elephant turn fast one way, even when running," and he gestured with his right hand. "Elephant strong. Kill lion. Strong- strong. Pygmy know forest elephant not turn fast other way," and he gestured with his left hand. "He turn big-big circle other way. Pygmy know which way elephant turn big circle. Lion not know. Pygmy stay on safe side elephant and stick big spear deep-deep in elephant belly. Long spear handle hit tree and rock while elephant run. Pygmy stay on safe side elephant. Three days, elephant die."

"That's very interesting, Paul," I exclaimed. "Now that you and I know the secret magic, I can kill an elephant with a spear."

"No, no, no," Samuel said quickly, and turned to look at me with horror in his eyes. "You and I not know which side elephant turn fast. Maybe right"—Paul gestured again with his right hand— "or maybe left," and he gestured with his left hand. "Only pygmy know. Pygmy know *secret magic.*"

"Okay," I said halfheartedly, "if pygmy knowledge is the secret magic, you and I now know the secret magic of the pygmy, except which way the elephant can turn to kill us. How does that explain the success of the Simba warriors against the army? Can the army only turn one way?"

Samuel did not answer, but stared straight ahead down the road.

I asked if the Simbas had spies in the army so they would know what the army would do. There was no answer. I asked if the soldiers were afraid of the Simbas and their spears. There was still no answer. I asked if the soldiers ran away because the Simbas were not afraid. Samuel glanced at me, and I thought I was on the right track. Finally I suggested that the soldiers believed their bullets would turn to water because of the magic which the fetish priests had given to the Simbas, and as a result the bullets could not hurt the Simbas.

There was a hint of a smile on Samuel's lips and he nodded, adding, "Simba chase soldier like pygmy chase elephant. Put spear in belly or back. In three day they die. Pygmy not afraid. He know elephant. Simba not afraid, he know soldier."

"I think I understand now," I said. "The Simbas aren't afraid, because they know they won't be hurt and that the soldiers will run."

Samuel grunted in agreement.

I asked why Tshombe's white mercenary soldiers weren't afraid. How come they could kill the Simbas?

"Simba not know white soldier and his gun. But white soldier know Simbas, and white soldier know his bullets kill, not melt like water."

I concluded that the Congolese soldiers and the Simbas believed that lead bullets would turn to water because of the magic, so the soldiers threw away their guns in fear. The white mercenaries knew their bullets would not turn to water so they were not afraid. Thus, knowledge was Samuel's secret magic. The white mercenaries knew their bullets would kill the Simbas, so when they shot the Simbas, the Simbas died. Knowing was the magic.

I had my talking drum, but I couldn't use it. I didn't *know* the children's rhymes or their songs; I didn't *know* the Otetela language. I didn't *know* the *madimba*'s secret magic—how to communicate with the drum—and I couldn't use what I didn't know. He was right about that. In Samuel's mind my secret magic was my knowledge of surgery and medicine, and only I could use it. I knew it wasn't magic, and I knew it wasn't really secret, but Samuel didn't know what I knew. And what I knew wouldn't be of value unless I used it, so I went back to the hospital to use what I knew and keep some people alive.

Eighteen
The Lions Roar

"The antelope that flees in fear from the lion's roar is brought down by the lioness hidden in tall grass."
—Bantu Proverb

My family went with me on my next visit to the Tunda Hospital because I wanted them to experience the forest, the Lomami River, and an isolated hospital lost in the heart of Congo. I wanted them to experience life there with me for a few days. Winkie packed a picnic lunch for the family, and we carried our jugs of water, cooking utensils, a Primus kerosene stove, and food for the two nights and three days that I planned to work there. We had received a fairly big supply of basic medicines from the Missionary Assistance Program in America, and we loaded almost everything on the roof of the Landrover. It had finally arrived to replace the truck as our family vehicle.

I drove, leaving Samuel and the assistant nurse behind, so there would be more space for the family. The nurse at Tunda could provide any help I needed. We passed through the forest and forded the small streams that crossed our dusty path. As the sunlight splashed through the canopy of green trees overhead, we laughed and sang. When we forded one of the small streams, we were enveloped by an enormous cloud of yellow butterflies. They enchanted us, swarming into the car and traveling with us for half a mile.

We stopped in a small clearing by the road to eat our picnic lunch. The butterflies, the few wildflowers, and the green forest were our world that day. The children played and ran in the grass with the wind blowing through their hair. My heart was content, my family was happy, and I was doing the work I had come to do. We saw monkeys swinging among the branches of the trees, and in one area a troop of baboons assured us there were no lions in the area. In the mid-afternoon we arrived at the Lomami River. It rushed and swirled around the exposed roots of the huge trees that leaned far out from both banks, shrouding the ever-changing light and shadows of the river's broad expanse. The ferry, which was really just a large raft fastened onto six airtight barrels, was tied to two trees on the bank and held against a makeshift dock with heavy ropes.

The ferryman emerged from his house and directed everyone but me to get out of the car while he directed me to drive onto the ferry. Winkie and the children then got onto the narrow spaces around the car. I had crossed the river here with Samuel and a nurse the first time I visited the Tunda Hospital, and I knew the ferry had no motor. A heavy cable spanned the river and was securely tied to trees on both sides. One end of another shorter cable was attached to a pulley that rolled freely on the heavier cable, and the other end of the short cable was hooked onto a corner of the ferry-raft. This arrangement meant that when the ferry was untied from the trees that held against the dock, it turned to a 45-degree angle to the current of the river. The current then pushed the ferry, our truck, and our family across the river while the cables kept us from being swept downstream. To cross the river in the opposite direction the ferryman simply hooked the cable to the adjacent corner of the ferry.

With the splashing sound of the current against the side of the ferry and the wind in my face, I fantasized that I was an explorer, the first white man to cross this river at this point. I looked down at the dark, swirling water a few inches below my feet and imagined crocodiles, snakes, and other dangerous creatures lurking there among the tangled roots and shadows along the bank. The moment seemed surreal, a tropical fantasy. My senses tingled with excitement and my mind was jumbled with thoughts of heroism and fear.

Our two-year-old, John, caught his foot between the boards of the ferry's platform and lost his shoe. I watched the shoe float rapidly down the river with the current. I was sorry to lose that shoe, because we had brought only one pair. Now Winkie would have to keep him inside the house where we would stay. I hoped there wouldn't be any hookworms on the floor.

Suddenly I was stabbed in the right buttock, right through my pants. I almost fell overboard but saved myself by clutching the car door with one hand and grabbing John with the other. I heard the distinctive buzzing sound of a tsetse fly. As the pain in my rear subsided, I was aware that the bite might have infected me with the trypanasomes that cause African sleeping sickness. This sickness was endemic here.

How quickly I went from reverie to anxiety! What if John had fallen into the river instead of just his shoe? What if I was now infected with African sleeping sickness and would waste away and die in a few months, leaving my family orphaned and my wife a destitute widow, just as I had dreamed in a nightmare long ago?

We reached the other side of the river and drove for another thirty or forty minutes through the forest with the sun sinking rapidly behind us. Then as we rounded a curve we suddenly saw the hospital. A small crowd of people was waiting for us in the fading light of evening. Winkie and Grace both gasped in wonder when they saw in the small clearing in the forest a brick hospital building two stories high.

It looked like a fairy-tale castle hidden in the shadows of the forest. The Congolese children stopped in their play to gaze as our Landrover roared out from among the trees. Statuesque women in colorful *panyas,* with babies tied onto their backs, gazed at us indifferently. The group of men in dark, torn trousers and dirty shirts turned and quietly watched our approach.

I greeted the nurse and the patients briefly and then unloaded the car. The nurse had already registered the waiting patients and was now leading them in a song and an explanation of how we would proceed. I was in a hurry to settle my family and get over to the hospital before it got too dark to treat the patients and to select those in need of a surgical operation tomorrow.

I heard John coughing violently in the kitchen where I had put our food and cooking equipment. I hurried to the kitchen and found John holding a water glass half filled with clear liquid. The open plastic kerosene bottle sat on the floor. I took the glass from John's hand and smelled it. It was kerosene. He had gotten himself a drink, but from the wrong container. We had not yet lit the kerosene lanterns and the darkness was deepening. I sensed the nearness of a roaring lion in my head, but I refused to panic.

Winkie appeared in the doorway and asked what happened. I didn't immediately answer until after I rummaged through our food box for the bread. Bread would absorb kerosene after ingestion, and reduce the vomiting. The greatest danger, as I recalled from a lecture in medical school, was for John to vomit up and aspirate the kerosene. That could cause a chemical pneumonia. He ate two large pieces of bread between paroxysms of coughs. I gave him some antibiotics and a spoonful of cough syrup, and the coughing decreased. I couldn't think of anything else to do for him, so I asked Winkie to give him some more bread and water in half an hour to dilute and absorb the kerosene. I went to the hospital to see the patients. Winkie listened to John's occasional hacking cough and prayed while she fixed supper for the other children and gave John more bread and water. When I returned much later that evening John seemed much better. His cough was gone the next morning and he was hungry. I thought he would recover, and he did.

On the next Monday, back in Wembo, I went to my morning clinic expecting Antoinette to have thirty or forty patients already registered and ready for me to see. Instead, there was another assistant nurse standing near my examining room and a large group of Congolese patients waiting to be registered. I asked the assistant nurse where Antoinette was. Antoinette had always been punctual and was an essential member of the clinic staff. When the assistant nurse only shrugged, I went to Papa Koi and asked him where she was.

He looked at me anxiously and finally said, "Antoinette cannot come anymore."

"Why? Is she sick? She has been a tremendous help to me."

Paul referred me to Rev. Musea, the church's district superintendent. The Batetela people avoid giving bad news if at all possible, especially to a white man. Papa Koi knew she had been fired and he didn't want to be the one to give me the news.

I was well acquainted with Rev. Musea and admired his leadership. He knew his people, knew the Bible, and was wise in the church affairs. What had Antoinette done that caused him to sack her?

"She is with child," Rev. Musea told me, "and she is not married."

I asked Rev. Musea how he knew this. He said that one of the other nurses had told him, so he called her before the church council on Saturday and she confessed.

"Who is the father?"

"She would not say. We asked her many times. I think it must have been someone for whom she cared a great deal."

"Is there any way that she can be forgiven and continue working here at the hospital?"

"Certainly she can be forgiven. God forgives anyone who confesses and repents of his sin. The church will forgive in the same way. She has confessed her sin, but did not show any sign of repentance and would not ask for forgiveness. Her example would be bad for the church. The people used to fornicate and nobody cared unless a baby was born. Then the father of the baby must accept his responsibility. But the Bible and the church teach that such a relationship outside of marriage was wrong."

"Couldn't Antoinette and the father get married now?"

"Certainly, but nobody knows who the father is except Antoinette, and she will not tell us. We cannot approve of such sin by pretending that we do not know of it. The father also must confess and repent. But how can we know who he is if neither he nor Antoinette will tell us?"

My face must have showed my concern, because I saw the pastor's eyes cloud with sadness. I understood the church's need for discipline in this matter, but I suspected that a woman as attractive as Antoinette would have loved someone who was as attractive as she, probably one of the male nurses with whom she worked.

"Do not worry for her," Pastor Musea said. "Her family will care for her and arrange a marriage. The baby will have a home and a father."

I hadn't really thought about what would be the best thing for the baby. I had only thought of what would be fair for Antoinette. Rev. Musea's concern for the baby was very African. Then he added, as though he thought he understood my concern, "I will find you another nurse to help with the consultations."

"That won't be necessary," I said quickly. "Papa Koi has already found a replacement."

I was surprised that Rev. Musea assumed that I, an American, would be more concerned about getting my own work done than about an unborn baby's welfare, or a young woman's future. He was perceptive about our American culture, and I was more American than I sometimes wanted to acknowledge.

My concern had really been about the injustice of having an adulterer working in a hospital run by the church, while his lover was fired from her job and banished from the church because of her forthright confession. There was no way that I could help Antoinette, and I saw no way that equal justice could be applied in these circumstances. At least the baby would be given a home and a father. It was rumored later that Antoinette's lover was indeed one of several married male nurses with whom I worked each day, and that he was a church member. But there was no proof, no confession, and no accusation.

Antoinette's family arranged a marriage for her, and she became the fourth wife of a polygamist in Lodja, many miles north of Wembo. The rest of her life would be spent tending babies, cooking meals over an outdoor fire, and taking orders from the other wives of her husband. I never saw or talked to Antoinette again, and I never learned the identity of the baby's father. I have a feeling that I really did not want to know or to be involved. I was American and I didn't think like, or really understand, the Batetela people as well as I had sometimes thought. It was an uncomfortable and helpless feeling. I recognized that we were in a dangerous country and that I was as vulnerable to the whims of politicians and friends as I was to the creatures of the forest. But I didn't know where the greatest danger was or what I could do about it. The Batetela might have said, *When the lion roars, he sends his prey fleeing toward the ambush where the lioness waits.*

Grace and Joy had school with Winkie each morning, but found the long afternoons boring. Grace read every children's book she could find in the afternoons, but Joy couldn't read well and pestered her sister to come play with her. Often the two of them would look for Madia and the three would play together. Madia was a few years older than Grace and had been deaf since she was four, but she could say a few words in French and knew many words in Otetela. She just couldn't hear. Somehow Madia, Grace, and Joy were able to communicate as they played, and Madia often told the girls about some of the customs of the Batetela people.

The three girls liked to play behind our house where the land sloped downhill to the forest and a stream. Our big German shepherd dog usually stayed near the children. On one occasion the girls were playing on top of an old brick oven behind our house when a poisonous black mamba snake slithered out from under a cardboard box that the girls had been pretending was a cooking stove. Madia recognized the danger and hissed like a snake and jumped off the oven to the ground. Grace followed her. Joy seemed paralyzed with fear—afraid of the snake, but more afraid of the big dog's barking. She stood on the brick oven and began to cry while Madia and Grace, now safe on the ground, shouted at her to jump.

Finally the snake slithered back under the box, and Joy climbed down. Papa Ngongo searched for the snake to kill it, but never found it. How could I protect my family from dangers I neither noticed nor expected?

On another occasion, some of the Congolese secondary-school students invited me to go swimming in the Lotembi River, which was only a few miles from Wembo Nyama and much smaller than the Lomami River. They assured me it was perfectly safe and that they had gone swimming there many times before. A swim was appealing and I thought this would be an opportunity for Grace and Joy to get some relief from the boredom and the heat. I asked the students if my little children could go along with me, and they told me it would be okay—the river was very safe. I still had reservations about possible dangers, and I didn't yet have confidence in my ability to recognize them in advance. A Congolese might say, *I could hear the lion roar,* and it caused me to be afraid. In my case I might not even hear the roar, but if I did, I still wouldn't know which way to run.

Grace and Joy couldn't swim well, and the water would be deep, so each girl wore a life preserver that kept her head above the water. As an extra precaution I took an empty forty-liter kerosene drum to use as a float for them to hang onto in the water. Winkie drove us all to the place on the road where a path would lead us through the forest to the river. She would drive down the road another half-mile where the road crossed the river, and wait for us.

Grace, Joy, and I tried to keep up with the excited students as they ran down the winding path among the trees, but Grace and Joy were small, and we fell behind. My main concern as we hurried along was to avoid letting the students get too far ahead of us. If the students were wrong and there were some unknown dangers, I thought we would be safer in a group than if we were alone.

The river was overshadowed by treetops nearly touching those on the opposite side, and only occasional beams of sunlight flashed through the deep shadows onto the fast-flowing water. The birds and monkeys made a ruckus that announced our presence as we reached the cool riverbank. The secondary-school students had already jumped into the water, shouting and laughing as they were carried downstream by the current.

I hesitated, still concerned. Swimming in this river no longer seemed to be such a good idea. But the alternative was not good either. It would be a long walk through the forest alone with my children, and a longer walk down the road to a bridge I had never seen. If we weren't with the students when Winkie met them at the bridge, she would be frantic. The students were almost out of sight around the bend of the river and there was no time to waste. We all jumped into the dark water, held onto the floating keg, and were caught by the current of the river. I couldn't see the students, but I could easily hear them shouting and playing in the water ahead of us. I kicked my feet and paddled with one arm, trying to catch up with them.

Then on the left bank, half hidden in the shadows of the roots of a tree, there was what appeared to be a crocodile. Only the top of his head and back were above the water. I watched as the current carried us rapidly toward him. Why had the Congolese not seen it and warned us? The crocodile began to move. I wanted to do something, but I was terrified and knew we were helpless. When we came closer, I saw that it was not a crocodile but only a partially sunken log, moving in the water. I was relieved but still anxious, and every log now looked like a crocodile, every stick a snake. I perceived danger but could not identify it. And I could not run.

Something underwater brushed against my foot and grabbed my ankle, but I kicked free. Maybe it was only the branches of a waterlogged tree. The girls clung to the barrel as I pushed it faster toward the sound of the voices. Then I heard the buzz of tsetse flies and saw one land on Joy's forehead. I splashed water into her face and the large fly flew away. But he came back. I splashed more water and the fly left, but again returned. My anxiety was turning into terror. God help us!

Fear transformed the beauty of the dark river and the cool air into a multitude of frightening dangers. The exposed roots and the shadows of overhanging trees alternately revealed and obscured the imagined creatures lurking under the water. I tried to swim faster toward the distant voices of the students. When we passed each bend, I saw ahead of us another tree-shrouded bend in the river. Where was the bridge?

Minutes passed as we floated with the current. Then the shouts of the students grew louder, and as we rounded another bend I saw the students climbing onto the bank, and there was the bridge and the truck. I pushed Grace and Joy toward the bank and we got out of the water. The students were laughing and teasing each other in Otetela, like the teenagers they were. I tried to act nonchalant, but I was shaking, not from the warm air or the breeze, but from relief. My knees were weak. We dried off and got back into the truck. Winkie drove us home. Grace thought the swim was great fun and Joy wondered why I had splashed water in her face, but I didn't want to talk about it. The experience was too fresh.

When Bull Elephants Fight

As the months slid by, the work at the hospital, the schools, and the church at Wembo Nyama became routine. The four young American young men who had come with the "Congo Team" to be teachers did their work under the direction of the Congolese superintendent of the mission school system, and I seldom saw any of them. I was officially appointed as the "adviser" to Rev. Musea, the district superintendent for the Methodist churches in the Wembo Nyama District. He and I had several warm conversations, but I didn't try to give him any advice. He would have to ask me if he wanted my opinion.

I was also the adviser for the superintendent of the churches of the Minga District, a less capable man than Rev. Musea. I visited the hospital at Minga every few months and saw the superintendent each time. On one visit he asked me to bring him a new leather belt from America the next time I came. I only smiled. He asked for new trousers to go with his new belt, then for a new shirt to go with his new trousers—all the while twisting his fingers through the holes in the trousers he was wearing. When I looked down at his feet he added, "And new shoes for my new clothes." He looked at my unsmiling face, and said "Thank you, *Uwandji.*"

I felt a twinge of guilt as I realized my constant dependence on these people for help and protection, both of which they freely gave me. The superintendent was not offended by my indifference to his requests. He smiled warmly, thanked me, and asked, "The next time you come? If God wills?" He and his people had little expectation— only hope.

The other American missionaries had left Wembo Nyama by June 1967 and the Congo Team of teachers had completed their second year of teaching and left. The Reids were in America and the Lovells were in Kindu. The Isleys had gone to some other place to study Otetela and I had not seen or heard from them for several months. We were the only foreigners there. Winkie operated the single side-band radio that was our link to Kananga and the other mission stations, and also taught and cared for the children and ran our household. I continued caring for the patients in the hospital.

It was a tense time. In May of 1966 Mobutu had summarily tried and executed a number of the leading politicians, including a former prime minister, for allegedly trying to overthrow the government. Tshombe, a former prime minister, had fled the country in fear for his life. In May of 1967 Mobutu began nationalizing the Belgian-owned mines. Union Minière was renamed "Société Générale des Minérals" and all the profits went directly to Mobutu. Afraid that Tshombe would return and lead a rebellion against the government, Mobutu had Tshombe tried, convicted, and sentenced to death in absentia.

Nobody seemed to know where Tshombe was, but there was a contingent of Katangese soldiers in Kisangani, thought by some to still be loyal to him. If the Katangese soldiers in Kisangani rebelled, they would likely go through or very near Wembo Nyama on their way south toward Katanga. We were in potential danger, and Bishop Shungu warned us in a radio message to stop traveling to other hospitals or dispensaries and to remain close to the Wembo Hospital and the radio.

We were the only foreigners in Wembo Nyama, and also the only white people within a hundred miles. We depended on Rev. Musea and Paul Koi to take care of us. When Wes arrived on his next flight, he told us to stop all radio communications or the Congolese army would become suspicious and confiscate the radios. The only news we received from outside of Wembo was what Wes brought back on his flights every week.

Winkie wanted to take the family back to America, but we still had more than a year left to complete our first term. I wanted to stay, and to trust the bishop and the Congolese at Wembo Nyama to take care of us and warn us of any imminent danger. Winkie thought I was a slow learner. Wes had asked us to signal him if everything was okay by opening our south attic window every time we heard the engine of his plane. That would tell him that he could land safely. If the window were closed, he would radio Kananga and tell them so they could do whatever they could to help us.

I did as he requested each time I heard the engine. Then I would drive to the airstrip and Wes would give me the mail and any other news he had. Sometimes John would ride to the airstrip with me and the three of us would stand in the shade under the wing of the plane and talk about the current status of Congo. John idolized Wes and was fascinated with airplanes. Wes was a great comfort to us, but my free-floating anxiety increased daily.

I studied a map carefully, identifying which roads would take us most directly south to Lusambo without having to cross any bridges. At Lusambo we would have to take a ferry across the Sankaru River. I prayed the ferry would be functioning if we needed it. We waited and kept working. Winkie trusted my judgment, but she was mostly concerned about the children. I thought I could hear a "lion's roar," but I didn't know when or which direction to run.

Nineteen
Exodus

"There is a time for everything..."
—Ecclesiastes 3:1 (The Bible, NIV)

Our friends Dr. Charles and Kay Bascom had been missionaries in Ethiopia and when returning to America with their children, wanted to come by way of Kinshasa. They gave us the date and flight number and asked us to meet them in Kinshasa if possible. Our children were close friends with theirs, and we were eager to see them. The bishop gave us permission to take a week's vacation. I was relieved to leave Wembo for a few days and talk to other Americans and learn if there was any basis for my apprehension.

On Wes's next flight he brought confirmation of our schedule from Kananga to Kinshasa on Air Congo. He would return to Wembo Nyama in three days on his way back from Lodja, and fly our entire family to Kananga, where we would spend the night before taking our flight to Kinshasa. It was essential that we be ready so he could reach Kananga before dark. The landing lights at the airport in Kananga were not in use at night. The local authorities feared that mercenary soldiers would use the lights to guide them in a night attack against the government. There were no radio beacons or navigational aids for airplanes in our area of Congo, so flying at night was out of the question.

On the appointed day the plane buzzed our house at 1:30 in the afternoon. I hurried home from the hospital and opened the "barn window" to let Wes know that it was safe to land. Then I drove to the airstrip where the plane was already on the ground and Wes was waiting in the shade under the wing.

"You're early, Wes," I yelled out of the window as I drove up to the plane. "Winkie's almost ready. Do you want to ride up to the house and get a drink?"

"No," he answered. "There's a bank of clouds coming in from the west and we'd better hurry. I'll just wait here."

I headed back to the mission station and ran inside the house to get the suitcases. I told Winkie to hurry because Wes was worried about the weather. She was in the bathroom arranging the curlers in her hair.

"Forget your hair, Winkie," I said as I grabbed the two suitcases and started for the door. Grace and Joy were already getting into the Landrover. "Put on a bandanna or something, but hurry," I called back over my shoulder.

With the suitcases in the car, I went back into the house to encourage Winkie to hurry. She had a bandanna over the curlers in her hair and a makeup kit in her hand. I hadn't seen her in curlers for months. She hurried out to the car with John and Rogé in tow. We were in high spirits, all laughing and talking at once. It was wonderful to see her laughing again. She was so glad to get away for a few days. Samuel drove us to the airstrip.

Wes loaded our suitcases and diaper bag into the pod under the belly of the Cessna and when we were all secured inside and Wes had done an abbreviated checklist, we bounced down the runway and into the air.

Winkie was elated. She had been on the verge of tears every day for weeks, but this sudden change and abrupt departure, even though it would be only for a week, was a great relief to her. We sang and laughed in childish excitement and that made the children happy, too. Winkie put her hand on my shoulder and shouted above the engine noise, "Do you think Kay will have any gray hair yet?"

I laughed and shouted back, "She would've gotten plenty of gray hair if she'd been in Congo."

The next day we took a commercial flight to Kinshasa. There were hundreds of Congolese soldiers at the airport, and nobody would tell us why. We spent one night in the Methodist guesthouse and met our friends the next morning at the Ndjili International Airport. The entire area was crawling with Congolese soldiers. We took the Bascoms to our guesthouse and fixed a meal of chicken, rice, bread, and instant coffee. Our celebration was muted by fears that something was seriously wrong.

The next day we learned that Tshombe had been captured on an international flight from Europe and had been taken to Algeria as a prisoner. The airport in Kinshasa had closed right after the Bascoms' arrival and all foreigners in Kinshasa were restricted to their homes. Rumors of an imminent military attack by Belgian mercenary soldiers filled the air. Was Tshombe really a prisoner, or was this part of his plan to confuse his enemies before he returned to Kinshasa? If Tshombe returned to Congo, the Katangese soldiers in Kisangani were likely to rebel. I anticipated trouble and violence in Wembo for a long time into the future.

But for the time being we were together with our good friends in the same house. We couldn't stop talking, sharing memories from medical school and from the years when we lived in the same house in Kansas City during internship. We recounted our experiences in recent years in Belgium and Congo and they told us about Ethiopia and the conflicts there. Their experiences in Ethiopia seemed even more discouraging than ours. Both of our families had been starved for fellowship, for somebody who really knew us, understood us, and loved us.

The airport at Ndjili was reopened three days later and the Bascoms left. We learned nothing more about Tshombe or the Katangese soldiers in Kisangani, but Rev. Mel Blake, our mission's secretary for Africa, arrived from New York the same day the Bascom family left. He believed the situation was critical and would consult with the Congolese leaders about what we American missionaries should do. The next day we were notified that the families of all American Methodist missionaries should leave Congo immediately, if possible. Winkie and the children got tickets and left in two days on a Pan American flight. They had only the suitcases they had packed for our holiday in Kinshasa. I would stay in Congo until after our church's annual conference in Lodja the next week. At that conference the Methodist church would decide what to do next. I was specifically interested in their plans for the Wembo Nyama Hospital, and whether they would keep me there. Winkie wanted me to resign from the mission board and return to America with her and the family, but I felt that I should stay until the bishop and the church made their decision. Winkie was not happy with the prospect of going to America without me, and wanted me to promise that I would join her after the church's conference, no matter what they decided. But I couldn't promise that. We tried to hide our fears and our anxieties from each other and from the children. We were miserable company.

The Pan American flight left on schedule with Winkie and the children on board. Because we had very little money, Winkie and the kids planned to stay with her parents and her sister in Kansas. Although I knew they'd be well cared for, I was embarrassed that I couldn't provide for them myself. My future in Congo looked as bleak as theirs in America, but I clung to the nebulous feeling that my moral and religious duty was to stay at my assigned post until relieved.

The next morning at the Union Mission House I met an American doctor named Bill Close. I introduced myself and told him I was a Methodist missionary doctor from Wembo Nyama in the Sankaru District and that I was going back to Lodja in a few days. Dr. Close said he had a private practice in Kinshasa, which I thought sounded strange. He looked at me curiously, sizing me up.

"How's the supply line up to your hospital?" he asked. "Got all the medicine and supplies you need?"

"What supply line?" I answered. Close gave me a knowing grin.

I explained that our mission had a little Cessna that flew supplies from Kananga to five other stations besides ours. When the plane came our way, every week or two, it carried supplies for four hospitals, a secondary school, thirty churches, and a primary-school system with five thousand students. He laughed good-naturedly when I told him that the plane brought us a shoebox of medicine every few weeks. I said that I improvised a lot and got along the best way I could.

He asked me what I needed, indicating that he might be able to get some urgent items for me. He sounded serious, and his blue eyes were bright and cheerful. He cocked his head a little to one side as he talked.

I tried to size him up. Who was he? He was about my height, five foot eight, with sandy-colored hair that tended to fall across his forehead, and he often brushed it back with his hand. He had an athletic build and seemed to be exceptionally self-confident.

I rattled off a few things that were needed—like antibiotics, hexylresorcinal, chloroquine, intravenous fluids, and plaster of Paris. He listened and looked at me, as though he expected me to say more, so I asked him if he could get the stuff up to Wembo Nyama. He nodded his head as though getting several tons of supplies up to Wembo Nyama would be simple.

I told him of my concern that the Katanga soldiers in Kisangani would rebel against their ANC officers, and return to Katanga, passing near or maybe through Wembo Nyama. I explained that Lodja was about 250 miles north of Kananga, and Wembo Nyama was in between.

He smiled and said, "I know where Kananga is and Lodja, too." He stood looking at me, then added, "Don't worry about the Katangese soldiers. They are already taken care of."

I didn't think he understood what was happening in the interior of Congo, and I asked, "What do you mean? How do you know?" I thought Dr. Close was just being pretentious and didn't know any more than I did. I wasn't sure I should trust him even if he was an American.

"I know a lot of things," he said. "I know that Lumumba was from your area, and so was Olenga, and Mulele. But President Mobutu is concerned about his people up there who've been left out."

If Bill knew that General Olenga and the other leaders were all Batetela, he really did know more than I had given him credit for. Victor Olenga's name popped into my head, and I wondered why I had never associated my operating room nurse back in Wembo with the Simba general until now.

"Is Mobutu really concerned about those people in the bush?" I asked. "Do you know him?"

Instead of answering my question, Bill said he had to get down to the hospital now and see a patient, but he might drop back by the Mission House later. He shook my hand again and left rather abruptly. I watched the confident way that he walked to his car. I wondered who he was, why he was here in Kinshasa in a private practice of medicine, and if he really knew President Mobutu.

Dr. Close stopped by the Union Mission House later that afternoon. He wanted me to see the patient in the hospital whom he had mentioned in the morning, and he drove me to the Danish hospital near the center of town. I had never visited any of the hospitals in Kinshasa before, and Bill assured me that this was one of the best. It certainly was a lot cleaner than any hospital I had seen in Congo, but it wasn't as well equipped as most American hospitals.

The patient had an intra-abdominal abscess and needed a laparotomy urgently. Bill asked me to scrub in with him the following morning. We operated the next morning, removed his appendix, and drained the abscess. As we worked we talked about the medical needs of Congo, and how those needs might be met. He seemed optimistic, even idealistic. I told him I had been training some of my mature nurses how to use antibiotics more rationally and to perform minor surgical procedures such as suturing lacerations, applying casts, draining abscesses, and better management of deliveries. Bill said that was exactly what President Mobutu wanted to support—the participation of Congolese doctors and nurses in providing good care of patients while being taught to do it themselves.

Dr. Close seemed to admire President Mobutu because of the president's distaste for bureaucracy as well as his concern for the ordinary people of Congo. "What President Mobutu wants is to have some American doctors who know how to work and who want to teach Congolese doctors how to work." As we left the operating room Bill told me, "This country needs dozens of American doctors." He then grinned mischievously and added, "Because the president doesn't trust most Belgian doctors."

Two days later I flew back to Kananga. The following morning

Wes flew Mel Blake's assistant from New York, two Congolese pastors, and me to Lodja for the Methodist Annual Conference. There were dozens of soldiers on the tarmac. Six Congolese soldiers were lying behind sandbags between us and the terminal, their machine guns pointed at us. They kept us in their sights as we walked to the terminal. I tried to look nonchalant and innocent, as if I had nothing to hide. Paul Koi greeted us at the terminal building, took me to a car, and drove me to the church where I would stay during the conference.

Gloom and uncertainty filled the conference discussions. The Congolese discussed and palavered every problem until they were all so exhausted they were prepared to agree to anything just to bring the meeting to a close. It was democratic in terms of everybody having a say, but it was tediously slow. Bishop Shungu sometimes cut the discussion short and took a vote because it was quicker.

Eventually the group discussed the wisdom of closing the Wembo Nyama Hospital and what that might mean to the people in the area. Most views were in favor of keeping it open, but the danger of leaving a foreign missionary there, namely me, was emphasized. The bishop asked me if I remembered the story of "My Elephant" that he had told us in Belgium several years ago.

I answered immediately in Otetela, *"Eluh, Uwandji,"* and everybody laughed and clapped.

The bishop repeated the story of "My Elephant" in Otetela for all of the delegates. Near the end of the story, when all of the villagers took hold of the vines and began to chant, the bishop stretched out his hand as though he were grasping a vine and began to chant, "Our elephant! Pull!" The point was, everybody had a stake in the decision and had to put aside personal interests in favor of what would be best for all involved.

The Congolese delegates joined the bishop in stretching out their hands. They mimed the bishop and chanted in unison with him, "Our elephant." And then they leaned back as though they were actually pulling and shouted, "Pull!"

With this show of unity, the bishop announced his decision that no foreign personnel would be assigned to Wembo Nyama until the political situation stabilized. The Congolese delegates continued to chant, "Our elephant!   Pull!" as evidence of their unity in supporting his decision.

I flew back to Wembo Nyama, packed up our family belongings and waited for Emanuel, one of the bishop's young assistants, to arrive with a truck to take our belongings and me to Kananga. I was to be temporarily assigned to a new hospital that was being constructed by the Presbyterian church. Wes flew the pastors and me back to Wembo before going on to Kananga. Emanuel arrived with the truck a few days later and helped me load our belongings. I said goodbye to the patients and families and shook hands with the men who had been our household helpers. Nobody cried and there wasn't any ceremony, yet a pall of sadness hung over the compound when Emanuel pulled away. How different my departure was from the celebration of our family's first arrival, and even from our family's departure just two weeks ago when I had laughed at the curlers in Winkie's hair.

I hadn't heard any news about Tshombe or the Katanga soldiers who had rebelled against the government. If the bishop or other authorities knew anything, they gave no hint of it to me. I assumed the rebel soldiers were already approaching Wembo Nyama from the north and I wanted to drive south toward Lusambo and on to Kananga as rapidly as possible. I did not want to be caught by rebel soldiers on a road in the forest, but if caught, resisting would be useless. I trusted Emanuel to get us through.

We drove carefully through the forested areas with sharp turns and little streams in the shallow valleys and then increased our speed when we reached the dry, grassy savanna. We passed through several small villages, each with a half-dozen or so mud huts with thatched roofs in varying states of repair. Our passage sent the chickens squawking in every direction. Little children with dirty white shirts stared at us with wide, frightened eyes, then raced back inside their small mud houses. Women with loads on their heads walked with stately grace between the huts, ignoring the clouds of red dust that trailed us. The men watched us with empty eyes and hopeless expressions. When the dust finally settled, it would be as though we had never passed by. Late in the afternoon we came to the Sankaru River and I saw the ferry tied to a tree on the far side.

Emanuel honked the horn several times, and a man emerged from one of the thatch-roofed huts across the river. He pushed a hollowed-out, wooden canoe called a pirogue into the water and paddled across, pulling up to the bank a few feet from where we were standing. He stepped into the shallow water and pulled his round-bottomed boat firmly onto the sand. Emanuel talked to him in a language that sounded harsh, like Lingala, and I knew we were now in the territory of a different tribe. After several minutes of talking and gesturing, Emanuel turned and told me the ferry was broken. "Ferryman say they fix tomorrow. He take you across river in pirogue, and you stay in house." He pointed toward the huts on the other side of the river. "I go with you and boy-chauffeur stay with truck."

The pirogue had four or five inches of water in the bottom. When I tried to avoid putting my feet into the water, the pirogue rolled and might have turned over if the ferryman had not steadied it. I put my foot to the center of the pirogue and felt the water run over the top of my shoe. Emanuel squatted on his heels behind me. We pushed out from shore and the pirogue rolled precariously from side to side, but reached the other bank with only our feet getting wet.

I stayed in a small thatch-roofed hut that night, sleeping on four small logs tied together in parallel fashion. I declined their offer of *manioc* and fish, and ate bananas instead. I was afraid to eat anything I couldn't peel. The next day they brought papayas and pineapples as well as more bananas. They worked all day on the engine of the ferry without success. It was nearly noon the next day before they got the engine running and retrieved the truck and the boy-chauffeur from across the river. I paid for the use of the ferry and the food I had eaten, and I added a generous *matabish* for my accommodations.

We drove all afternoon and for an hour in the dark before we saw a faint light ahead of us. We slowed and found two kerosene lanterns and two large logs blocking the road.

Emanuel and I got out and stood in front of the headlights so that we were visible. There was no moon, and the forest was silent except for the cicada. A deep voice boomed out of the darkness very near us.

Emanuel answered in Lingala, and I recognized a few words. "American" and *"Docteur."*

I heard a rifle bolt open and shut. Several voices whispered in the dark. Then there was silence.

I said softly to Emanuel, "We almost made it."

Twenty
The Vestibule of the Church

"Our misfortunes are never out of proportion to our capacity to bear them."
—Yoruba proverb

My heart was racing. I looked around, but couldn't see anything. In my anxiety and fear, the light of the kerosene lanterns and even of the stars in the sky seemed to have disappeared, swallowed by the African night and the glare of our headlights.

Emanuel turned slowly from the voices in the dark and called for Paul to come out into the light.

Paul stepped from behind the truck and walked into the light. He had silently climbed down from the truck without being heard or seen, but he had not run away. The soldiers were surprised by Paul's presence, and began to talk in loud and threatening voices. I noticed that neither Emanuel nor Paul seemed intimidated or frightened. That encouraged me.

Finally, Emanuel turned to me and said, "Soldiers take us to commander." We got back into the truck with one soldier in front by me, and another in back with Paul. We drove about a mile farther down the road and stopped by the bright light of a Coleman lantern. There were three tents visible just off the road and at least four soldiers in the uniforms of the Congolese National Army. The soldiers who had accompanied us talked with the officer in command. I picked out the words *"missionaire"* and *"docteur"* in their conversation again.

The officer smiled at me in a vaguely hostile manner, extended his hand, and spoke in French. "Your passport. I take you to headquarters."

I held my passport so he could see it with his flashlight. Instead, he turned the beam of the light into my face and eyes and snatched the passport out of my grasp. *"Merci,"* he said in an unfriendly voice. He beamed his flashlight onto the passport for a few seconds, and then beamed it back into my face. When he turned his light away, my passport was gone.

One soldier got into the back of the truck with Paul, and the officer sat in the cab next to me. Emanuel had watched everything but had said nothing. We drove three or four more miles before we reached a cluster of small houses. If this was the outskirts of Kananga, these soldiers were loyal to the Congo government. If it wasn't Kananga, they were Katangese rebels still in their army uniforms. As we continued, I noticed more houses and shops and I thought it must be Kananga. I began to relax. We stopped in front of a house with electric lights and a large group of soldiers lounging around it. The officer took me inside the house and told me to sit down near three soldiers. Emanuel stood by the doorway. The officer went into a room that looked like an office. He returned a moment later and said, "Come tomorrow. Ten o'clock." I was dismissed.

We left the truck and our boy-chauffeur parked among the soldiers, and Emanuel led me down the dark streets to the house where Winkie and I had stayed with our family nearly two years ago when we first came to Kananga. Joe Davis, the bishop's assistant, greeted us and told me the bishop wanted to see me.

Bishop Shungu was sitting behind his desk. When he saw me he stood up, greeted me, and extended his hand.

"I'm glad you made the trip safely, Doctor. I was told the soldiers at the edge of town intercepted you. No problem. Emanuel will look after your things, and I'll speak to the general tomorrow. You will get everything back in good order."

I told him that they'd taken my passport.

He wasn't upset, but said he would get it back for me in the morning. He told me to stay here in Kananga for a while, and see if I could help out in the new Presbyterian hospital that was several miles north of town.

I didn't sleep well that night. The next morning the bishop told me that I didn't need to see the general and that he would take care of everything. Joe gave me the key to an old Volkswagen and I drove to the Presbyterian hospital.

The hospital was still under construction and I spent ten minutes wandering around the nearly vacant hospital before I found someone who told me the hospital wasn't yet functioning and there was nothing there for me to do. I didn't see the bishop that evening, so I reported to Joe. He suggested that I check out the government hospital here in Kananga.

That evening I wrote a letter to Winkie and mailed it the next morning. Then I drove to the government hospital. There were no doctors there, but I found a nurse who told me that on some days a doctor would come in around noon, but he never stayed long. The patients wandered in and out of the hospital because there weren't any medicines and the patients couldn't pay for them even if they had some. A few patients slept in the hospital, but most stayed with relatives in Kananga.

The registry book indicated that fifty patients were in the hospital, but there were only two patients physically present on the ward when I was there. There were chickens and mangy dogs wandering through the wards and delivery rooms, and the operating room was filled with big empty boxes, indicating that no operations had been done for a long time. Nobody seemed to care. The diagnostic laboratory did not have even rudimentary functional equipment or reagents for the technicians to use. The salaries for personnel were irregular and never adequate, so the personnel often chose to stay home and work in their gardens or see a few private patients in their homes. Working in the government hospital would be impossible for me.

When Bull Elephants Fight

When I reported to Joe, he suggested that I consider seeing patients at the Methodist church building and using the medicines in the Methodist medical depot. I got Emanuel to help me. I could then understand why Dr. Hughlett had sent so little medicine to Wembo Nyama for me: there wasn't much in the depot. In any case Emmanuel and I helped ourselves to what we could find. Dr. Hughlett had returned to America several months earlier.

We started a little clinic in the vestibule of the church with a few effective medicines like chloroquine, acetaminophen, penicillin, and chloramphenicol. Several boxes of sample medicines, which churches in America had collected from various American doctors and sent here, provided medicines like Lasix and barbiturates. Joe found me a nurse to help part-time, and Emanuel served as my translator for Otetela to French.

I only saw six patients the first day, and the Congolese nurse who helped me collected a few francs for registration and medicines from each of them. The following day there were a dozen patients, including two with infected lacerations. Within a week I was seeing twenty to twenty-five patients every day. I began to feel better about myself because I felt useful again.

I wrote letters to Winkie almost every day and mailed them at the post office. I didn't know if the letters ever reached Winkie, but I never received any letters in return. I felt certain the problem was with the Congolese postal service.

Over two months after my family left Wembo Nyama I was on my way to the post office to mail another letter to Winkie when I saw two American soldiers. They drove their jeep toward me. The soldier with the sergeant's stripes on his shoulder got out and walked toward me.

"Are you an American?" he asked, with a mid-western twang.

"Yeah, I'm an American," I said. "Why?"

"We're looking for some American doctor around here. Look here at this name and tell me if you've ever heard of him," the soldier said, holding out an official-looking paper.

I looked at the name underlined in the letter. I was really surprised by what I read. It was my own name. "Sure," I said. "I know him. That's my name. What do you want with me?"

Instead of answering my question, the soldier asked if he could see my passport. I explained that the ANC soldiers had confiscated it. He asked more questions, trying to confirm my identity, such as what state I was from, and if I knew any senators.

"I sort of know Bob Dole from Kansas. My sister-in-law has worked in his campaigns." That must have convinced him. His face spread into a wide, friendly grin.

"You must be the one," he said. "Are you well? Any problems?"

"Yeah, I'm fine. Why are you looking for me?"

"Hell, I don't know. I just take orders. Is your family here? Your wife? Any kids?" he asked.

I explained that they had left a few months ago and that I wished I had gone with them. The sergeant grinned and said he wished some senator would get him out of Congo and send him to Paris. All three of us laughed.

As the sergeant turned to leave, I remembered the letter to Winkie in my pocket and called after him, "Hey, do me a favor, will you?" As he turned around, I pulled the letter out of my pocket and gave it to him. "Get this in the mail system somehow, will you? I've written my family every day for over a month, but I don't think any of the letters ever got out of the country. I haven't heard from my wife since the family left."

The sergeant agreed, took the letter, and climbed back into the jeep. They made a U-turn, stirring up a small cloud of red dust, and drove two blocks before turning left onto a side street. I never saw them or any other American soldiers in Kananga again.

The jeep and the American soldiers were gone, and the warm sense of camaraderie faded. The episode began to seem as if it had been a dream. Why in the world would American soldiers be here? Maybe there had been a coup in Kinshasa. Maybe Tshombe had taken over. The orange-colored dust settled on the motionless palm trees as I stood in the empty street and watched a barefoot, bare-breasted woman with a pan of plantains on her head as she ambled down the side of the road. In the shadow of a wall I saw two old men with a board on their knees, playing a game of checkers. Three dirty, half-clothed little boys kicked a deflated ball back and forth. I thought about America, and a wave of nostalgia and loneliness swept over me. I was trapped here in the dust and the everlasting heat, away from those I loved.

When Bull Elephants Fight

"What was that all about?" Joe Davis asked as he walked toward me. He looked neat and cool, his hair combed and a friendly smile on his tanned face. But his shoes were dirty and they stirred up more dust with each step.

"Did you see a jeep and two American soldiers here a minute ago?" I asked, testing the reliability of my memory. He nodded. I told him the American soldiers had been looking for me. He didn't know why the soldiers were here, but he said the bishop was pleased with the clinic in the vestibule of the church. He added that he would notify the American Embassy in Kinshasa that I was here, because the embassy wanted to know the location of all Americans in Congo. He walked away, stirring up the dust again.

Weeks went by and nothing changed. No letter from Winkie. No follow up from the military. Emanuel obtained medicines from the medical depot and together we opened the sample packages and put the pills in labeled boxes. His cheerfulness and genuine desire to help encouraged me. Paul's dedication in staying with our truck of belongings at the Congo Army's storage area day and night, rain or shine, showed impressive patience and loyalty. I had never appreciated him adequately at Wembo Nyama. I didn't even know if he had a wife or family.

During the lonely evenings and weekends I remained in my room, reading and reflecting about loyalty. I didn't really care much about administrative structures, the mission board, or even the church organization in Congo. It was the people who were important—people like Paul and Emanuel doing their jobs without being noticed or encouraged. I admired them and wished that I had some of their qualities. Bishop Shungu, Joe, and the other missionaries were extraordinary, but these other unrecognized people did their jobs without fanfare—they were the apple of God's eye. I remembered tall, skinny Victor Olenga whose uncle was a general in the Simbas' rebel army. He had reliably run the operating room at Wembo and assisted me in many operations. Maybe my duty had been simply to encourage these people by just being here. Maybe our working together to treat the thousands of ordinary Congolese was really helping them in what they wanted to do.

I thought again of that African proverb about elephants fighting. There seemed to be no end of "bull elephants" in Congo. Bishop

Shungu and other Congolese would have to deal with the bull elephants. I didn't know how and didn't want to learn. It was the Congolese people who had touched my heart—the people I had worked and lived with—and they were tough. They had gotten along without me before I came, and I knew that they could get along without me after I was gone. I wasn't essential here, but Winkie and our kids needed me now and I wasn't there for them.

I had tried to explain to Winkie in a letter several weeks ago why I would stay here. I told her I still had a job to do. I had been called, I had prepared, and I was now here fulfilling my duty. Duty to whom? The bishop? To my wife and family? It didn't really matter now, because I had no choice. Without a passport I couldn't leave anyway. And I had a growing certainty that God wanted me to be faithful in my responsibilities to my wife and children first and foremost at this time of their need. I didn't remember exactly what I had written to Winkie that night, but it was something like this:

I know that you and Dad Stewart certainly understand responsibility, discipline, and the need for a man to do his duty. I'm learning about discipline and duty now. If and when I am sent back to Wembo, I hope it will be safe enough for you and the children to return. I miss you, but for now I am stuck here, and will remain where the bishop assigns me...

But since I had written that, my perspective had changed. My primary responsibility and duty was to God and my family. My career as a missionary and obedience to the bishop were secondary. I would leave Congo the first chance I got. I wish I had never written that letter.

Twenty-one
Escape

*"Hope is the confidence that something good which you
cannot control will happen to you."*
—Anonymous

I slept soundly the night after I decided that my duty was to
take care of the family God had entrusted to me. I was awakened at
dawn by the banging of pans in the kitchen, punctuated by the
raucous laughter of the cook and the sentinel. I heard the Congolese
women talking as they swept the leaves and frangipani blossoms off
the path with palm branches. Some other women, farther away
from my window, were singing and laughing as they prepared their
morning tea. The Congolese have a deep sense of community and
draw strength from each other's presence, laughing and singing in
the early morning.

There was excitement in the vestibule of the church even before
I arrived, because the general who commanded the Congolese army
in our province had come to the clinic to see me. An entourage of
eight men, including two bodyguards with automatic rifles,
accompanied him. The general was fluent in French and even knew
some English. His eyes were bloodshot and he moved his head

carefully as though in pain. He had a severe headache that had persisted, even worsened, over the last two weeks. The native doctors had given him some medicines, which had not provided relief. The general first told me that somebody had put a curse on him, but on second thought he said his food had been poisoned. He knew that Western doctors had a low opinion of witch doctors and their treatments, and the *wechi* doctors felt the same way about foreign doctors. I wasn't surprised that he had gone to the *wechi* before coming to me. It was common. I had often heard the Congolese say that "white man's medicine is good for white men, and black man's medicine is better for black men." But if the *wechi's* medicine didn't work, most Congolese wouldn't hesitate to go elsewhere. Severe pain can cause a man to disregard traditions he grew up believing in, as the general revealed by coming to me.

"Nothing stops the pain in my head," he told me in French. "It gets worse every day." He gestured as though he was pounding his head, and grimaced in pain.

My examination of the general showed that he had high blood pressure, but no fever. I doubted that he had malaria, but I gave him chloroquine and acetaminophen because malaria was so common and I had no laboratory to rule out this diagnosis. But I thought the real cause of his headache was his high blood pressure, so I added a diuretic and a tranquilizer to the other medicines. I instructed him to cut back on salt and work. "Sleep ten hours each night for the next three nights," I told him and I instructed him how to take the various medicines I had given him. He paid close attention to my specific instructions, as though there might be some magic associated with both the medicine and my words. Misdiagnosing and mistreating such a prominent patient as the general could have very serious consequences in Congo. I told him to return for a follow-up exam in two days.

In the meantime I checked to see if I could find better anti-hypertensive medicines than the Lasix and Valium I had given him. When the general returned two days later, he was clear-eyed and all smiles. His headache was gone; he had slept ten hours each night. His systolic blood pressure was 60mm lower than it had been two days earlier. I told him that he was living with too much stress and worry. I wasn't sure whether he had suffered from hypertension or malaria, or maybe both. But I repeated my advice to give up salt, avoid as much stress as possible, sleep at least eight hours each night, and take the medicine I gave him for another week.

He laughed loudly, and said, "I like salt on all my food." But he said quietly, "If you say stop, I'll stop." And then he smiled and said slyly, "At least I'll use less salt," and again laughed loudly. He thanked me with great enthusiasm.

When he stood up to leave, he turned toward me and laid my passport on the desk. I stared at it with surprise and uncertainty. He and his entourage left the room, stirring up a commotion as they left the church. There it was. My passport. I opened it to be sure it was mine, and I saw that a *"laissez-le passer"* was also stamped and signed in the passport. I could travel all over Congo, leave the country, and return again whenever I pleased. I was freed!

I couldn't concentrate on my remaining patients. I kept thinking about running down to the Air Congo ticket office and buying a ticket home, but I didn't have enough money and I was a white foreigner. I didn't care what the bishop or anybody else thought. I didn't care what the mission board in New York thought. I was getting out of Congo and going home as fast as I could. My loyalty to the bishop and the mission board had been completely subverted by this opportunity to leave. I would inform the church authorities of my decision. I wouldn't ask for permission.

As soon as I could get away from the clinic, I went to the bishop's office, but he was out of town and wasn't expected back for several days. I talked with Joe Davis, who indicated that if I really wanted to leave now in order to take care of my family in America, that was probably the best thing for me to do. He would tell the bishop. If the situation at the Wembo Nyama Hospital did not improve in the next month, he would ship our truckload of belongings to us in Kansas. I like to think he understood my decision. He had children too.

Early the next morning I went to the Air Congo ticket office with my enthusiasm more subdued. I had no money for a ticket and I hoped I could get a ticket here in Kananga for a flight to Kinshasa and have it charged to the Menno Travel Service. David Lundblat, the manager of Menno Travel in Kinshasa, was sympathetic to missionaries and he had arranged the tickets for Winkie and the kids when they had returned to America a few months earlier. The Air Congo clerk contacted the Menno Travel office in Kinshasa and they authorized the ticket and guaranteed payment. The clerk filled out the paperwork and gave me the ticket for Saturday's flight.

I sent a telegram to David in Kinshasa, thanking him for his help in arranging a ticket for me on the first plane to New York. I wanted a two-day layover in New York and then a flight to Kansas City. I needed to talk to the Methodist Board of Missions, and I thought I had better do it when I passed through on my way home. I would have a hard time finding the money to fly back to New York later.

I returned to my room and packed my suitcase. My plane wouldn't leave until noon the next day, so I would see patients in the morning and thank the nurses and Emanuel. I would let them all know that I would be leaving.

When I arrived at the airport before noon the next day, a large crowd of would-be passengers had already gathered. My heart sank—I thought the airline must have oversold the flight. When the announcement was made to board the plane, I walked onto the tarmac as confidently as I could. I was allowed to board the plane, but it wasn't until we were airborne that I relaxed.

We were allowed to deplane in Kinshasa and walk to the terminal in the afternoon heat. Inside the terminal it was even hotter.

The driver from the Union Mission House spotted me, the only white face in the crowd. We located my suitcase and made our way to the area where his old Landrover was parked. I had forgotten to make a reservation at the Union Mission House, but David had made one for me. I still could hardly believe all of this was happening.

As soon as I set my bag down, I called Menno Travel Service. They were closed for the weekend. My emotions had been down and up and down so many times in the last few days that my stomach was cramping with anxiety. Tina gave me a glass of iced tea and I sat down and tried to relax. Half an hour later David came to the Mission House looking for me. What a relief. He greeted me warmly, handed me a large envelope, and said that he had everything arranged and it would all be charged to my account in New York with the Methodist Mission Board. I opened the envelope and pulled out my airline tickets.

I would fly out of Brazzaville, the capitol of French Congo across the Congo River from Kinshasa, at ten o'clock in the morning on Air France. I would have nearly ten hours in Paris before I would board another Air France flight to New York, and arrive there mid-morning Monday. I would have until five in the afternoon on Tuesday in New York before taking TWA to Kansas City, arriving about eight in the evening. It made me dizzy to think that I would be home with my family on Tuesday.

"It's all worked out," David reassured me. "If you would like, I can send a telegram to your brother, Ronald, in Kansas City so that he can meet you, and let your wife know when you will arrive. I have his phone number from our files." He paused and looked at me. "Is that okay?"

"It's better than that, it's perfect," I said with gratitude.

"But there is one small problem," David cautioned. "Air France doesn't land in Kinshasa, so you'll have to take the ferry across the river to Brazzaville. The first ferry will leave Kinshasa about 7:00 A.M. from the dock. Be there by 6:00. There will be a big crowd trying to cross. Do you know where the dock is?"

I didn't, but Tina said the driver for the Mission House did know and could get me there by 6:00. David handed me the tickets and said there would be an airport bus at the dock where the ferry tied up to unload on the Brazzaville side of the river. He gave me two ten-dollar bills for possible expenses in New York, wished me well, and left.

I hardly slept that night. At 5:15, I had a cup of coffee and a piece of toast. At 5:45, I headed for the dock. A crowd had already gathered there. The Congolese are known for their aggressiveness in pushing and shoving in crowds to get where they want, and I was prepared to do my share of pushing and shoving to get on the ferry.

A dozen soldiers got off a truck and spread themselves among the crowd. Mine was the only white face there. One of the soldiers walked up to me and pointed his gun at my suitcase. He said, "Drugs." I opened my suitcase and spread my arms wide in invitation. He dug through my things and finally lifted up a shirt and looked at it admiringly. Then he looked at me.

I smiled and nodded. He took the shirt and I took the suitcase and began worming my way through the crowd toward the gate between the dock and the ferry.

Another soldier stepped in front of me. I opened the suitcase and he took a shirt. I nodded and smiled. I picked up the suitcase again and pushed and shoved my way toward the gate. A third soldier stopped me and took his time going through my suitcase. He took a pair of khaki pants. Before I could close the suitcase, a fourth soldier stepped in front of me. It was 6:30 and the ferry was loading passengers. The crowd was moving slowly toward the gate. The fourth soldier took a pair of trousers and a shirt. I pushed between people and managed to work my way more vigorously toward the gate. I kept several people between me and two other soldiers, and thus was more protected from further hassles and delays. Finally I got to the gate and gave the attendant my ticket and boarded the ferry.

At ten minutes before 7:00 the gate was closed. Many people were left on the dock. The diesel engines started and in a few minutes we began moving upstream close to the shore. The rapids of the Congo River dropped one thousand feet from Kinshasa to sea level at Matadi, and the river carried four times more water than the Mississippi at New Orleans. I hoped those diesel engines were powerful enough to overcome the current, and I hoped that somebody had remembered to fill the fuel tanks this morning.

The ferry slowly turned away from the shore and into the current. Abruptly the direction of the ferry changed and we began drifting rapidly downstream. When the powerful current hit the ferry broadside, I thought we were going to tip over. "Oh God," I whispered. "Not now. I'm so close." But the throb of the engines increased until their roar was almost deafening. The ferry trembled before it straightened around with the prow angled 45 degrees upstream and the current forced the ferry slowly across the river. In fifteen minutes we docked on the Brazzaville side.

I found the bus, showed my passport, and gave the driver my ticket. We sat there until most of the seats were filled, then started for the airport. Every passenger had several large suitcases and one or two boxes, but I only carried one small suitcase and it was almost empty.

At the airport I followed the crowd into the terminal, showed my passport and ticket at the Air France counter, and checked my suitcase. I waited hours at the boarding gate. Finally, after showing tickets and passport again, we were allowed to board the plane. Shortly after takeoff I fell asleep. That night I was in Paris, and I dozed in the airport until my morning flight to New York.

Customs and immigration checks in New York were easy. I ate breakfast and drank some American coffee. I would call Winkie at her folks' house later because it was still early morning in Kansas. I took a taxi to the Methodist Board of Missions at 475 Riverside Drive. I couldn't wait any longer to talk to Winkie. I found a phone booth and dialed the long-distance operator.

The operator asked for the number I wanted to call, and I explained that I wanted to make a person-to-person call to Mary Ellen Youmans, collect. I gave her the number of my father-in-law, the retired colonel who had never wanted me to take his daughter to Congo. The operator asked my name so she could request whoever answered to pay for the call. I told her, but it made me feel cheap.

There was a long pause, and then I could hear the phone ringing. A male voice answered, "Hello."

The voice of the operator responded, "Is this 918-344-4148?"

"Yes, it is." It was the voice of my father-in-law.

"I have a long-distance call from New York for Mary Ellen Youmans. It is Roger Youmans calling collect. Will you accept the charges?"

I held my breath. There was a long pause, and a sound somewhat like a sob. Then Col. Stewart stammered, "My...my son...has come home!"

I half-choked and couldn't keep from crying. This man, a responsible father and career soldier, had called me his son! This colonel with lifelong discipline loved me, his delinquent son-in-law. A conscientious objector to war! I felt like the prodigal son returned. I wiped the tears away with the back of my hand.

"Yes. Yes. She is here. I accept the charges. Let me call her."

The line was quiet for nearly a minute. Then I heard Winkie's voice. "Roger? Is that you, Roger?"

"Yes. It's me. How are you, Winkie? And the children?"

"Everybody is fine. I just got a letter from you yesterday. It came as military mail. What has happened? Where are you?" Winkie choked up and I could hear her sobs of happiness and relief.

I explained that I had given that letter to an American sergeant to mail for me several weeks ago, but that now I was in New York and would be in Kansas City tomorrow afternoon. I told her the airline, flight number, and arrival time, and she assured me she and the children would be at the airport to meet me. We talked for several more minutes before I realized how much this call would cost her dad. Her last words were simply, "Thank you, Roger, for coming home. I need you so much."

Twenty-two
Starting Over

*"We are who we are in good measure because of what
we have learned and what we remember."*
—Dr. Eric Kandel, Nobel Laureate

I awoke in a strange bed with the sunlight streaming through a
window. It took me several minutes to remember the reception at
the airport the night before in Kansas City when I saw Winkie and
the children again. I had been too tired and had fallen asleep again
in their apartment while Winkie was putting the children in bed.

"Winkie?" I asked, still half-asleep.

She smiled. "I wondered if you would ever wake up." Then she
laughed, and her eyes glistened. "Would you like a cup of coffee?"

I rubbed my eyes, and nodded my head. The house was quiet,
and when I asked where the children were, she told me that it was
almost noon and the girls were in school.

I slowly realized that I had never been in this house before. We
had driven to Manhattan, Kansas, last night from the airport in
Kansas City, and this was the apartment Winkie and the kids had
been living in for the last few months while I had been in Kananga.
I sat up in bed and Winkie said, "Brush your teeth and take a

shower while I fix you some coffee and toast." She was smiling and began humming softly as she left the room.

As I walked into the kitchen, John and Rogé were at the table with cookies and milk. John looked at me as if he wondered who I was. A few months seems a lot longer when you're a kid than when you're an adult. I would give him a few minutes to get used to my being home again.

Grace and Joy got home from school in the afternoon and began shouting and yelling as soon as they saw me. "Daddy, Daddy!" I grabbed them both at the same time and hugged them as they laughed and kissed me. Then Emily, their cousin, bounded into my arms and all four of us fell down laughing and hugging.

The kids dropped their books and lunchboxes, grabbed a handful of cookies, and were back outside playing before I had adjusted to their presence. John was looking out the screen door and Rogé walked over to stand unsteadily beside him. I knelt behind John and put one arm gently around him and the other around Rogé. Neither one of them stiffened or withdrew. It was enough for now.

After the kids were all in bed that night, Winkie and I talked. Winkie's sister, Cathy, and her husband, Gerry, had given Winkie a thousand dollars when the little money we had in the bank had run out, and they had let her use one of their cars. That money was gone now. I had gotten almost a thousand dollars in back pay from the mission board in New York. Winkie wasn't as concerned about our lack of money as I was. She believed the hard times were over now that I was home.

I slept late again the next morning. The girls were at school and the boys were playing in the living room. Winkie had already cleaned up the kitchen. I staggered out of the bedroom still wearing my pajamas, and even after two cups of coffee, all I wanted to do was go back to sleep. I lay down on the couch and fell asleep feeling guilty that I hadn't come home two months earlier, and guilty because I had abandoned the medical work I was responsible for in Congo.

"Roger, Roger." It was Winkie waking me up. I had fallen asleep and it was one in the afternoon. "I have to go to the grocery store and I need some money for gas and for groceries." I looked at her, then at my watch. It was noon. "Come to the store with me, please."

As we walked down the aisle of the grocery store we talked about the last two months. It had been far harder on my family than I had realized. I had been sure that our relatives and friends would take care of Winkie and the children, and they did. The problem for Winkie was that she didn't know if I would ever come back to her again—she had only received one of my letters. She had been consumed with uncertainty about the future, plus lack of money and responsibility every day for four dependent children.

"Our children looked like ragamuffins, refugees from Congo," Winkie said and looking at me, added, "and right now, so do you." The best part was that she was laughing and teasing me.

That night after supper I told Winkie and the kids about that morning at the ferry in Kinshasa where I gave my clothes away, trying to get onto the boat to come home. In mock seriousness I told them that tomorrow after school we are going to go shopping for some new clothes for me. I was assailed by a chorus of "What about me?" and "Me too," from Grace and Joy, and we all laughed. I felt as though I was truly back home. "Of course, we all need some new clothes," I said, and Grace and Joy clapped their hands and danced around the room, laughing. That evening we told stories from our memories of Congo, about the dog, the airplane, Uncle Wes, and swimming down the Lotembi River.

Cathy's husband, Gerry, suggested that I call Dr. Allbritten, who was still chairman of the department of surgery at the medical center, and let him know I was back in town. Maybe he knew of a place that needed a surgeon. It was a reasonable thing to do, but I had to psych myself up before I could make that call. I hadn't really practiced American-style surgery since I had finished my training three years ago. On the other hand, Dr. Allbritten had trained me and thought I was an excellent resident. Besides, he would know all of the communities in Kansas that were looking for a surgeon. I called him.

Dr. Allbritten offered me an academic appointment and surgical privileges at the university hospital so I could begin a referral practice of surgery. Later on I would be appointed the director of the emergency service of that hospital with a salary four times higher than I had ever received before.

When we had a family meeting after supper, I told the children that I had a new job working in the medical center in Kansas City.

Grace quickly asked, "Are we going to move again, Daddy? That will mean another new school, won't it?" I shouldn't have been surprised. Every move has a profound impact on the children and they are always most concerned about how it will change their lives.

"The school may be close enough so that you won't need to ride the bus," Winkie said. "We'll have to see."

Before anything more could be said, Joy interrupted, "Are we moving tomorrow?" Winkie quickly reassured her that it would be a week or two.

The school was three blocks from our house. Grace and Joy quickly made new friends and walked to and from school every day. Grace won a contest at school and brought a puppy home from the litter of the teacher's dog. America is a wonderful place and our schools seemed almost like heaven on earth.

I had to remember that American medical care and hospitals were not run the same way that hospitals in Congo were, where relationships were more important than efficiency. Here performance was the top priority. I was eager for surgical patient referrals, and they came slowly. I focused on improving the quality of care given to critically injured patients, and I also wanted to demonstrate and measure the improvement. In cooperation with the chairman of orthopedics, we installed a video camera that would record the activity during the initial care of patients in the emergency room. This was an innovative step back in 1967, and no serious thought was given to the medical-legal ramifications of such recordings in Kansas.

After a week of these recordings, we showed a video of the management of one severely injured patient in our emergency room at our weekly in-service trauma conference. The hall was packed with nearly two hundred doctors and medical students. Most of those in attendance had worked in the emergency room at some time. Everyone could see the mistakes recorded in video. It was awful—confusion and delays, somebody stepping on the oxygen tube, somebody else on the suction tube while the anesthesiologist was trying to clear the blood out of the patient's mouth. The EKG changed dangerously, and the intern couldn't get an IV started quickly. The audience sat in stunned silence after the showing.

The staff had not realized how poor the performances of their interns and nurses sometimes were in the emergency room in the first few minutes of a major trauma resuscitation. They quickly gave their support to rapid improvement in the training of emergency care personnel and made emergency care a priority for the resident doctors. Higher standards were quickly established and additional personnel were recruited. Attention to the details of quality care rose sharply. I don't intend to imply that the care provided by the university's ER when I first started there was worse than any other ER in the city. On the contrary, it was significantly better, but in 1967 emergency care was a neglected area of medicine in America. During the next two years I had the opportunity to survey the emergency rooms of all twenty-eight hospitals in the city.

Dr. Richard Brose was recruited from the University of Pennsylvania to work with me to improve the entire system of emergency medical care in Kansas City. A citywide emergency-care improvement plan was developed and implemented with the cooperation of every emergency room, fire department, and police department in each of the governing jurisdictions of the metropolitan area. We sent each medical student out with an ambulance at least once so they could appreciate the skills needed at the scene of an accident and understand the difficulties faced by emergency medical technicians and police. Our results were published and appreciated.

About 2:00 A.M. one night a woman was admitted on my surgical service with an infected gallbladder with stones. In the operating room I removed her gallbladder and wanted to take an X-

ray (cholangiogram) to be sure there were no stones in the common bile duct, but the radiology technician could not be located. After repeated paging for the technician without any response, I broke scrub and brought the portable machine used for such X-rays into the operating room and took the X-ray myself while my resident injected the dye. The X-rays showed that there were no stones in the common duct, so I re-scrubbed and closed the incision. As the patient was leaving the operating room, the X-ray technician arrived.

He had been tied up in the delivery room when I called, and came as soon as he finished. I thanked him a bit sarcastically, pointing out that he was too late to help. The X-ray I had taken was of good quality and my interpretation had been correct and the patient did well.

But the chairman of the radiology department criticized me for using equipment that only his personnel were authorized to use. I had overstepped the radiology department's jurisdiction. The matter ended in a standoff, and underlying hostility persisted. I thought I was a mature operating surgeon, defending my responsibilities to my patient, and the radiologist was only defending his turf. I did not like confrontation and was not happy with our strained relationship.

The volume of patients coming to our emergency room increased rapidly. We had resident doctors in five specialties— internal medicine, surgery, pediatrics, obstetrics/gynecology, and psychiatry—in the hospital day and night with a priority to see urgent patients in the emergency room. We also had several interns and fifteen medical students working in the ER area all day and rotating night duty seven days a week. All patients were to be seen by a nurse immediately upon arrival, by a physician within fifteen minutes, and if necessary, by an appropriate specialty resident within another twenty minutes.

The head nurse for our emergency service had been running the area for many years, even before I was a medical student, without much supervision. On several occasions she failed to follow the standard protocol that I had written in the *Emergency Service Manual*. The manual had been created in consultation with all of the clinical departments, and had been approved by the hospital administration. I asked that she be transferred to another area of the hospital. The director of nursing service challenged the transfer, but I persisted, and the hospital administration backed me. But the nurse whom I had transferred had been my friend for many years, and she felt that I had betrayed her. I lost her as a friend, and I also lost the support of the director of nursing services. I regretted the arrogant way I had handled the situation. I needed to improve my administrative skills and develop thicker skin. My role as an academic surgeon and as the emergency service director was going well, but I did not like the anger, defensiveness, and stress of interpersonal conflicts.

I enjoyed my comfortable lifestyle at home, and Winkie enjoyed and adapted well to her American suburban life. The girls were doing well in school and their brothers were happy, healthy kids. I had much more leisure time with my family than ever before, but my life lacked some of the intensity and significance that our life in Congo had provided. Perhaps I was still drawn by the overwhelming need for medical help in Congo, or maybe by the camaraderie we shared with the people who had worked in the hospital and in our home. We even seemed to be a more closely knit family while we were there. But perhaps that was only my imagination. I was restless.

Part III

The Kinshasa General Hospital

*"No matter how long the night,
the day is sure to come."*

—Congolese proverb

Twenty-three
The Impossible Dream

"Art is long, life is short, judgment difficult,
opportunity fleeting."
—Johann Wolfgang von Goethe

I ignored the letter that came in the autumn of 1969. Dr. Bill Close, the surgeon I had met in Kinshasa just after Winkie and the family left for America, wanted to visit me to talk about Congo and a "wonderful opportunity" to return to Congo and teach Congolese doctors. I didn't respond to the letter, but I thought about it. His proposal sounded like wishful thinking to me.

I would have loved to work with Congolese doctors when I was at Wembo Nyama. I knew Winkie didn't want to ever go to Congo again, and I enjoyed what I was doing at the medical center, even though I didn't get into the operating room as often as I would have liked. I had a specialist in internal medicine as my assistant director of emergency service now, and I expected to do more surgery.

A few months later I received a telephone call from Bill. He was in New York and wanted to come to Kansas City in two days and talk. He was asking permission to visit our family. I told him he was welcome, but I wasn't interested in going to Congo myself. He came anyway.

Winkie answered the door, and there stood Dr. Close. "Good afternoon," he said deferentially. "You are Mrs. Youmans, I presume."

"Yes, I am. And you must be Bill Close," Winkie said warily, taken aback by Bill's courtliness. "Won't you come in, please? Roger is expecting you."

Bill came in, greeted me warmly, and gave me a firm handshake with the comment that I looked more rested than when he last saw me in Kinshasa. Then Bill turned toward Winkie and took both of her hands in his and looked into her face. "You have an extraordinary husband, Mrs. Youmans, and now I am so glad to meet you."

He referred to our experience in Wembo Nyama, and mentioned the hospital at Sona Bata. He was kindly and expressed interest in our family in a dignified and polite way. But I was suspicious, and didn't want to say anything that would suggest any interest in Congo. I sensed that he was on a mission now, and once the formalities were over and he was seated with a cup of coffee in one hand and a homemade cookie in the other, he came to the point.

"I don't think you ever visited inside the Kinshasa General Hospital, Roger, but it is a disaster that can't be described. President Mobutu has asked me to recruit a medical staff and clean up the mess and give his people a place to get decent medical care. I could certainly use your help."

I declined politely but thanked him for his thoughtfulness, and suggested that what most governments wanted, including the Congo government, was more money so they could do things themselves in the way they wanted. I had no doubt that the Kinshasa General Hospital needed a lot of help, even though I had never been on any of the wards.

"Of course they need money," Bill said emphatically, "but people who think more money will automatically improve medical care are part of the problem. Such people need to be replaced." Bill didn't seem to have any difficulty being blunt.

I didn't believe that any American would be allowed to fire a

Congolese doctor or nurse in Congo, no matter how incompetent he or she might be. But Bill insisted that President Mobutu loved his people so much that he had given Bill the authority to do whatever was necessary to improve the hospital. "The General Hospital doesn't cure disease," Bill insisted, "it causes disease. I worked there as a surgeon for over a year. It was bad then, but it is even worse now.

"The president knows quality, Roger, and he knows that the Kinshasa General Hospital is not quality. Patients just go there to die. It's filthy. The employees eat the food they're supposed to give to patients. The foreign doctors who are supposed to direct patient care don't even see the patients. They just leave the nurses on their own. It's terrible!"

It sounded so bad I couldn't really believe it. I had worked in rural mission hospitals in Congo where salaries were low, medicine was scarce, and the patient's family provided the meals, but the nurses didn't steal food or medicine at those hospitals, and the doctors saw the patients regularly. An American would think those bush hospitals were awful, but patients did pretty well there. I doubted if Bill was in a position to judge fairly.

"The patients and their families ought to complain," I said.

Bill scoffed. "Complain? Complain to whom? The doctors and administrators already know what is happening, and they don't care."

The situation sounded hopeless. I knew that without capable administration and honesty nothing much could be done to help the patients. I asked Bill what he thought he, one person, could do in such a situation, and I noticed Winkie out of the corner of my eye signaling, *No!* I was showing too much interest. We sat quietly for several moments.

Bill finally broke the silence. "I wouldn't touch it, Roger, but the president gave me authority to get rid of any employee who wouldn't work or who stole. But I need some doctors like you to help me. The president will provide all the money we need. He is committed to helping the people."

I laughed in spite of myself. "He gave you, an American, the authority to get rid of the Congolese doctors and nurses who don't show up for work or aren't honest?"

"I can't fire them, but I can have any of them transferred to some other place," he said good-naturedly. I thought he was enjoying my incredulity and what he thought was my naiveté. His boyish smile and laughing eyes were telling me, *Hey, there's no problem.*

Maybe Bill did have such authority from Mobutu. If he could pay the nurses and doctors regularly, many of them might want to work harder. But the Congo government had repeatedly promised to pay salaries regularly, and seldom did. I thought Bill's confidence in the president was misplaced. Mobutu was a dictator. He sounded more naive than me.

"They will learn to give better treatment to patients if they have respect for those who teach them," Bill said. "That's why I'm here asking you to help, Roger. I know how you worked at the Sona Bata Hospital. You're the kind of doctor we need at the General Hospital. I need you to work with me, and to help me find other docs like yourself."

His praise of me seemed excessive and I reacted with skepticism. I wouldn't encourage an American doctor who didn't know tropical medicine and French to go to Congo, and I probably wouldn't encourage them to go to Congo now, anyway. I really didn't see how I could be of any help to Bill. I shook my head.

Bill persisted. He told me that there were some American doctors who had worked in Congo but had to leave and return to America because of the health or education needs of their families. He said these doctors said they would return if their families could be well cared for. There was already an American School in Kinshasa, he said and there will soon be a dozen American doctors there who were specialists. Looking me in the eye, he said, "I want you to come and be the chief of staff at the hospital, Roger."

I squirmed with discomfort. I thought about the students and resident doctors I was training right now at the University of Kansas, who had expressed an interest, even a desire, to help people in Congo. They had no idea how hard it was just to survive there.

"There are lots of young American doctors," Bill said, "who want to treat patients who are seriously sick, but who could be saved with good, unsophisticated medical care." Bill seemed to know what I was thinking, because he added, "They're idealistic. They don't have to be religious fanatics to have a mission in life. Help me find some of those guys."

I didn't respond.

"Forget the formal education stuff," Bill continued. "Orient the American doctors to Congo and show them how old-fashioned compassion, good judgment, and a few modern medicines can work, and we'll save thousands of lives. Belgians speak French and they know tropical medicine, but many of them don't give a damn. They don't have compassion or the work ethic we need. We need American doctors."

I was skewered by his insights and words, even though I knew he was exaggerating the Belgians' lack of care. I had known a number of Belgian doctors who were superior physicians.

"I couldn't ask any missionary doctors already in Congo to leave the hospital where they are already working to come help us in Kinshasa," I said defensively. I noticed Winkie wince, and realized that I had said "I," and "us."

"You tell me what you need, Roger, and I can get it for you."

Winkie's face blanched. No, I wouldn't subject Winkie to Congo again, and Bill was acting as though I had already agreed. Bill's promises seemed so exaggerated that I didn't think I could trust him. Nobody could provide the things that Bill was promising, could they?

There was a silence, then Bill continued. "I'll leave a contract here for you and your family, Roger. Twenty-five thousand a year plus housing and a car, for two years. You and Winkie think about it. Sign it and mail it to me tomorrow or whenever you decide. You want to help the Congolese people. Here's a golden opportunity that you will probably never see anywhere else, ever again. The sick people in Congo need doctors like you. You can guarantee the security of the doctors who join you, and security for their families, too. Their housing area will be fenced in, the gate locked, and reliable guards on duty. I have the president's assurance on all of this, or I never would have come to Kansas City to ask you to leave the situation you have here."

I glanced at Winkie again, and she gave me a "don't do it" look. "Thank you, Bill, for remembering me," and I stood up as I continued, "and for coming all this way to offer me a job like this. It would be a challenge, maybe an overwhelming challenge. I know the people of Congo are living in desperate poverty and terrible sickness, but I don't believe that even President Mobutu has enough money, or the will, to do all the things at the General Hospital that we have been talking about. It would take years, maybe generations, to train Congolese doctors and nurses in both medical techniques and compassion. And because of their deep tribal prejudices it would probably take a lot longer than that. The problems are overwhelming."

"Exactly, Roger. We will recruit some bright young doctors who want to make a difference, like the ones you've been training here in Kansas City. Only men of faith like you would believe that God could give the strength and wisdom for such a challenge."

I had never heard him talk about "faith" or "God" before. I suspected it was a gimmick, to use religious words to sway my decision. He seemed like a smooth-talking and tough-minded realist now, with a political or economic angle he was working in Congo. I doubted if I could even work with him. But if Mobutu gave even half the authority and money Bill expected, maybe we could shape up the hospital and be a blessing to thousands, maybe millions, of people.

I was ambivalent, and ready to dismiss it all. Such an effort couldn't possibly be sustained long enough to be effective, and I didn't believe Mobutu was sincerely interested in medical care for the Congolese. It was just another impossible dream. But, what if...

Bill broke the silence. "I've already set up a special organization called FOMECO (Fond Medical de Congo), and its purpose is to carry out the improvement of healthcare in Kinshasa first, then the entire country. We will start small, Roger, but Mobutu is already building thirty new houses for the doctors, and I already have over a million dollars in the FOMECO bank account in Belgium. Congo has a lot of minerals, and the profits are going to the government now, not to the Belgians. Some of that money will be used to help the Congolese. I know Mobutu well, and he will put whatever we need into FOMECO whenever we need it."

Bill gave me a stamped and addressed envelope with the contract inside. We shook hands. He conveyed his wife's greetings to Winkie, and thanked her for her hospitality. He was very gracious.

"Bill, do you remember the first time I met you at the Mission

House in Kinshasa back in '67?" I asked as we stood by the door.

"Sure I do. Why?"

"Do you remember telling me not to worry about those Katanga soldiers up in Kisangani that rebelled and were about to start south toward Katanga? You said they were 'taken care of.' What did you mean by that?"

"Yeah, I remember that. I just meant that they had changed their minds and surrendered to Mobutu's officers in Kisangani. They were put under arrest for a few weeks. Why?"

"It doesn't matter now," I answered. "It's just that you didn't explain back then when I asked you what you meant."

"Well, Mobutu has the whole country under control now, including the Belgians who are still there. He wants to give good medical care to his people, and we can help him do that."

As soon as he was gone, Winkie looked me full in the face and said she didn't leave anything in Congo, and there was nothing there she wanted. "I mean it, Roger. You remember the long hours and frustrations of an even smaller hospital." She paused but I didn't say anything, so she continued, "You know as well as I do that Mobutu is a dictator and will do whatever it takes to stay in power. Even if he were to give Dr. Close everything he promised, and you know he won't, we might find ourselves in Congo with no money and no way to get out. Think about your children, Roger."

She was right, of course. It would be foolish for us to even think about returning to Congo. But we thought about it anyway.

Winkie understood my fascination with the possibilities to be found in FOMECO. It was part of my unfinished childhood dream, and maybe even a kind of penance for leaving Congo the last time—especially now that I knew that there had never been any real danger from the soldiers at Kisangani. Would I have left Congo so abruptly and returned to my family if I had known the military crisis was over?

In the next several weeks Winkie reminded me several times that the natives in Africa weren't the only black people who were facing hard times and injustice. During the late sixties black Americans were involved in peaceful marches and rallies, and some not-so-peaceful race riots in our cities. The Black Panthers were violently confronting the white establishment. Martin Luther King had been assassinated. Robert Kennedy was dead. Voter registration programs and the nonviolent confrontations of the NAACP had been met with violence and murder.

Winkie and I were sympathetic, but only marginally involved in the struggle for justice for the blacks in America, mostly through our church organizations. Bob Williams, one of my college fraternity brothers who now lived in Kansas City, spent time with me sharing about the need for our active participation in the struggle for racial justice. He was more active than I, but he seemed to understand how I recoiled against the confrontational style and violence of the activists. Lavannes Squires, another fraternity brother and my former roommate, was now in the banking business and not involved in the violence of the civil rights movement. Yet the murder of Martin Luther King had caused him to have doubts about the true intentions of the white community.

But it was Bob who was really angry at society and whites, though he always excluded me from his anger. Mostly he was angry at the whites who owned the drug store where he worked, because black employees were paid lower salaries than whites for the same work. When layoffs occurred, the blacks always went first. His pain was based on reality. I told him about the needs of the Congolese and about the General Hospital in Kinshasa. Bob was interested when I said that I might help Bill recruit Americans to work there. He wanted to go as a pharmacist. We were still *brothers*.

Winkie did not want to put our children through another move, and definitely not a move back to Congo, even if it was to a big city with an American School. She didn't want to risk our being separated again. She remembered the loneliness and helplessness at Wembo Nyama and the uncertainty generated by an unstable government. I shared her concern, but in my heart there remained a growing remnant of empathy, a residual desire to help the people suffering in Congo. Bill's impossible dream, combined with Bob's interest in going to Congo with me, gave substance to the question in my mind. Should I go back to Congo a third time—and take my family with me?

When I talked to my associates at the medical center about possibly going to Congo again, their responses were either, "Why would anyone do that?" or "You mean for a week or two, don't you?"

Finally, after several weeks, I signed the contract with FOMECO, but I didn't mail it. If it were ever to be mailed, Winkie would have to mail it. I put the signed contract in the envelope and placed it back on the piano. I told Winkie that she could throw it away if she wanted.

She agonized for a week. Then one day she said to herself and to John and Rogé, who were watching her, "We might just as well die in Congo as in America." Then she mailed the envelope. She had decided to stay with me no matter where I went or what I did. And she would bring our children. We would go together.

The night she told me that she had mailed the contract, I felt like celebrating. It was as if she shared the "impossible dream" even though she knew as well as I did, and probably even better, the frustrations and anxieties that would stem from following that dream. It seems strange to me now that I was so eager to return to Congo, so sure of what we as a family should do.

Twenty-four
Mobutu's Kinshasa, 1970

*"A monkey wanted to cross the river, but he
couldn't swim. He asked the crocodile if he would
carry him across the water, but not eat him. "
Of course I will. Get on my back."
In the middle of the river the crocodile rolled over
and began to eat the monkey. "But you promised
not to eat me," cried the monkey.
"Of course I did," replied the crocodile, "
but this is what crocodiles always do."*
—African Folk Tale

Confirmation of my employment by FOMECO came quickly
after our application was mailed. I reserved our airplane tickets and
informed FOMECO of the date and number of our flight. I
completed my contract with the medical center in June, sold our
car, rented out our suburban house, stored most of our belongings,
and packed the rest in suitcases. Our family and friends took us to
the airport, celebrating the start of a potentially large-scale

humanitarian medical mission to Congo. When we arrived at the airport in Kansas City, the Pan American ticket agent told me that FOMECO had not yet paid for our tickets to Congo. I was deeply embarrassed and angry that I had been so gullible and had believed Bill's "impossible dream" pitch.

We had already burned all of our bridges behind us. Dr. Friesen, professor of surgery at the medical center, invited us to stay in his house while we figured out what had happened. It required two days and many local and international telephone calls before we learned that Dr. Close's administrative assistant, Mr. Troger, had arranged for all international FOMECO flights to be made on Belgium's Sabena Airlines. I had not been informed of this, but I now complied, grudgingly, and the new tickets were immediately prepared for us on Sabena. We left the next day.

Our arrival in Kinshasa was very different from any of our previous experiences. As we stepped off the plane, Mr. Troger, his wife, and several Congolese greeted us on the tarmac. They took our luggage and escorted us rapidly through passport and health checks, picked up our suitcases, and led us past customs without a search. We were escorted to a new Peugeot that took us to our new home on Binza Hill.

This was an exclusive neighborhood with huge old mansions, all of them surrounded by walls eight feet high and built by the Belgians but now occupied by Congolese. We could see the green tile roof of our home looming above the walls topped with barbed wire and broken glass. The yellow stucco house was two stories high and had several garages. Mr. Troger drove up the short driveway to the locked iron gate and honked the horn. A barefoot sentinel dressed in dirty khaki trousers and a torn T-shirt ambled toward the gate, fumbled with the lock, and finally swung the gate open. The sentinel locked the gate behind us.

"Is this where we will live?" I asked, awed by the size of the house.

Mr. Troger grinned. *"Oui,* this is your new house. You like it?" His Belgian English was clearly understandable, but it definitely did not sound American.

"It's so big," I answered. "Who takes care of this yard?" I swept my hand in an arc to indicate the land surrounding the house.

Mr. Troger laughed. "The gardener will do it."

The sentinel carried our bags into the house. Two marble steps led up to the front porch and a wall of eight-foot-tall doors and windows—all covered with re-bars to prevent thieves from breaking in. The living room had the air of an empty museum, with marble floors and a marble staircase going to the second floor. The room was at least thirty feet long and twenty-five feet wide, with a fourteen-foot ceiling, and there were rich crimson draperies covering the tall windows. The dining room was cavernous and the sound of our footsteps echoed. The kitchen was large, with tiled counters and a double sink. An electric refrigerator and gas range were the only appliances.

"What do you think?" Mr. Troger asked. "It is okay, yes?"

I was awe-struck. We went upstairs and discovered three huge bedrooms and a large bathroom, all with fourteen-foot ceilings.

"There is another apartment on the other side of that wall," Mr. Troger explained, pointing to the solid wall on the south side of every room. "It's like yours, but the redecorating is not finished yet. The other American surgeon will live there. Dr. Burrus, he comes soon."

The sentinel had deposited all of our bags in the house and was standing outside by the gate. "Mr. Lacher will bring you your car tomorrow," Mr. Troger said. "My wife put some food in the kitchen and dishes in the cabinets. Rest well. I'll see you in the morning." He shook hands with Winkie and me, waved, and drove off. We were now the guests of FOMECO, funded by President Mobutu.

We wandered around the house in a daze for a few minutes, and then Winkie began fixing some supper for us. There was irradiated milk, butter, sugar, bread, cheese, instant coffee, and a round box of Quaker Oats in the kitchen. We saved the oats for breakfast. Supper was simple, but we were tired and not particularly hungry after the long trip from Kansas City. We bathed the children, read them stories, and put them to bed.

An hour after we had gone to bed, I was awakened by screams from the room where Grace and Joy slept. I jumped out of bed, fumbled for the flashlight, and stumbled into the hallway.

I found the light switch in Grace's room with the help of the flashlight. Grace and Joy were both standing on Joy's bed, screaming and pointing at Grace's bed.

"What's the matter?" I asked. Then I saw the biggest cockroach that I had ever seen. It was at least four inches long, and it was sitting insolently on Grace's pillow. I took the girls by their arms and guided them into our bedroom.

Returning to the girls' room, armed with a shoe, I attacked the cockroach. He escaped onto the floor where I was able to hit him with the shoe. I cleaned up the mess with toilet paper and flushed it down the toilet, then cleaned my shoe.

It took almost half an hour to assure the girls that everything was now safe.

Later Rogé woke up crying, and I heard men shouting. Light was pouring through our room. I sat up rubbing my eyes, and then realized that it was morning and that the workmen had arrived to continue painting the outside of the house. John called for his mother between sobs. We got up, washed in cold water, dressed, and had our Quaker Oats and coffee for breakfast.

In due time Mr. Troger arrived and took us to the immigration office where we registered and began the process of converting our tourist visas into renewable, two-year resident visas. Then Mrs. Troger took Winkie to the grocery stores while I stayed with the children and explored our new house and yard. Congolese workmen continued painting the outside window frames and shutters on our side of the house while others worked on the inside of the apartment next to ours.

About two in the afternoon all of the work on our house stopped and the workers left. It was the end of their workday. A short time later some Congolese workers arrived in our neighbor's yard, on the other side of our wall, and began hammering and sawing, apparently working on a house that they owned or hoped to own. They also had a large garden of corn, squash, and other vegetables that I couldn't identify. Their garden occupied more than half an acre of their yard. They paid no attention to me or to the children.

Mr. Lacher brought our new car to us in the late afternoon. All the documentation had been done on the car, which had a sticker in the front window with a red cross that identified me as a doctor, and identified the car as belonging to FOMECO. It was ours to use however we pleased. Winkie fixed a great supper and we all slept soundly that night.

The next few days were spent investigating the American School of Kinshasa and making arrangements for all four of our children to attend. Little Rogé was old enough to attend the kindergarten. Winkie did more shopping. We met several other American families. Some were with the U.S. Air Force, others with our embassy. Grace had a classmate whose father was an American businessman directing the construction of an electric power line that was to stretch from the Inga power station on the Congo River below Kinshasa all the way to the copper refining plants in Katanga nine hundred miles away. Other classmates were children of missionaries.

A couple of days after our arrival in Kinshasa, Bill took me to see his clinic. He was the director of the Medical Bureau of the Presidency, and his medical office was in one of the large new buildings on Mount Galiema, inside the presidential compound. In addition to being President Mobutu's personal physician, Bill also took care of the medical problems of the elite paracommando guards who were based on Mount Galiema. There was an X-ray machine, a small laboratory, and a cardiac defibrillator in his office, which was as clean and well equipped as any medical office in America. Bill had an American surgeon and a Congolese doctor working for him in the clinic. The American doctor was retiring at the end of August to return to America, but the Congolese doctor would stay on. Bill invited me to take the American doctor's place and see private patients with him in the office, in addition to working in the General Hospital. Mrs. Troger, Bill's nurse, spoke excellent English. It was an attractive place to work, but I didn't come to Congo to find an attractive place to work. We stopped by Bill's house, located between his office and the president's house, so he could introduce me to his wife, Tine, before he drove me back down the hill to the hospital.

The following week Bill asked me if I would go up to Kisangani (formerly called Stanleyville) on Friday to meet President Mobutu and his *bureau politique* aboard the president's boat. I didn't want to meet a bunch of would-be politicians. I wanted to get started doing surgery and taking care of patients in the Kinshasa General Hospital and wanted Bill to deal with the politicians and the government.

When Bull Elephants Fight

Bill was a smooth talker and he knew the president and the important Congolese who might be involved with the hospital. He laughed at my reluctance and concerns, reassuring me that he would take care of the politicians. He wanted me to take care of the patients and to ensure that the quality of the medical care provided by the staff didn't get diluted by the huge number of patients to be cared for. He told me he had already arranged for the best Congolese doctor, who was also the most honest administrator in the country—a Dr. George Bazunga—to be the hospital director/administrator.

The meeting with the president was special because Bill wanted the president and the Conseil to know who I was. If I needed anything, I was to just tell Dr. Bazunga or Bill and it would be provided. "You are only responsible to me," Bill said. He respected my aversion to politics, but reminded me that we were going to need a lot of money to improve and run the hospital, and we had to work within the way the Congolese think and work. Although such social affairs, especially in French, would make me uncomfortable, it would be important for the Congolese authorities to have confidence in me. Bill made the arrangements for my flight to Kisangani and for a berth on the president's boat.

I wondered what Bill meant by the phrase "the way the Congolese work," but I didn't ask. I doubted if Mobutu's confidence in me was really important as long as the president had confidence in Bill, and Bill had confidence in me. But I also wondered why Bill, a white man, had such a privileged relationship with Mobutu? I didn't have any satisfactory answers.

A Congo military plane flew me to Kisangani on Friday. Our flight path provided me with an overview of the Congo River, which I had never seen before. Beyond Mbandaka the river curved east until we came to Kisangani. Navigation by landmarks on the ground, specifically the river and the towns along its banks, was safer and more reliable than flying over hundreds of miles of rain forest. Bill met me at the airport and flew me in a military helicopter to the president's boat, which was tied up to a private dock on the river. He quickly introduced me to a half-dozen Congolese politicians who were part of Mobutu's *bureau politique,* and had my bag taken to my berth. I told Bill afterward that I didn't understand the names of the various members of the *bureau politique* and I certainly would not recognize their faces if I saw them again, but Bill brushed my concern aside, saying these men weren't important anyway.

I was taken to the president's suite almost immediately after arriving. The rooms were crowded with overweight Congolese men enjoying cocktails and jovial banter as they socialized with each other. The trim, tall figure of President Mobutu with his leopard-skin hat made a sharp contrast to the others. Bill and I were the only two white faces in the crowd. Mobutu noticed us immediately and moved toward us, carrying a champagne glass in his left hand.

"Mr. President," Bill began in fluent French, "I would like to present to you my cherished colleague and the director of the medical staff for FOMECO. He will assist me in recruiting our medical staff and improving the care of the Congolese citizens in the General Hospital. The Professor, Doctor Youmans."

I couldn't help smiling at the flowery introduction. President Mobutu also smiled, the corners of his eyes crinkled, and his perfectly white teeth gleamed in the artificial light of the cabin. He apparently didn't smoke. He extended his hand, and I responded with a firm handshake.

His brown eyes were alert and seemed to be laughing. "You are American," he said in English. "I am glad to have another American doctor to help Bill." He looked at Bill and began speaking in Lingala.

Bill answered in Lingala and laughed. Then he looked at me and switched to English. "He knows that you have been a missionary in Wembo Nyama and in Sona Bata, so he asked if you would like a drink or are you still a Protestant missionary?" He paused a moment, then added, "Catholic missionaries usually drink, but Protestant missionaries usually don't."

I was surprised that President Mobutu knew anything about me, and that he had a sense of humor. "I am a Methodist surgeon, and I am most pleased to be here," I answered in French. "I hope that I can be of help to your people by my service in the hospital, but I do not drink. Thank you very much, Mr. President."

Mobutu turned aside quickly to shake the hand of a Congolese man who had walked up and greeted him. President Mobutu clapped him on the shoulder, laughing freely. They exchanged comments in Lingala, and the other man walked away. I was struck by Mobutu's height; he was over six feet tall, much taller than most Congolese men. I was even more impressed by the grace of his movements and the ease with which he could talk to three people in three different languages about three different things, all in the course of two minutes.

"Do you play checkers, Doctor?" he said to me.

"Only a little," I answered, "but Bill told me you are a master at checkers and you play very fast."

"Yes, but Bill takes much time. Life is too short to waste. I prefer fast decisions," he added. "Perhaps we will play fast checkers sometime, yes?"

"I would like to," I said. But President Mobutu had already turned away to greet somebody else, and the two men took a few steps away from Bill and me and engaged in a serious discussion in Lingala.

I stood at the side of the room and watched President Mobutu move from one guest to another, conversing freely and laughing gently with each of the men. He shook hands, occasionally slapping a shoulder, often engaging two or three men in conversation at the same time. He appeared relaxed, confident, and genuinely interested in each person. If he knew and remembered as much about each of them as he seemed to know about me, he must have an extraordinary memory, and if he was as ruthless as everyone but Bill thought he was, he could be a very dangerous man. I was comfortable in his presence, but hoped he would never ask me to play checkers with him. This was not my kind of crowd.

I didn't attend the subsequent meetings on the boat, and I seldom saw President Mobutu after that first brief encounter. The general atmosphere aboard the boat was that of a party with considerable drinking. I had a private berth where I stayed much of the time, reading *Black Skin, White Masks* by Frantz Fanon, while Bill socialized and attended meetings. He was very much an extrovert. I wished I could be as much at ease in social situations as Bill and the others were, but I was not only shy, I was also unsure of my competence in French after not using it for three years. As for Lingala, I knew only a few phrases.

Several days later I visited the Kinshasa General Hospital. I was curious. I tried to look over the walls, but I couldn't see anything but the rusted metal roofs of the buildings. Dozens of men stood in the street outside the gate, talking with each other and casually watching me, and four women sat on the curb with large pans of bananas, pineapples, peanuts, and mangos between their feet. Plastic bags had blown into the mounds of garbage that were piled against the outside of the hospital walls. Signs painted on the wall warned people not to urinate there, but I saw two men ignoring the signs. The air was sultry, and heavy with the stench of rotting food. A vendor of boiled cassava wrapped in leaves leaned on his cart. Patrons chewed what they had purchased while they talked, laughed, and occasionally spat on the ground. Halfway around the outer wall was a park with a dilapidated sign identifying it as a zoo. A collection of cages was overgrown with weeds, but the zoo wasn't totally abandoned. Three crocodiles lay in the muddy water of a small lagoon, partially submerged like logs in a swamp.

A small Congolese man in a ragged uniform, whom I assumed was the keeper, opened the gate and slowly walked inside of the fence surrounding the crocodiles and the lagoon. He carried half of a goat loosely tied to the end of a fifteen-foot pole as he walked slowly toward the motionless crocs, stopping about fifteen feet from the first one. The keeper slowly swung the piece of goat on the end of the pole until it was three feet from the motionless croc. Suddenly there was a violent splashing, and the croc leaped from the water, clamped his jaws on the goat, and fell back into the water while swallowing the meat. He then lay there motionless as before. It happened so fast I wasn't sure what had actually occurred. The waves in the water became ripples, and then the water was still. The keeper walked slowly out of the enclosure. The flies buzzed around my face, the mid-day sun burned down on the rippling circles of muddy water, and the three motionless crocs.

The keeper returned with another piece of goat on the pole and approached the second crocodile. I watched closely as the second croc changed from a half-submerged log into a thrashing mouth with huge crooked teeth, snatched the goat, and fell back into the water. It all happened in less than a second. I watched the third croc take a chunk of goat just as the first two had. What might happen to me if some dark night I walked around the outer wall of the hospital and the crocs had gotten through that fence? I shivered in the hot sun.

I went back to my car, shaken by what I had just seen. I wondered if the harmless-looking General Hospital might also surprise me with unexpected quickness.

The next day Dr. Close took me on a brief tour of the hospital, and introduced me to several of the nurses. He walked jauntily through the front gate with his usual confidence, casually greeting the sentinels in Lingala. Inside the walls there were rows of single-story pavilions on each side of a covered walkway running six hundred feet from the front gate to the far wall. We didn't see any doctors working except Dr. Paul Beheyt, a Belgian cardiologist, who was gentle and gracious, and spoke very good English.

The fetid smell of rotting food hung on the air inside the hospital walls as heavily as it had on the street outside, but was now mixed with the foul smell of backed-up sewers. Piles of garbage lay against the walls of several pavilions. Paint was peeling off the window frames and doors. Congolese patients and visiting relatives stood at the sides of the walkway and looked at us with blank, hopeless expressions. I noticed some fresh paint on several windowsills of one of the pavilions, and there was some construction going on near the wall at the end of another one.

Bill indicated the newly poured cement. "They're building the six new operating rooms and a doctor's lounge there. I have an engineer supervising some urgent repairs and painting," he added, pointing his chin toward some freshly painted window frames.

We entered the emergency room in Pavilion #2, where I saw two men in dirty uniforms and one woman in a much cleaner uniform. One of the men was entering the names of patients in a book, and the other was scolding a group of Congolese who had come in just ahead of us. One of the new arrivals had his left hand wrapped in a bloody green cloth. The woman in uniform, apparently the nurse in charge, was listening to a child's chest with her stethoscope. She looked up at us, then quickly pulled the stethoscope from her ears, and smiled in our direction.

"Bienvenu, mon docteur," she called.

Bill responded to her cheerful greeting in French with energy and enthusiasm. They had worked together ten years ago when Congo first became independent. It was during the time when Col. Mobutu and Dr. D'Arenberg had searched through the prisons of Kinshasa to identify and treat the medical problems of many of the high-profile prisoners, and Bill was working in the Kinshasa General Hospital. Col. Mobutu appreciated the way Bill treated patients and his confidence in Bill's courage, integrity, and judgment grew over time.

Later, Mobutu became the general in command of the Congo army, and eventually became the president of Congo. At that time he appointed Bill as his personal physician, and as the director of the Medical Office of the Presidency. Now Bill was the director of FOMECO and had the authority to hire and fire the personnel in the Kinshasa General Hospital, or at least to get them transferred.

The emergency room of this huge hospital was pitiful. There was no emergency equipment—no ambu bags, no suction machine, no defibrillator, and no electrocardiograph. I asked the nurse where the laryngoscope and endotracheal tubes were, and she said such things were in the operating room. I didn't see any thermometers or alcohol. They did have stethoscopes, one blood-pressure cuff, and a pan of surgical instruments soaking in a disinfectant solution. Two dead flies and three mosquitoes floated on the surface. I supposed that proved the solution was lethal.

In the holding room a dozen patients were lying on cots or on the floor. Another nurse's aide was scolding a semiconscious patient who was lying in the diarrhea that had just filled his pants. The odor was nauseating.

We left the ER in Pavilion #2 and stepped out onto the covered walkway just as a tropical rainstorm broke. It began with a flash of lightning followed almost immediately by a deafening clap of thunder and splashing drops of rainwater. A sudden blast of wind swept between the pavilions, bringing waterfall-like torrents of rain. Before the second bolt of lightning and roar of thunder came, shouting erupted as dozens of visitors in the area ran for cover, carrying various bundled belongings and covering their heads with their hands. Again and again the lightning and thunder pummeled us. The water arced off the roofs turning the puddles between each of the buildings into muddy lakes. It was impossible to carry on any conversation. Wet women and children lined the walkway trying to keep out of the rain and at the same time stay out of the way of the two white men. Those who couldn't push their way onto the covered walkway stood in the mud under the eaves.

In Pavilion #9 more than sixty patients wandered around or sat on their beds. Most of them were barefoot and had dirty and bloody bandages on some part of their bodies. A few of them were lying quietly on their beds, and they looked very sick.

A woman stood outside under the eaves trying to get a patient's attention inside. The patient walked over to the window and received a pan of rice covered with sauce, which was passed through a gaping hole torn in the window screen. The window screens on both sides of the pavilion all had huge holes torn in a bottom corner so that family members could pass plates of food into the patients.

We left the pavilion and toured the two operating rooms. In one room an operation was in progress. The second operating room served as a storage area for tables and for anesthetic machines that were probably no longer usable. The rain stopped almost as suddenly as it had started, and the silence was ominous. The sudden violence of the storm followed by eerie silence made me think again of the crocodiles at the zoo just outside the hospital walls; placid at first and then suddenly, devastatingly violent, followed quickly by peace that again seemed benign. Would Congo always be like this?

Bill nudged me to follow him.

"Are they all doctors?" I asked, gesturing toward the men standing in the light around the operating table.

"No, the one with his back to us is a scrub-nurse, and the one at the head is a nurse anesthetist. The anesthetist is good," Bill said. "We'll keep him. The other two guys don't know what they're doing. They'll have to go."

The magnitude of what FOMECO hoped to accomplish here

seemed patently impossible. Why would any of the employees, including the anesthetist, want to work harder and longer hours unless they were paid more, or motivated and inspired in some other way? I didn't know then that most of the employees had not been paid for months and some for over a year, because the government didn't have enough money. They hoped that some day their back pay would be given to them. In the meantime they would hang around and scrounge food from wherever they could, sometimes even from the patients. Why not hang around? There was no other work available in Kinshasa that paid a salary.

When Bill dropped me at our house, I noticed that our neighbors were working on their house, and that their hose was connected to our outside water hydrant. They were running our water onto their garden all night, every night. I had asked them to stop using our water, but they pretended not to understand. I called our sentinel over and explained that I was paying for the water, and that I did not want the neighbor's hose connected to our hydrant again. I removed the hose while the sentinel watched, and threw it over the wall into our neighbor's yard. The neighbor seemed surprised, and when I went to the wall to explain that I was paying for the water, they appeared not to understand.

"Do not run the water from my house into your garden," I shouted in French to the neighbors. "No more. Understand?"

They didn't understand. The next morning the hose was connected to our hydrant and it was watering our neighbors' garden and their construction site. I removed their hose and threw it back into their yard. I told the sentinel that if he saw the hose connected, he should turn it off and throw it back into the neighbors' yard.

Two days later, on a Sunday when our family returned from church, we found that our house had been broken into and our radio, tape recorder, and record player had all been stolen. We could live without them, and I knew that the police would be of no help in recovering them, so I didn't even waste a day filing a useless report at the police headquarters. Our sentinel did not see how anyone could have broken into our house except for the time when he was washing up in back of the house about nine in the morning. I thought about those crocodiles in the zoo.

Dr. George Burrus and his family moved into the other half of our huge duplex with their five children, and our two families quickly bonded. George had a warm, jovial personality and a quick sense of humor. He loved life and enjoyed playing with his children. He and his family had gone to India as medical missionaries years ago, but one of their children had died there, and so they had returned to America. He still had a tender spirit toward the sick and a genuine compassion for the poor people of the world, which he disguised with occasional gruffness. Dr. DeBakey in Houston had trained him in cardiac surgery. He had been a short-term missionary-surgeon at a little hospital at Boshwe, on the Kwilu River, when he'd met Bill, who told him about FOMECO and the General Hospital, and invited him to join us. George had been the only foreign doctor at his mission station, but he was willing to leave his assignment and join us in the General Hospital to do general surgery and share night calls with us.

The first day that his kids and our kids were all in school somebody broke into our house again, but we didn't have much for them to steal and we couldn't be sure whether anything had been stolen. I told George about the break-in and he talked with the sentinel. George had learned some Lingala words and he used them frequently when he was upset with a Congolese. He didn't know much French.

A few nights later George woke up in the night and saw somebody in his bedroom. The man ran away, and George chased him with a baseball bat, being careful not to follow too closely in case the intruder had a gun. The intruder escaped and our sentinel claimed that he had neither seen nor heard anything. The sentinel was fired and replaced.

A couple of mornings later George discovered that his car was missing. He had left it locked inside our walled and locked compound, and with a sentinel on duty. We reported the robberies and the stolen car to Dr. Close, who said he would take care of the matter. All of our sentinels were fired and new ones were hired, all through the agency of Dr. Close. From then on nobody used our water, and nobody stole anything from George or me again. I knew that the word had gone out that the president and his personal bodyguards, the paracommandos, would protect us. I liked the protection FOMECO and the presidency afforded us, but I was uncomfortable being so closely identified with the president. I had entered into an ambiguous relationship with the general population of Kinshasa, and with Bill and with the presidency.

In the small villages of Sona Bata and Wembo Nyama I had been safe, living and working among people who appreciated me, who wanted me to be in their midst. They wished me well. In Kinshasa, the teeming capital city, I would be appreciated within the confines of the hospital and the operating room, but in the city beyond the hospital walls I would become a white foreigner, rich and powerful, while they, the citizens, were poor, sick, hopeless, and desperate. Living in Kinshasa with its undercurrent of hostility, and working to change the huge General Hospital would be a new kind of challenge.

Twenty-five
A Cesspool of Sickness

"You are as young as your hopes,
and as old as your despair."

—Anonymous

On my first day at the General Hospital I was immersed in its sickness and apathy. Dr. Kennel, an American cardiologist who had just arrived, went to the hospital with me. He wanted to get acquainted with Dr. Beheyt, the English-speaking Belgian doctor I had told him about, and he planned to spend the day working with him.

I couldn't find any surgeons in the hospital, so I picked a surgical pavilion and began seeing the patients by myself. The young nurse on the ward seemed pleased and offered to help me. She gave me the patient charts, such as they were, but the charts were illegible and of almost no help.

"Dr. Makala is the surgeon for this pavilion," she told me, "and Dr. Mvunu works with him, but he is traveling." I remembered that "traveling" is a figure of speech. It didn't mean that he was literally traveling, but only that he was on leave. I asked if Dr. Makala would come to the hospital today, but the nurse didn't know.

When Bull Elephants Fight

Down the length of the pavilion's double row of beds, about thirty on each side, I could see more than twenty patients with pus soaking through their dressings. I had smelled the stench as soon as I entered the pavilion. I wasn't sure what to do, so I began by removing the putrid dressing from the first patient. He had an old fracture of the femur and a wound in the thigh that was infected. The pus from the wound dripped onto the floor when I removed the dressing. I asked for a clean pair of gloves.

"We don't have any gloves here," the nurse said. "You must get them from the operating room. But they may not have any either."

I should have anticipated this, but I was caught by surprise. I asked for some sterile water, alcohol, and gauze dressings.

The nurse returned after several minutes with a small brown bottle of alcohol, a fairly clean-looking washcloth, and a tin cup of water. Gloveless, I washed the pus from the skin and poured a little alcohol on the wound.

"Do you have some sterile dressings?" I asked.

"Yes," she answered in the way Congolese do when they want to please the questioner. Then she added that they used to have those things, but they are gone now.

"How do I dress this wound?" I asked.

She produced a pair of scissors, cut the dirtiest half of the dressing off, and handed the cleaner portion of the dressing back to me. I was appalled, but took it and covered the wound.

When I asked for adhesive tape, she said there was no tape. I tore the end of the dressing I had placed over the wound and tied the tails of the dressing around the patient's leg to hold it on. Chronic infection of the bone like this would need a surgical operation to clean out the dead tissue, and then a long course of antibiotics. "What antibiotics is this patient on now?" I asked.

"He is on penicillin, but his family stopped bringing it here for us to give him many weeks ago," she said. I looked at her in disbelief. "Doctor, if you can get these things for us we will be very grateful." She knew very well how patients should be treated, but did not have any way to do it.

"Do you have a culture report on this drainage?"

"A culture has not been ordered, Doctor."

"Do you have some place where I can wash my hands?" I asked.

She nodded and led me to the end of the pavilion where the makeshift nursing station was located. She pointed to a pan half-filled with water.

"Do you have any soap, or a towel?"

"The soap is finished," she replied. "Here is a towel."

She held out a very dirty, but dry towel for me to wipe my hands on after I had rinsed them.

I went to the operating room to get some sterile dressings and bandages, and I hoped that I might be able to get some adhesive tape and betadine or iodine solution for cleaning and dressing the other infected wounds.

"We don't have any bandages," the nurse in the operating room told me. I thought he had not understood my French, but when I repeated my request, he shrugged his shoulders. "The surgeon brings the dressings when we run out," he said.

"Where does the surgeon get the dressings?" I asked.

"I don't know." After a pause he suggested, "Maybe from the nuns in the delivery room. They always have bandages."

"Will you go get some for me now?" I asked.

"They won't give them to me. Maybe if you go ask, they will give some to you."

There were a lot of patients on this pavilion who needed dressings changed, and I was beginning to understand why they had not been changed more often. I went to the delivery room in the maternity pavilion to get some clean bandages from the nuns there. They were sympathetic. They knew how bad the care was on other pavilions. But they had none to spare.

"What can we do?" the sister said, shrugging her shoulders. "This is their hospital. We try to keep the maternity clean, which is the only place we work. It is very sad."

I was speechless and helpless. What on earth could I, or any surgeon, do in a hospital like this? They didn't cure disease here; they watched it spread.

After a brief silence, the nun spoke sympathetically. "A few Congolese nurses are capable and work hard, but salaries are always late and we are given no supplies. The cost of everything goes up, but salaries stay low. The Congolese get discouraged. Inflation is terrible." She shrugged her shoulders again. "And no hope," she added. "Here, I give you a little." The dressings were long strips of cloth, torn from bed sheets, and rolled up.

"Thank you, Sister," I said. "Excuse me, please, but do you happen to have a little piece of soap that I might have so that I can wash my hands?"

She beamed in amusement. "Certainly. We have plenty of soap. We don't even lock it up. After all, what could somebody do with soap that is bad?"

I forced a smile and accepted the dressings and the soap, and left. I was frustrated and angry about the conditions in the hospital, and impotent to change them. How could I work here under these circumstances?

Dr. Makala, the Congolese doctor for the pavilion, had just come onto the ward. He was a young, stocky man, probably only a year out of medical school. He gave me a broad, winsome grin as he introduced himself in broken English. His eyes danced with both amusement and pride. He could speak English even if the new Americans couldn't speak Lingala or French.

"Is this your pavilion?" I asked in English. I was so upset and angry about the pus-soaked bandages and infected surgical wounds that I couldn't think of how to express myself in French.

Dr. Makala answered in French, having understood my English, but not able to easily express himself in English. "I am the surgeon for this pavilion." He paused and waited, but I didn't say anything. I couldn't think of anything positive to say about this filthy place. Dr. Makala continued, "The nurses will not help. Look at the dirty dressings. I ask them to change the dressings, but they never do it. Everything gets infected. Now that you Americans have come, everything will get better, yes?"

I thought he was baiting me. Surely nobody could do much in this impossible situation. "Making things better will take a long time and a lot of money," I said as my anger subsided and my French returned. "More importantly, it will take some very capable and conscientious people."

Dr. Makala laughed a bit cynically. "I've been trying conscientiously for over a year, but the nurses won't work. Can you Americans bring us some good nurses?"

I assured him that we would bring some nurses and more

doctors from America, but made it clear that we wanted to keep all of the good, hard-working nurses and doctors here so we can make this a better hospital. He was interested in what I was saying, but his eyes looked at me skeptically. I didn't want to unnecessarily offend anyone, so I asked him if he could identify some of the doctors and nurses who come to the hospital early and work hard all day.

His eyes clouded and he looked at me as if I were naive and foolish. "There are no doctors in the world that do that," he said. "No doctors here, or at the university or anywhere else, do that. Especially if they are not paid."

I had wanted to stimulate him, not offend him. He was the only Congolese doctor who was here with me. I needed his cooperation and help. I looked down the line of sick patients. These patients had no influence over their future, and they had no advocate to speak for them, no way to change their wretched condition. I would become their advocate now. Bill would be their advocate, too, I hoped.

"Dr. Close will help with the administration and find some money to buy the essentials and to pay the salaries of the employees," I said, "and I will work with you and the nurses to keep these pavilions clean and clear up all of these infections." I waved my hand at the patients, who were all watching us as if their fate rested with us, and it did indeed. I asked him to take me around and tell me about his patients.

He gave me an ingratiating smile before addressing the nurse beside him. "Nurse, bring your charts and go with us and tell us how your patients are this morning."

"Excuse me, Dr. Makala," I apologized, "I neglected to introduce myself. I'm Dr. Youmans." I extended my hand and he shook it, grinning broadly.

"I know who you are, Doctor Youmani," he said, adding an extra syllable to my name, as most Congolese did. He continued, "You are welcome. I heard on the radio yesterday that you would be in charge of the American doctors who were going to work here with us. You are all welcome." He was still smiling, but I was not comfortable with his acceptance of the existing conditions on this pavilion. I considered trying to express my thoughts, but I was afraid that my French would fail me and I would only offend him again.

I explained to Dr. Makala that I was the new chief of surgery and the new director of the medical staff, and that I wanted to work with the medical staff already here. We would bring in some foreign doctors and nurses to help, and it was our purpose to improve the care of patients in this hospital. I asked him what he thought was the most important step to be taken first, because I wanted to enlist his help in correcting the problems. I thought post-operative wound infections would be one obvious choice.

Dr. Makala saw the problems quite differently. "I believe that the salaries are so low that we cannot get good nurses to work here, and the doctors are paid so little they must carry on a practice outside the hospital so they can feed their families. If you can do something about the salaries, Dr. Youmani, everyone would work hard and the care would get better."

He was watching my face, as Africans do, to see my reaction. I met his gaze, and told him Dr. Close and the president would work on that problem, and that I would focus on the problems of patient care. I should have known to expect that salaries would be his first concern, but I didn't. I turned to the nurse and asked her about her salary.

She hesitated, then said, "I am paid the same salary I was paid when I started two years ago, but now the money only buys half as much as it did then. Some of the assistants and cleaners have been paid nothing for over a year. They come to work, and sometimes they get something to eat here. They have no other place to work, so they come here to work without pay."

I wasn't sure what to say. I shook my head and said, "The salaries will get better," before asking for the next patient's chart.

The nurse handed me a dirty, torn sheet of paper with the patient's name on it. I saw Dr. Makala's signature, but I couldn't read the list of medicines that the patient was receiving, or was supposedly receiving. "Penicillin" was legible on the paper, so I asked if the patient had received it today.

"No, Doctor. He was told that his family must buy the penicillin, a syringe, and a needle, and bring them to us, but they never brought any."

The temperature graph had only one temperature recorded, and that was for two weeks ago, the day of his operation. "What was his temperature this morning?" I asked, as I handed the paper to Dr. Makala.

The nurse answered, "We don't have any thermometers, Doctor. They took his temperature in the operating room. They have a thermometer there."

I was unable to respond to such a simple statement that revealed such poverty of essential equipment. After a moment, I turned to Dr. Makala. "Tell me about this next patient, Doctor."

Purulent dressings covered the patient's infected hernia incision. For the next two hours Dr. Makala and I discussed and examined patients on the pavilion. We talked about surgical technique and sterile operating conditions. Mostly, I was learning about the limitations under which the doctors and nurses worked.

Dr. Makala excused himself at two o'clock in order to keep his appointments with private patients in his office at home. I washed my hands with soap in a pan of cloudy water and dried them on the dirty towel the nurse handed me. I walked to the doctor's changing room in the old surgical block and retrieved my sandwich and bottle of water from the shelf where I had placed them when I had first arrived in the morning. I began to reflect on my morning's experience and to consider why I was here in this cesspool of sickness.

I had come with the intention of helping the sick Congolese people and perhaps teaching some of the Congolese doctors, but I had underestimated the magnitude of the problems that I would encounter. I had seen fifteen patients on one pavilion during four hours of making rounds this morning, and there were at least twenty more pavilions in the hospital. Kinshasa had a population of nearly three million people and five major hospitals. This hospital was a collection of twenty-two single-story pavilions sprawled over six city blocks. It had two thousand beds, twice as many as the other four hospitals combined. Belgian nuns ran the maternity service here, which was clean and efficient. They delivered a hundred babies every day. It was certainly a bright spot compared to the surgery service I had seen this morning.

I was numb as I sat there on a bench just outside the empty operating rooms, with the confusing babble of voices and languages outside the window on the walkways. The stench of mold, rotting food, and human waste drifted in through the window. I held my half-eaten sandwich in one hand and the bottle of water in the other. The sick patients, the hopelessness, and poverty exceeded anything I had ever seen or imagined before. This was the hospital where the Congolese who lived in poverty came and often died. My puny efforts seemed ridiculously futile.

I finished my sandwich, took another drink of water, and walked over to the cardiac pavilion where I found Dr. Kennel talking with Dr. Beheyt. They were sitting together in Dr. Beheyt's office discussing a patient's X-ray, while the patient and eight others sat on a bench outside the office. When I began to express my frustration, Dr. Beheyt smiled sympathetically and reminded me that there was only so much that anyone could do.

"I've been here most of my career, more than twenty years with the Belgian government's *Aide Technique Belge,*" he said. "But it is not possible to do much here now. I haven't been able to do any research since independence. Now I just stay in my office and see referrals and manage a few patients on the pavilion. I'm glad to have a colleague like Dr. Kennel here to discuss cardiac problems with me. Don't be discouraged, Doctor. Step by step. It is all anyone can do now."

Dr. Kennel agreed that the hospital's needs were overwhelming, and hoped I could find somebody competent in surgery to help me.

"That won't be possible unless some new personnel can be brought in," Dr. Beheyt said sadly. "There are no competent surgeons here."

"Dr. Burrus and his family moved into the other side of the duplex where we live," I said, " but I don't know when he's coming down here. Dr. Close told me he would work in the office up on Mount Galiema with him, but I hope he comes down here at least some of the time. I just spent the last few hours with Dr. Makala. He thinks he is a surgeon because he knows which end of a knife to hold."

"He is bad," Dr. Beheyt commented dryly. "Dr. Mvunu is much better, but he isn't trained either. At least he tries hard. Have you met him? I think he has been on leave. Maybe he isn't back yet."

The little chat with colleagues did encourage me, and replaced some of my discouragement with faint hope. The hospital was a disaster, but just because I couldn't do everything didn't mean the situation was hopeless. Back at the surgical pavilion I continued making rounds with the nurse, who was able to tell me about each patient and seemed encouraged because I was interested. I had used all of the clean bandages the nun had given me, but I planned to ask Winkie for an old sheet when I got home, and I would tear it into long strips for bandages. I would borrow some sterile dressings, adhesive tape, and some iodine from Dr. Close's office on Mount Galiema. Tomorrow I would try again.

Twenty-six
Transformation in the Hospital

"The trampled 'grass' began to grow again."
—Congolese pastor's comment

I returned the following morning, better prepared to see patients. I brought dressings from the torn sheet, some soap, and a clean towel from home. Yet, after working all day, I still felt I had hardly made a dent in the problems on the surgical pavilions. What little encouragement a few patients and a nurse may have received from the day's efforts would evaporate if not accompanied by some radical changes in patient care. I had worked all day on a different surgical ward. No Congolese doctor ever showed up during the day, and I was discouraged. Dr. Close and Dr. Burrus came to the hospital that afternoon and wanted to look around the hospital with me.

"The sewer system is blocked," Bill said. "I've checked the records. The sewers and septic tanks were installed in 1925 and the tanks have never been emptied or the pipes repaired. Whenever the toilets or sewers got stopped up, they just quit using them."

"It smells to me like some people didn't get the word," Dr. Burrus said, holding his nose.

"Replacing the septic tanks and sewer lines will take two or three months. They'll start next week," Bill promised, and headed down the walk.

He stopped us at the hospital kitchen and looked in through the door. "We need to feed the patients at least one meal every day as soon as possible, and give them some tea and bread each morning. That will show the people that the president cares about them, and that's as important as fixing the sewers."

"I saw some hot rice and sauce brought out of the kitchen several times today," I said, "but the aides ate it instead of the patients."

Bill stopped in his tracks. "I won't have that! Get the name of any employee who eats food intended for patients, and the names of two witnesses, Congolese preferred. I'll fire anybody who has been seen doing that."

I saw bigger problems here than lack of meal service. In the bush hospitals the families always provided the patients with food, but we had medicines and concerned nurses there, and here we didn't. "Is Mobutu really serious about this hospital?"

"You bet he's serious, and so am I. The president really cares about his people."

George spoke up before Bill could continue. "How about the emergency room and the operating rooms, Bill? I sure wouldn't want any of my family to be treated in them."

"We've already started on the operating rooms, and the ER will be next. See." Bill pointed toward some new construction.

Bill's main job was going to be meeting Mobutu's expectations for the hospital, and that meant meeting Mobutu's ideas of good care for the patients—good food and sanitation. My main job was going to be to see that the quality of patient care improved rapidly, and that the patients were pleased with it. But to accomplish this, somebody would have to enforce the changes and the higher standards. We needed an authority figure here, a Congolese doctor or administrator who could deal with the nurses, salaries, and medical supplies on a daily basis so the FOMECO doctors could focus on patient care and the training of nurses and doctors.

I asked Bill to find us a Congolese administrator who could

discipline the personnel and create some integrity in the hospital. And that would mean paying salaries regularly, and getting rid of some of the lazy and corrupt personnel. "We can't improve medical care under the conditions here now," I said. Bill agreed with the need for aggressive changes and said Dr. George Bazunga would be transferred to FOMECO to be our hospital administrator and general director. "He's honest and knows how to work with people," Bill said in his authoritative way. "We'll wait till he comes for some of these changes."

I nodded, unconvinced but hopeful. This was the second time Bill had referred to Bazunga, who he thought was exceptional. I hoped this was true and that he would get here soon. I told Bill the biggest problem I had personally encountered so far was the hundred patients with infected wounds that I had seen on the wards in the last two days. "The hospital doesn't even have sterile dressings or iodine, not to mention medicine," I said. "We can't improve care if we can't demonstrate it." He invited me to go up to his clinic with him, and he would have his nurse give me a personal supply of things to use until things in the hospital improved.

We walked a little farther before Bill continued with his usual optimism. "We'll get to the personnel problems after Dr. Bazunga gets here, but in the meantime we've already started the new operating rooms, and we'll move ahead with renovating the emergency room, and maybe an intensive care unit at the same time."

But I still saw the personnel problems and the lack of care and the incompetence as more urgent than construction, and impulsively said so. Bill became a little angry.

"Personnel will be replaced when Bazunga gets here," Bill said irritably, his face getting red. I had gone too far in pressing my complaints. But Dr. Burrus immediately volunteered to come down to the hospital and help me as soon as his family was settled— assuming, of course, that Bill would let him go from the Galiema office.

The tensions faded and we continued talking as we walked down the center corridor. I was actually much encouraged by Bill's confidence, enthusiasm, and energetic comments about the coming changes.

When Bull Elephants Fight

"Just let me know who are your best people and who are the worst," Bill said. "Dr. Bazunga will do the rest. You guys take care of the patients and teach the Congolese who are willing to learn." I could at least do that, I thought, as we turned and headed back to Bill's car and then to his office. I got a little stash of supplies from Bill's nurse to clean up a few of the surgical wound infections on the pavilion, but nowhere near enough.

It was after six when I got home. I had supper and went back to the hospital to spend a few hours in the emergency room just to see how it functioned after dark. I had already spent most of the day working my way through a second surgical pavilion before Bill and George arrived to tour the hospital. It had been the same as the day before—infected wounds with dirty dressings, illegible charts, and discouraged patients. But today the nurse on the ward was neither interested nor helpful, and no Congolese doctors showed up.

I stayed in the emergency room and observed that the sentinels locked the gate to keep people out and only made exceptions for patients who they thought would die before morning. That was what they had been instructed to do. When a patient was brought in unconscious about ten o'clock, I examined him, but there were no laboratory or X-ray facilities to help me make a diagnosis, and no drugs in the ER to treat a patient if a diagnosis could have been made. His blood pressure was only 60 and we had no IV fluids to give him. I had him put in a holding bed. He died in less than an hour, and I went home depressed.

The quality of patient care did improve, especially after Dr. George Burrus came down to the hospital full-time and Dr. Bazunga took over the administration. A couple of other American-trained surgeons arrived within a month, and we all worked flat out. We could see improvement, and we encouraged each other. We came in early and went home late. We ate our sandwiches and drank our bottled water whenever we could. We covered the emergency room and kept it open all night. Dr. Bazunga arrived during that first month and he was everything Bill had promised. The attitude of many of the nurses improved, and some began to show an interest in learning new ways to do things. Some of the doctors who were there when we arrived, including six of the young Congolese doctors, were open to learning, but others preferred to be transferred to another hospital. Dr. Bazunga and Dr. Close arranged it. Of the six Congolese doctors who were kept, three left later during the first few months because they were needed elsewhere in Congo and the work at the General Hospital was too demanding.

I met with Dr. Bazunga three or four times a week, and together we met with Dr. Close at least once a week. We worked on the multitude of problems inherent in running any big hospital, and encouraged each other. We made a good team, and we quickly became close friends.

The medical staff at the General Hospital was trying to adopt many of the standards of American medicine and apply them in Congo, but we had European, Asian, and Congolese doctors whose views helped us, and sometimes forced us, to be flexible in our approach. We also had ten times more patients every day than any of us had ever tried to manage in America. It was a daily struggle, and we were all learning and changing.

We used what we had, and in the first month that FOMECO ran the hospital we did 650 major and minor operations, and had very few infections. The nurses were amazed and became increasingly willing to follow our directions. We used local anesthesia much of the time, and found that the Congolese anesthetist whom Bill had pointed out the first day was excellent in both attitude and skill. We kept him busy.

We had hoped to have the new operating rooms and emergency rooms built before the end of 1970, but they weren't ready until the end of January the following year. Seeing the construction in progress gave us hope, and hope generated the energy to make more progress despite the inadequate facilities that we worked with every day.

The Congolese in Kinshasa quickly recognized the change in the hospital. Many patients recovered in a few days and went home, operations were not followed by infections, doctors and nurses were available in the emergency room all night, and the nurses and other hospital personnel were friendly and helpful. We weren't really what could be called a modern hospital, but the improvement was so obvious that patients and their families came to us with growing confidence, expecting that they would be treated and would return home stronger and healthier. Articles appeared in the newspapers describing the sudden and dramatic change for the better in the Kinshasa General Hospital. The president was pleased with FOMECO, and Bill was satisfied. Salaries were paid regularly, and a 10% premium was added to the salaries for all of the Congolese employees in the hospital. Additional foreign doctors were arriving each week, and the best Congolese nurses in the city wanted to transfer to our hospital.

The newly arriving American surgeons and I worked twelve hours a day in the hospital and took turns in the emergency room all night every third night. But sometimes the progress didn't seem proportionate to the hours expended or the sleep lost. The morning after my first full night in the emergency room I counted over one hundred mosquito bites on my body. Given the fact that we were always only a few feet away from two thousand patients who carried malaria parasites, it is likely that dozens of the bites I received did transmit the malaria parasites to me. But the chloroquine I took every week kept me from developing clinical symptoms.

Whenever the emergency room was quiet, I would walk through the other pavilions to see how the patients were doing. After the first couple of nights the sentinels began to allow an increasing number of sick patients to come inside the hospital gate, and the aide at the emergency room door would call us for every patient who came. Because the nurses and other personnel were paid regularly, the stealing of instruments, medicines, and other equipment decreased tremendously. The nurses who didn't want to work hard were quickly replaced by those who did, just as Bill told us they would be.

More young American doctors arrived in early 1971—specialists in internal medicine, pediatrics, orthopedic surgery, and plastic surgery. They settled their families in the newly constructed houses in Mimosa, and within a few days after arrival each doctor was given a car to drive, and began putting in nine or ten hours a day in the hospital. The doctors carried their water bottles and lunches with them and ate what they brought whenever they had the chance.

Our medical staff's attention was focused first on finding out what was actually happening on the assigned pavilion and then doing whatever it took to improve it. Our second focus was on the emergency room because without our constant attention there, the enthusiasm of the ER nurses waned. One of the expatriate doctors, usually a surgeon, stayed in the emergency room every night. At first I was personally involved in keeping the ER appropriately stocked and in reducing the number of items being stolen, but several Congolese nurses soon responded to our efforts and accepted those responsibilities themselves. We encouraged the nurses not only to allow sick patients to enter the emergency room at night, but to retrain the sentinels to assist the patients who arrived and to admit the patients into the ER during the night instead of making them wait until morning.

The president had arranged with Belgian contractors to build prefabricated houses near Mount Galiema, and he gave them to us for FOMECO employees to use. Within a few months most of our expatriate doctors had good homes, and Winkie and the other medical wives who could speak French welcomed each new family and helped them become oriented to Kinshasa. Most of the newly arrived wives didn't know French or where to buy things, and most of them had never been overseas. The more experienced wives took the new ones shopping and helped them enroll their children in the American School. Within a year nearly half of the students in the American School were children of FOMECO employees or of American missionaries. Most of the teachers in the American School had been recruited from California schools and were familiar with the California curriculum, so the American School in Kinshasa followed that curriculum. Our girls renewed friendships with kids they had known in our previous years on the mission field, and began to pick up some Lingala expressions as they socialized with the other students. They enjoyed their teachers and did well academically. It was an exciting and happy time for us.

We were able to hire some European nurses who were in Congo as missionaries or whose husbands were employed in Congo in some capacity. They were a big help in teaching the Congolese nurses how to improve the cleanliness of the various pavilions to European standards. But women, even white women nurses, were not given the same degree of respect that white doctors were, and the expatriate nurses found the pressures of trying to change the way the Congolese nurses worked very stressful. Only the tough-minded expatriate nurses survived. One of our best American nurses became hooked on narcotics and was sent back to America where she fully recovered. Another was killed one night while joy-riding on a motorcycle. One of the European nurses attempted suicide. But positive changes occurred and the patients benefited in spite of the difficulties.

Dr. Bazunga handled the Congolese nurses and doctors who resisted the longer hours and higher standards, and I did my best with the Americans and Europeans who found the frustrations in Congo much greater than they had anticipated. Dr. Bazunga replaced many of the administrative personnel with new personnel who were eager to work and help him implement changes.

Major building and renovation projects established functioning sewers and toilets. New water pipes were laid, and electric and telephone lines were strung through the pavilions. By mid 1971 over fifty patients were seen in the emergency room every night, a dramatic improvement from the year before. But the growing number of patients to be cared for and our struggle for quality care took its toll. Each morning the doctors and nurses returned to the hospital to find that some aspect of excellence they thought had been established had disappeared in a swamp of new problems and recurring old ones.

The emergency room was the most difficult area to manage. The patients usually came at night when our personnel were tired. The patients were usually in need of urgent attention, and our staffing at night was minimal because most of our medical and nursing staff did not want to work at night. It was under such circumstances that solutions had to be improvised to deal with the unexpected. What Dr. Ngema and I faced one night after a long day of work is an example. There had been a fight with knives, and a group of men had fled in a car, but crashed. Two of them had sustained minor head injuries and multiple deep lacerations of the face, hands, and arms. The other two had only a few superficial lacerations of their arms. Dr. Ngema began sewing up the two men with superficial lacerations in the emergency room using local anesthesia. I took the other two patients to the operating room for repair.

There was no anesthetist in the hospital at night, so we used intra-muscular injections of ketamine, which blocks the patient from sensing any painful stimulation but does not complicate occult head injuries or cause the patient to sleep. Unfortunately, it does not cause muscle relaxation. The patient can breathe and move, but can't feel pain. The only disadvantage reported in the medical literature was that sometimes adults had a transient psychotic reaction, but we had never experienced such a complication.

After getting both of these large, muscular men to lie quietly, each on his own table in the operating room, I injected each with ketamine. I explained to them in French, and had the OR nurse explain in Lingala, what I was doing and what they could expect. They both drifted off in an inebriated sleep. I began operating on one patient, and when Dr. Ngema came in he began repairing the lacerations on the other. Both patients slept with no awareness of pain.

After about an hour, the man Dr. Ngema was working on suddenly sat up on the operating table and stared wild-eyed around the room. As he bellowed and yelled, the patient on my table woke up and tried to get off the table. Both instrument trays flew across the room and instruments clattered on the floor. One nurse ran from the room to summon help while Dr. Ngema, the remaining nurse, and I tried to restrain and reassure the patients. By the time help arrived, both patients were standing up and looking around the room apprehensively, and Dr. Ngema was on the floor. Brute force and reassurances in Lingala finally soothed the patients and they lay down on the tables again. We waited until they were both asleep before we resumed our procedures. They slept until we finished and had the dressings taped in place. When they finally woke up, they thanked us and walked out of the operating room. The following day they and their companions left the hospital without any memory of the chaos they had caused in the operating room.

That night Dr. Ngema decided to become a pediatrician instead of a surgeon. He wanted to deal with smaller patients. I could hardly blame him.

Twenty-seven
Authentically Zairian

It was called authenticity: Joseph Desire Mobutu,
Congo, and the Kinshasa General Hospital
became Mobutu Sese Seko, Zaire, and
the Mama Yemo Hospital.

We had come a long way by that mid-morning in 1971 when the news media descended on the General Hospital. The new water and sewer systems had been completed, the new surgical block was in use every day, patients were getting two meals a day, salaries were paid on time, and most important of all, the quality of care had vastly improved. The nurses and doctors, both expatriates and Congolese, worked long hours and morale was high. Dr. Close had obtained the funds and the Congolese personnel we needed, and Dr. Bazunga was a good, fair, and tough administrator.

Back in November 1970, three months after FOMECO took over the General Hospital, we had only twenty-four expatriate doctors (mostly American trained specialists) and eight Congolese doctors. Even by that time the changes were impressive—the average length of stay dropped from thirty days to ten days in the surgery department where the 355 beds had an average of 105% occupancy. In addition, the nine doctors on the surgery service staffed an outpatient clinic that, in the month of November, treated nearly two thousand patients.

By the time the news media came to the hospital along with the politicians, the other clinical services had expanded and improved significantly, even if not so dramatically. We had reached a plateau of medical care that was not dependent on sophisticated technology, but on cleanliness, attention to physical signs, sound judgment, and sterile technique. Our laboratory and radiology services were basic but dependable. I believed that we were now ready to train Congolese doctors in the basic medical care that we were demonstrating.

The news media of Kinshasa had been mentioning the dramatic changes in the Kinshasa General Hospital for months, and before noon on that morning in 1971 the first newsmen arrived at the front gate of the hospital. The street was remarkably clean in the bright morning sunshine. There was no garbage piled against the outside walls of the hospital. The food vendors had been banished to the adjacent streets, leaving a growing crowd of curious Congolese in front of our gate. Then came the police, with sirens screaming, and they moved the people away from the gate. After the police, the Mercedes sedans and limousines arrived, bringing members of Mobutu's cabinet and several members of his *bureau politique*. Finally the president's limousine arrived, surrounded by another squad of motorcycles with loud sirens, and stopped in front of the hospital's gate. Joseph Desire Mobutu, president of the Democratic Republic of Congo, stepped out of the limousine and was greeted by Dr. George Bazunga.

The dignitaries were surrounded by newsmen taking pictures and running the television cameras mounted on their shoulders, seeking to record the president's actions while the reporters asked for quotes for publication. The president's head and leopard-skin cap towered above the other dignitaries, projecting strength, and his carved walking stick added dignity to his naturally graceful movements. Dr. Bazunga led the president through the hospital gate and down the central walk between the pavilions. Mobutu waved to the crowd, smiling broadly, and the crowd cheered. Families of patients filled the space between the pavilions and watched the "Guide," the "Father" of their country who had "transformed" their hospital. A small, grinning six-year-old boy stepped up onto the walkway in front of Mobutu and held out his hand. Mobutu stopped, bent down, and shook the boy's hand.

"Are you getting enough to eat?" the president asked.

The boy grinned even wider, flexed his biceps, and nodded.

The president put his hand on the boy's shoulder and glanced up, smiling at the television cameras, the flash bulbs, and the journalists. Dr. Bazunga was in the background smiling benignly, but as I looked around I did not see Bill Close. This was Dr. Bazunga and President Mobutu's hour, and the president was demonstrating his care for his people, as his mother, Mama Yemo, had often urged him to do. For the moment President Mobutu was basking in the adulation, honor, and love of his people.

A short time later the president left. The ministers and other dignitaries followed, trailed by the photographers and reporters. The crowd dispersed, and we went back to work. Dr. Close had fulfilled the promise he'd made to me at my house in Kansas City over a year ago. He had spent hours with the president and had brought the president's authority and money to FOMECO and to the hospital. Dr. Bazunga had shuffled personnel and installed discipline, a sense of responsibility, and honesty to the administration of the hospital. Our medical/surgical staff of doctors and nurses had exceeded all expectations in providing higher levels of care to ever-increasing numbers of patients.

We were doing "medical center surgery" now. The boy whom Mobutu had greeted was two weeks post-operative from Hirschsprung's Disease, an intestinal disorder. Dr. Burrus had surgically closed the patent ductus arterioses in several other patients, and repaired a tracheo-esophageal fistula in yet another. Dr. Johnson was routinely stabilizing femoral fractures with intramedullary rods and sending the patients home in a week. Our surgical care had come a long way in a very short time. The Kinshasa General Hospital was already one of the best hospitals in central Africa, and it was also the largest.

Shortly after Mobutu's visit to the General Hospital, the senior students at the Lovanium University medical school in Kinshasha organized a strike, demanding better food and dormitories. The dean of the medical school appealed to the minister of health, and the minister of health, who had no funds available, submitted the problem to the president. Mobutu, eager to have the young Congolese student-doctors trained to the quality of care provided at the Kinshasa General Hospital, simply drafted the entire class of thirteen senior students into the army and assigned them to work in the General Hospital under the direction of FOMECO. These young Congolese medical students had received an adequate theoretical background in medical science, but had received almost no hands-on training. We were to train them for a year, much like interns are trained in American teaching hospitals, and then they would be posted to various other hospitals throughout Congo.

The American doctors were thrilled with an opportunity to teach and train these young Congolese doctors. I assigned several students to each of the major specialties and rotated them every three months. The presence of the students complicated the lives of the doctors, but encouraged the various services to conduct formal teaching rounds and an educational conference each week, in addition to their daily ward rounds. As for the two doctors who had been with us since FOMECO started, we now informally regarded them as residents in the specialty of their choice. Dr. Mvunu chose surgery and Dr. Ngema chose pediatrics, and both were given progressively more clinical responsibility.

The American and European doctors, who had been so stressed by the increasing volume of patients, were glad to have help even if it meant spending time teaching and preparing for clinical conferences. The morale of the staff improved.

Ten years ago at Sona Bata my dream had been to train Congolese doctors, and now I saw that dream fulfilled. As for the Congolese doctors, they were delighted not to be taking basic training in an army camp. Unfortunately, the time required for scheduling and carrying out the training of these interns made it necessary for me to resign as chief of surgery. I appointed Dr. Cal Johnson, our orthopedic surgeon and a former missionary in Congo, as my replacement. As chief of staff I had an ever-increasing number of new responsibilities.

Dr. Burrus's contract with FOMECO was nearly finished, and he began preparing to return to Nashville and resume his private practice of cardiac surgery. In anticipation of his departure, he had sold a bookcase to a Congolese friend, and asked me to help him deliver it. The bookcase was too large to fit in Dr. Burrus's VW minivan so we had to tie it onto the roof, and it was dark by the time we got it securely tied down. I went with him because it was always safer to have two people in the car after dark in case there was an accident. The Congolese are excitable, and a crowd of bystanders might beat, or even kill, the driver who appeared to have caused the accident.

George knew how to find his friend's house in daylight, but at night and without street signs and rarely even streetlights, it was hard to see the landmarks. The first turn was easy, and then ahead of us I saw a liquor store with several men standing in front of it. One of the men unexpectedly stepped into the street in front of us without looking.

George hit the brakes hard and the tires skidded just before the sickening thump, as the minivan hit the man and knocked him fifteen feet down the street, where he lay unconscious. At the same time the ropes on the bookcase broke, and the bookcase slid off the roof and skidded toward the man lying in the street, stopping before it reached him.

I jumped out of the van and ran to him. I could see by our headlights that he was breathing, and I did not see any blood or other obvious evidence of serious injuries. A crowd of Congolese quickly materialized, talking, questioning, and sometimes yelling as they surrounded us, apparently demanding explanations in Lingala.

I grasped the man under his arms, and a Congolese, who I supposed was his friend, lifted the victim's feet to help me get him to the van. The noise of the crowd had increased and some people were pounding with their fists on the sides of the van.

We got the injured man's shoulders and hips inside the van, but we had trouble getting his legs in because our efforts were not coordinated. George was yelling in Lingala, but nobody seemed to pay any attention. I was scared.

I yelled at George to get in the van and drive to the hospital. I yelled again, "George, let's go. Now!"

I was afraid George and I would be attacked by the crowd, maybe even killed. George had been looking at the bookcase, but now he returned to the van and climbed into the front seat behind the wheel. A Congolese climbed in the passenger seat beside him. I finally got the injured man's feet into the van and was reaching for the door handle to close it when several men grabbed my wrist and tried to pull me out. I braced my shoulder against the doorframe, resisting those who were pulling my hand. The Congolese in the van with me was trying to help me close the door. George had the motor running and I was yelling for him to go. We slowly moved forward. The hands holding my wrist slipped off. We gained speed, and the crowd—and the bookcase—were left behind. The cargo door of the van slid shut. George drove us to the hospital.

At the hospital we put the injured man on a gurney and took him into the emergency room where a Congolese nurse and doctor took charge of him. George moved the van while I told the doctor and nurse what had happened. The American doctor on duty came into the emergency room, and I left, hoping the crowd from the accident scene would not come to the ER, at least not until I was gone. George called Dr. Close and told him what had happened, and Bill said he would take care of it.

The next morning the injured man was awake and moving all of his extremities. X-rays had shown several broken ribs but no other injury. George and I were relieved. Nothing further was ever said or done about the accident. There was never a mention of it in the newspapers. The injured Congolese was discharged in several days and the new owner of the bookcase went to the scene two days later to recover it. George took his family back to America as planned.

About a month later Bill told me that the president had asked him to fly up to Gemena with two doctors from the university for a medical consultation on President Mobutu's mother, Mama Yemo, who was dying of heart failure. Bill said he had to stay in Kinshasa with the president and asked me to make the trip in his place. Mama Yemo refused to come to Kinshasa for treatment, and the president didn't want to force the issue if nothing further could be done for her.

At seven in the morning on the appointed day, I went to the N'djili Airport in Kinshasa where I was to meet and accompany two Congolese colleagues from the university medical school. The terminal was deserted and I looked for somebody to tell me where I would board the plane for Gemena. Nobody there knew of any such flight. Over an hour later a large four-engined plane taxied out of the military hangar near the far end of the runway and proceeded down the runway and took off. I assumed that it was my plane and it had left without me, but the plane circled and landed, and without stopping, it took off again. Then I saw an Air Force officer walk by the door and I asked him if this was the place to wait for a military flight to Gemena today.

"Yes, sir, that plane taking off now is going to take some doctors there today." He pointed to the plane I had been watching. It was circling for another landing. I asked why the plane kept taking off and landing, and the officer laughed. "The pilot has never flown that plane before," he explained, "so he's doing a few practice touch-and-go's. He'll park right out there to load up in a few minutes."

I noticed two well-dressed Congolese men approaching me whom I did not recognize, but I hoped they were the colleagues who were to accompany me to see Mama Yemo.

"I'm Dr. Youmans," I began, extending my hand, "and I'm to fly to Gemena today on a medical mission, and I assume you are, also."

"Yes, yes, we are going to Gemena this morning," they acknowledged. They each then formally introduced themselves to me, and we shook hands. They continued talking to each other in Lingala. I interrupted them to ask if the large plane now approaching the door was our flight.

"Yes," they murmured together, and one added, "That is our plane." They resumed their conversation in Lingala and I remained silent.

About thirty minutes later a young military airman came to us and introduced himself as our host for the flight, and led us to the airplane. The engines were running while we boarded the huge plane and I could not hear anything our host or my colleagues said. There were no other passengers, so we sat down and buckled our seat belts. I was anxious about our pilot's lack of experience in this plane, but hoped he could make at least a few more safe landings.

I had a window seat, and watched the landscape below as we climbed above the Congo River. I could not see the rapids but southwest of the Malebo Pool, I saw the large island in the river as we turned north from Kinshasa following the river. In about fifteen minutes I could identify Bolobo by the reflections of the metal roofs of the oldest mission hospital in Congo. Soon I saw the mouth of the Kwilu River flowing into the Congo from the east. At least four of our FOMECO surgeons had worked in mission hospitals along the tributaries of the Kwilu, and another had left Bolobo to work with us. The dramatic improvement of the Kinshasa General Hospital was in large measure due to these and other doctors who had spent years in bush hospitals before leaving them to work in Kinshasa. I know more Congolese had been helped by our collaboration in Kinshasa than would have been helped if we had all stayed at our rural mission hospitals, but I was sorry for the loss of medical staff from these rural hospitals, and wondered how the abandoned hospitals had fared without their doctors. I felt a twinge of guilt, but fell asleep.

When I awoke, the river looked almost like a lake, many miles wide with numerous small islands. We had crossed the equator, and were following the river east. About an hour later we landed in Gemena. A group of soldiers met us and immediately took us to the president's estate, a large house with a well-kept yard.

The leader of our delegation outlined the protocol that we were to follow. Mama Yemo's personal military physician would translate our medical questions from French to Lingala for Mama Yemo, and then translate her answers back to us. Our leader would then examine the patient and tell us what he found. It was an unnecessarily formal and long consultation. It took us nearly two hours of polite conversation and gentle examination of our patient before we could agree on what we learned in the first fifteen minutes. She was dying of heart failure, and probably of kidney failure as well, and was receiving appropriate treatment. She would gain no additional benefit by being transported to Kinshasa. I found the entire exercise somewhat futile.

In October of 1971 Mama Yemo died, and the name of the General Hospital was changed to the Mama Yemo Hospital in her honor. President Mobutu had a statue of his mother placed inside the hospital, and a large sign placed above the hospital entrance with the new name.

At about the same time, President Mobutu announced the new national policy of "authenticity," which meant, among other things, that the name of Congo would change to Zaire, the Congo River would be the Zaire River, and even the money would be called *zaires*. The acronym FOMECO remained the same, but the letters would now stand for *"Fond Medical de Coordination."*

At heart, the policy of authenticity entailed throwing off the European influences. The names of cities were changed and Coquilhatville became Mbandaka, Luluaburg became Kananga, Stanleyville became Kisangani, and Elizabethville became Lubumbashi. Later, even personal names had to be changed to authentic African names. Mobutu changed his western name, Joseph Desire, to the African name *Sese Seko Kuku Ngbendu Wa Za Banga*. Although the English translations of his new name varied widely, the new name clearly implied extraordinary power.

Neckties, an innovation of foreigners, were forbidden for Zairians. A new style of suit, referred to as the "Mobutu suit," was introduced and quickly adopted by Zairian and foreign businessmen. New ID cards were mandatory for all Zairians, with their new African names on the cards. While these changes did not directly affect us at the hospital, there was a definite change in the attitude of soldiers and police toward us when we were outside the hospital compound. The new attitude was tolerant but tinged with hostility.

I tried to focus on medical care at the General Hospital, now called the Mama Yemo Hospital, but there was no way to ignore the anxiety of the Zairian personnel who worked daily with me. They were not sure how much of their lifestyle was to be affirmed as authentically Zairian, and how much was to be rejected as foreign. The Belgians, even the doctors on our staff, were subjected to more hostility than Americans, but they were sometimes more assertive of their rights.

Dr. Close reassured me that the authenticity program of the government did not apply to FOMECO's staff, but when an infant died during an exchange transfusion, the Belgian doctor caring for the baby was arrested and imprisoned. The baby's father was a high-ranking officer in the army. Dr. Close was able to obtain the doctor's release from prison and deportation from Congo, reminiscent of the collaboration in 1960 when the then Col. Mobutu and Dr. D'Arenberg identified foreign personnel in prison and secured their release.

The ambiance in Kinshasa was rapidly changing. The people, and even government officials, appreciated the improvement in the Mama Yemo Hospital, but the resentment against foreigners would not be tolerated for long. Dr. Close remained the director of the Medical Bureau of the Presidency and of FOMECO and he remained a close friend and confidant of President Mobutu. The American and Zairian personnel at the hospital continued to work together, but the camaraderie was strained.

Twenty-eight
A Thousand Patients a Day

"He who has begun his task has half done it.
Have courage to be wise. Begin!"

—Anonymous

Our hospital's success bred its own problems. The hordes of patients in our general outpatient clinics, our specialty clinics, and our emergency room seriously strained our efforts to improve the quality of our care. The better our treatment, the greater the number of patients who came to us, and the bigger the problem became. We were now seeing more than a hundred patients in the emergency room every twenty-four hours. The influx of new outpatients seen in the hospital clinics increased to over two thousand patients each day. The people of Kinshasa demonstrated their appreciation for our services through the progressively increasing number of outpatients until our staff and facilities were overwhelmed.

A trained nurse had for years supervised several nurse-aides in seeing the patients in the general clinic, located adjacent to the hospital but outside the walls, but there were no physicians directly involved in the general clinic and there were no written guidelines for the nurse to follow. The general clinic had only a few medicines that could be given to patients—solutions of vitamins, chloroquine, acetaminophen, and cough syrup—and seldom were all of them on hand at the same time. Dr. Bazunga and his assistant administrators were reluctant to place large quantities of any medicines in the general clinic, because the medicine always disappeared and the records were never accurate. Hundreds of patients went to the general clinic each day, but most patients tried to bypass that clinic by going directly inside the hospital walls to obtain treatment in the emergency room or in a specialist's clinic.

Many of these patients waited outside the specialist's consultation room and when the door opened for the previous patient to leave, they would slip in ahead of the twenty or thirty patients waiting with referral slips. The Congolese can be ingratiating with broad smiles and smooth talk, and an American doctor who wasn't fluent in French or Lingala would accept them as their next patient. Other patients went directly to the emergency room and mixed with the true emergency patients and flooded the area, making it difficult to give sufficient attention to those with genuine emergencies.

Nearly a thousand patients sought care inside the hospital walls and mixed with the visitors who came to see hospitalized family members. The Congolese nurse helping the doctor sometimes accepted a *matabish* from patients to get them into the doctor's office. The doctor was then frustrated because he saw and treated so many patients who had no serious illness, and there were always more patients waiting outside his door. These doctors were helpless to control their own clinics.

The walkways inside the hospital became clogged with thousands of people each day who were visiting family members and mixing with the outpatients who were trying to see a doctor. It was chaotic.

This situation was an aggravation to the doctors and to the nurses, and the administration could not find a way to bring acceptable order and efficiency to the process of screening patients so they could be seen by the appropriate specialist, and not be mixed in with the family members, visitors, and unscreened patients.

A large part of the problem was caused by Mobutu's insistence that all foreign doctors working for FOMECO had to have higher qualifications than the Zairian doctors, and thus FOMECO only had specialists on its staff. Foreign specialists did not want to be bothered by patients outside of their specialty field, and a general practice doctor would have been a better choice. Enabling an appropriate doctor to see the patients was further complicated by the fact that at least three-fourths of the patients had simple medical problems that did not even require a doctor's care. These patients could be treated very well by a nurse following a few guidelines as long as the nurse had an adequate supply of medicine, and the patients could be persuaded or compelled to see the nurse instead of a doctor. Equally important to FOMECO and the president was the need to have all of the patients who came to the hospital satisfied with their treatment, if possible. The control of patient flow depended almost entirely on our clinic nurses, and the nurses could not be controlled adequately because of the virtual absence of written consultation requests and the resistance of the patients, nurses, and doctors to any disciplined procedures regarding outpatient care.

I spent hundreds of hours over the course of a month working with Dr. Bazunga, the director of nurses, and various doctors, trying to devise a way to appropriately handle the thousands of outpatients who mixed daily with the families and visitors of the hospitalized patients. We asked the Belgian company, Eurosixtem Hospitalière, for guidance, and they spent weeks observing our clinics, reviewing our medical records, and talking with the administrators. I had previously spent three years organizing an expanded emergency service at the Kansas University Medical Center, but the problems here were different, bigger, and we had fewer resources with which to work. I did not know how to deal with all of these problems.

The consultants from Eurosixtem Hospitalière suggested that the general clinic outside the hospital be expanded and called the Family and Mass Patient Care clinic (FMPC clinic) with several tiers of triage designed to protect the doctors and nurses in the hospital from the crushing load of outpatients. There was no working consensus on how to do this, and nobody was willing to tackle the problem or attempt to implement a solution. The situation was overwhelming, and getting worse each week. Patients complained; families complained; nurses, doctors, administrators, and even the Eurosixtem consultants, complained.

Without initial opposition, and with dubious approval, I initiated a rigid subdivision of the new FMPC clinic by creating printed forms for the nurse-aides to use for each new patient coming to the first tier of the clinic, referred to as the screening clinic. The forms listed ten symptoms, with a space for the aides to mark the symptom as present or absent. The aides were given a color-coded key, based on the symptoms, of the seven most common syndromes among the Zairians in Kinshasa. The aides also had a color-coded list of two medicines that were to be given for each syndrome. The patient would be seen by the supervising nurse only if the patient (1) had an injury, (2) was a small child, (3) was pregnant, or (4) had symptoms that did not fit any of the seven common syndromes.

We found that 65% of the patients coming to the FMPC clinic could be treated satisfactorily in the screening clinic this way without involving a supervising nurse, and the flow of medicines could be controlled by comparing it with the records of the patients' symptoms. Any patient whose symptoms persisted the next day was to return to the clinic, bypass this first screening clinic, and see one of the supervising nurses, who would treat or refer the patient to the physician assigned to the FMPC clinic. Only the physician could refer a patient to one of the specialists in the hospital. The doctor used a special prescription blank that he signed, rubber-stamped, and designated as his referral.

The number of new patients to be seen by the specialists in the hospital was thus reduced to fewer than one hundred per day. Any physician in Kinshasa could write a consultation request and send a patient directly to a specialist in the hospital. This arrangement seemed to be satisfactory to the doctors and nurses, but the patients persisted in trying to bypass the system. Fences had to be set up to channel new patients to see the nurse-aides, and to channel returning patients with persistent symptoms to see the supervising nurse in the clinic, separately from the new patients.

The system wasn't perfect, and was not received enthusiastically, nor was it always followed by patients or doctors, but some order was established. I was saddened by the presence of fences that made treatment of patients so impersonal. But I was pleased that so many patients were getting effective and prompt relief from the most common diseases in Kinshasa, and that other patients were seen and treated by a supervising nurse or doctor within twenty-four hours. Most of all, the specialists working inside the hospital walls were relieved of many patients with common illnesses that could be treated by nurses. As a result, they could concentrate on patients needing their specialized care.

The young doctors needed to see how a clinic could be organized to provide adequate care to a large number of patients and still leave the doctor time to focus his attention on the sickest ones. Supervising nurses giving routine care to many patients allowed the doctor to give better care to patients who benefited from a more specific diagnosis confirmed by laboratory studies. I was glad when I was able to disentangle myself from the details of the FMPC clinic and have Dr. McCullough handle them.

I'm sure that some patients were not properly treated, and that bribes were still sometimes used, but ten thousand patients were given treatment that relieved their symptoms each week, and hundreds of sicker patients were diagnosed and treated each week by fifty doctors and their nurses. We rotated the newly graduated doctors through the various specialty clinics and through the FMPC clinic in order to broaden their experience.

The first group of young Zairian doctors completed their year of training with us, and served the remainder of their time in the military as physicians in various hospitals in the interior of the country. A new group of just-graduated Zairian doctors was sent to the hospital for us to train. The president was pleased with FOMECO's work, but the next challenge was as uniquely different from our staff doctors' previous experience as the FMPC clinic was.

Twenty-nine
On the Ubangi River

*"Never give up what you have seen
for what you have heard."*
—Swahili proverb

Even before 1970 President Mobutu and Dr. Close had plans for extending medical care to the interior of Zaire. My first awareness of the plans came when Bill began talking about a sister boat of the president's yacht. Bill showed me the old, rusty riverboat lying in the shipyard located in a small harbor of the Zaire River. I was not impressed. Workers were welding new beams and plates onto the rusty frame of the derelict to rejuvenate her. Months later I attended the christening of the new riverboat hospital, named the *Marie Antoinette* after the president's wife. The boat had been outfitted with new engines, air conditioning, and other equipment, and became an impressive riverboat, now to be a floating hospital. A Zairian captain had already been engaged and a Zairian crew hired, but the boat remained in the harbor another month after christening while workers finished the interior and installed an operating room, X-ray machine, and other medical equipment. During that time Marie Antoinette died and a new name, *Mama*

When Bull Elephants Fight

Mobutu, was painted on the bridge over Marie Antoinette's name.

Dr. Bazunga and I were responsible for stocking the pharmacy and supplying the nurses, technicians, and doctors to staff the boat for each cruise on the Zaire River and its tributaries. I chose two doctors, a Zairian and an expatriate, to rotate on each voyage, and Dr. Bazunga selected the nurses and assistants.

The press and national radio and television stations focused on the boat as the newest evidence of the president's concern for the health of his people in the interior of the country. I shared the president's concern, but thought a similar amount of money spent to improve the support system for the hundreds of hospitals and dispensaries already in the rural areas of Zaire would be a much more effective and efficient way to help the people. Probably others agreed with me, but none publicly expressed it. At least Mobutu's plan was better than spending the money on his luxurious lifestyle and that of his family and his cronies.

In December 1971 I went on the second long voyage of the *Mama Mobutu.* We went north on the Zaire River to the Ubangi River, then north on the Ubangi to the town of Zongo on the border of the Central African Republic. It was a twelve-hundred-mile round trip that took almost three weeks to complete.

The river was very broad at the Maleba Pool (formerly known as Stanley Pool), but narrowed to several hundred meters farther north. We kept near the Zairian side of the broad river where the current against us was the weakest. North of Kinshasa I saw commercial farms interspersed with thatched mud houses and miles of tall trees leaning out over the river. Farther north small fishing villages, each with pirogues pulled up onto the riverbank, added variety to the wall of the green forest as we slowly passed by.

The increasing heat and humidity soon forced me to leave the outside deck for the air-conditioned interior. Moving from stern to bow I wandered through the well-appointed examining rooms, the laboratory, physical therapy room, the twenty-bed hospital ward, and the delivery and operating rooms. Moving back toward the stern on the other side were the treatment rooms, nurses' lounge, pharmacy, and waiting room. It was a small but first-class floating hospital all on the first deck.

The kitchen, dining room, toilets, and sleeping quarters for the medical personnel were on the second deck. The third deck had a large general-purpose meeting room, a heliport, and an observation deck. The fourth deck was the officers' quarters and the bridge. I didn't tour the crew's quarters that were below the first deck.

In the early afternoon we passed the mouth of the huge Kwa River, fed mainly by the Kwilu and Kasai, as it emptied the water it had brought from the interior of Congo. I thought about the Sankaru River that emptied into the Kasai, and the time I crossed it in a waterlogged pirogue, fearful of pursuing soldiers.

The rain forest became increasingly dense on both sides of the river as we moved north of the mouth of the Kwa River, and the shadows of trees blended into the darkness of the water. I saw monkeys playing in the trees and several times I saw crocodiles lying in the mud of small streams that cut through the bank, making eddies where they joined the river. There were hundreds of water hyacinths floating in the river here. I had been told that an American missionary threw hyacinth seeds into the river to beautify its brown water years ago. The hyacinths now foul the propellers of riverboats.

We passed the hospital in Bolobo, but the original mud-and-thatch hospital built by the British Baptist missionaries in the 1880s has been replaced by a modern hospital. The doctor had left that hospital to help us in the Mama Yemo Hospital. Our gain had been Bolobo's loss.

A small cluster of pirogues launched toward us from Bolobo, bringing fish, bananas, *manioc*, and mangos to sell to our captain. The villagers tied their pirogues to our boat as we continued upstream, and haggled with the captain over the quality and price of their offerings.

Late in the afternoon our boat hit a sandbar. The captain had to reverse the engines several times to break the boat free. I thought again of Conrad's description of traveling up the Congo River eighty years earlier in his book *Heart of Darkness*. If I were forced to spend a night in the rain forest that bordered the river as he had, I doubt whether I could have survived. Radios, searchlights, and SONAR had taken some of the mystery out of the Congo River since Conrad's day, but the river and the forest are still dangerous.

In growing darkness the captain turned on his searchlights and scanned the riverbank for a place to tie up to some trees for the night. It was not safe to continue in the dark. A spot was found, the boat moved close to the riverbank, and lines were tied to trees. Half an hour later dinner was served in the dining room and an auxiliary generator provided air conditioning and lights.

Dr. Mvunu sat across from me at dinner that evening. He was tall and broad-shouldered, with a slow smile and thoughtful brown eyes. He was both conscientious and intelligent, about thirty years old, and still single. He had assisted me in the operating room many times and I looked forward to getting better acquainted with him. He had been an excellent student in the Catholic schools in his village, and the nuns had encouraged him to study for the priesthood. But after Congo's independence in 1960 he took the opportunity to go to medical school, and enjoyed it. He had joined the army after graduating and was assigned to the General Hospital where I first met him.

I invited him to take responsibility for the medical aspects of this trip and he eagerly accepted. After dinner he began organizing and instructing the nurses and technicians, and checking the supplies and medications.

The next morning I visited the bridge and watched the captain navigate the channel between sandbars, calling down instructions based on his observations of the color of the water. He showed me the map of the river channel, but assured me he didn't need any map. He could identify the channel by the color differences of the water, but the brown river water all looked the same to me.

The Zairian nurses relished this opportunity to see parts of their own country they had never seen before. There were crocodiles lying on sandbars absorbing the early morning sun and its energizing warmth. Monkeys chattered and played in the trees. After breakfast we left the Zaire River and entered the Ubangi River. We saw several hippopotami, and a few minutes later we approached the first village where we would see patients.

At Wembo Nyama the Batetela had used talking drums to tell villagers when the doctor would arrive, but this time a radio had informed the villagers when the Mama Mobutu Hospital riverboat was due, and now the boat's whistle announced our actual arrival. A crowd greeted us on the riverbank, and Dr. Mvunu and I went ashore to greet the government officials and the chief at the village. We invited them to come aboard first in honor of their position in the village. The chief, an old, skinny man, led the way. Although he was much less impressive-looking than the government officials, he was clearly more respected by the villagers. The government officials, who came aboard pompously, gave the impression it was their influence that had brought the hospital riverboat to this village.

After taking care of the prominent people of the village, we treated the other sixty villagers. The most common ailments were malaria, diarrhea, and anemia just as in Kinshasa. But there were also more leg ulcers, hernias, severely infected lacerations, and more patients with pneumonia and bronchitis than we usually saw in Kinshasa, but nothing particularly exotic. Our laboratory was of little value due to our brief stay.

We finished the clinic work within an hour and a half of our arrival, and admitted three patients—two for surgery and one with diarrhea and dehydration—before moving on upstream to the next big village. We stopped at three or four villages each day, repeated the same formalities with the local chief and government officials, and diagnosed and treated similar diseases. Every patient was given some medicine, just as we had done for the patients at the rural dispensaries of Sona Bata and Wembo Nyama. Patients who were sicker, usually with severe diarrhea and dehydration, were admitted to our hospital-boat to undergo laboratory tests and receive intravenous fluids. Patients who needed simple surgical procedures, usually hernia repairs, were also admitted and operated on in the evenings.

The few seriously ill patients who needed a longer period of treatment or sophisticated laboratory studies remained on board until we returned to the Mama Yemo Hospital in Kinshasa. Every time we took a patient with us we also had to take several family members as *aides de malades*. The riverboat was heavily loaded with patients and families when we finished our last clinic at Zongo.

The medical care provided by the riverboat hospital seemed small compared to the expenses of building, equipping, and operating it. The boat had provided a brief vacation for the doctors and nurses and respite from the demands of the Mama Yemo

Hospital. The experience expanded their knowledge of a remote part of their own country. The riverboat hospital may also have given hope to the villagers, but not much long-term benefit. These people would become sick again, but the riverboat hospital would not return for a long time. We actually reached only a small fraction of the people along the Ubangi River, and the treatment was, of necessity, superficial and very expensive. The riverboat was probably a political boondoggle to widen Mobutu's popularity outside of Kinshasa. But even so, it was better than completely ignoring the people in the interior.

After we had completed the final medical clinic at Zongo, in the far north of Zaire, Dr. Mvunu and I sat in my air-conditioned cabin and evaluated our seventeen days on the riverboat while the crew and our staff prepared for our return to Kinshasa. We had treated over two thousand patients, and had performed eight surgical operations. We were taking twenty hospitalized patients and twelve post-hospitalized patients down-river to their villages. Including the *aides de malades,* we had nearly one hundred passengers on board in addition to our medical personnel. There were six other patients we would take to the Mama Yemo Hospital where they could receive more definitive diagnostic tests and treatment.

I had not accumulated any valuable statistics about health problems of the population living along the banks of the Ubangi, but we had brief medical notes on each patient we saw. Dr. Mvunu questioned the medical value of the trip. "Do you believe the patients we've treated are going to be healthier next year because we came?"

I shook my head, and he continued, "Why did you spend all of this money on the boat and bring us up here? Is the boat just a political thing?"

That kind of talk could be dangerous, so I looked up and down the empty hallway, then closed the door and sat down again. We had already talked about public health projects and other health teams or individuals who might follow up our quick trip. I knew such follow-up was unlikely to happen. I knew it wouldn't happen in my lifetime, and Mvunu's conclusion was similar. He said pessimistically, "Nobody who has any education or knows anything about medical care is going to be dumb enough to stay way up here in Zongo long enough to teach anybody anything."

I was looking out the window watching three boys about ten years old playing soccer in the dust of the main street of Zongo. They didn't even have a ball. They were just kicking a tin can with their bare feet. But they were intense, engrossed in their game, pushing, running, and laughing in a cloud of red dust. One boy tripped and rolled in the dirt and the other two stopped playing, helped him up, and the game resumed. Mvunu also watched.

"Dr. Youmani," he said, "you're a religious man. I used to be, but I'm not anymore. I'm in the army now and I go where they send me. That's why I'm here. But why in God's name are you here? Why are you wasting your time on this trip?" I didn't respond, so he continued. "I think it's because the man who is paying you said for you to come, and that same man stole his money from other people." He stopped waiting for my response. Did he mean Dr. Close? No. I thought he meant the president.

I told him I came because of compassion for these neglected people who had so little. They were sick, poor, and hopeless. I wanted to see what we actually accomplished with this floating hospital, but I did not express my disappointment aloud.

"Those kids playing in the street are happy just playing together," Dr. Mvunu said, "but they've no idea what other possibilities exist. I used to be just like them when I was a kid. Right now, they don't even care about their future. If the kid that just kicked gets an education like I did, do you think he would come back up here to live? Come back up here to teach or help those guys he's playing with now? Hell no, he wouldn't. He wouldn't even remember their names if he could help it."

Dr. Mvunu obviously had not been impressed with the benefits of the voyage either. "When you leave, Dr. Youmani, and the money runs out, we're all going to be back where we started. Nobody is going to come up here and live in this town to help these people. I've got an education and I've got my health, so why in the hell would I ever come here again? I'll just take my salary and never look back."

I remembered what Dr. Mvunu had told me about preparing to be a priest until Zaire's independence opened the possibility of medical school, and I asked him why he had spent so much time in school when he was a kid. He said his mother told him he'd never be happy without an education, and school was easy and fun, but he never thought a Zairian could be a doctor until Lovanium University opened its medical school and accepted him. He would have been happier in medical school if he hadn't been so poor, he said, but now that he was a doctor and the army paid his salary, his situation was better. He thought his mother had it wrong. Education wasn't enough to make him happy; he needed his health and money, too. When I told him I had known lots of people who were educated, healthy, and rich, but were still unhappy, he laughed. He said it would be enough for him, and then corrected himself by adding, "But not if I had to live here. I'll take the education, the health, and the money, but I'll take it all in Kinshasa. "

Six of my assistant nurses from Wembo Nyama had come to Kinshasa and applied for work as soon as they heard I was there. Very few educated Zairians wanted to live in the bush; even those without an education wanted to live in Kinshasa where they imagined they would find work and get rich.

Dr. Mvunu watched me as I thought about my own life. Maybe I had wasted my years here in Zaire treating malaria and hernias when I could have put my education and training to better use in America. What did I have to show for my time and effort? As I began to reflect on the years at Wembo Nyama and Sona Bata, I thought about some of the patients I had treated who would not have lived if I hadn't been there. What would I have done with those years if I hadn't been out there in the bush? I didn't know. Nobody knows what might have happened if they had made other choices. I had genuinely enjoyed the camaraderie of my work with the doctors, nurses, and pastors, and the satisfaction of seeing gratitude in the eyes of my patients, but maybe I could have found that in America, too. A great satisfaction came from seeing men like Dr. Mvunu come into their own—become more than what they had been. But that didn't sound like much. I had rather hoped that Dr. Mvunu would have more compassion for others, but I was glad to have been at least a part of his life.

The whistle of the riverboat signaled that we were starting back to Kinshasa. We both went out on the deck.

My family was on the dock when the *Mama Mobutu* arrived. I waved to them and they waved back. A skinny Zairian man, probably one of the *aides de malades,* approached me on the deck as I waved to my family.

"Thank you, Dr. Youmani, for what you are doing for my people," he said in French that was difficult to understand. Why couldn't Dr. Mvunu have said such a thing?

His clothes were well worn and ill fitting. He had spoken with a lisp. I nodded and smiled faintly. He said he wanted to give me a gift of appreciation, but I told him it wasn't necessary. My mind was on Winkie and the kids, but I wanted to affirm him and his generosity, and a small memento might be appropriate.

"The captain has it up in his cabin," he told me, "and I can't get it for you now. Could you come back later this afternoon?"

When I asked what kind of gift it was, he seemed hesitant to tell me, but finally did. He said he had caught a baby deer and brought it to Kinshasa. He wanted to give it to me for my children to enjoy. "It's all I can give you for all of your help," he said.

He persisted and looked at me with sad brown eyes. I didn't remember helping him at all, and I shook my head. I had no way to carry a baby deer in our little car. "I have my children in the car now. Can you keep the deer until tomorrow?" I asked.

His face broke into a radiant smile filled with hope. "Yes, yes. I noticed your wife and children there on the dock. You are a very fortunate man. God has blessed you. I will keep the deer until tomorrow at noon and I will meet you here. Thank you, Doctor, for accepting my small gift."

The gangplank had been placed on the dock. I shook his hand and said, "I'll see you here at noon tomorrow, and I thank you." I walked down the gangplank and onto the dock. When I looked back, the man was gone.

I hugged Winkie and the boys and Joy, but Grace was at cheerleading practice at school. We were in the car when the Zairian who was going to give me the deer tapped on the roof.

"Excuse me, Doctor, but I will need to give the captain something for transporting the gift here and for feeding it. Could you lend me a few *zaires* to pay for his expenses?

"Will ten *zaires* be enough?" I asked, as I pulled my wallet from my pocket.

"Oh yes, I think that will be enough."

I gave him the money, and he thanked me profusely. "Tomorrow," he said as I drove away.

"What was that all about?" Winkie asked.

I had intended the deer to be a surprise, but now I had to explain. The children were full of questions. "How big is it? What does it eat? Where is it now? Will it sleep in our garage?" Then Joy said, "Let's name it Bambi." They talked about Bambi all the way home. They made plans for the spot in the yard where the gardener should put the pen.

The next day I returned to the dock at noon. The riverboat was gone and the area was totally deserted. I waited for half an hour before I was fully convinced that I had been the victim of a scam. I had been duped. I was embarrassed that I had been so gullible, but I guess that paying ten *zaires* was better than becoming cynical. My hope for a gift had been dashed like the hopes of so many Zairians. It was clear to me that we were all in this together.

Thirty
Confrontation and Choice

"To see what is right and not do it is cowardice."

—Confucius

My double challenge at FOMECO and the Mama Yemo Hospital during my third year as chief of staff was to maintain what had been achieved: the standard of care for the enormous number of patients who came every day, and the standard of training for Zairian doctors. The emergency room had been remodeled, an intensive care unit had been added and equipped, the laboratory had technicians and instruments, and the Mama Yemo Hospital had an excellent reputation in the city. Our achievements were widely recognized and we were the hospital of choice for Zairians.

Blood transfusions had demonstrated a cultural difference between FOMECO personnel, with our objective view of blood, and the Bantu—more specifically, the Zairians—with their spiritual view of blood. Both views are complex. Western medicine recognizes that the value of whole blood for transfusion in patients who have suffered blood loss, and recognizes various types of blood are incompatible with each other if transfused. In addition, it recognizes that there are many identifiable fractions of blood that

267

are helpful in a variety of specific medical conditions. The common Zairian view of blood is essentially magical. Zairians would not give their own blood to a stranger, much less a potential enemy, who might thereby gain magical power over them. Similarly they would not accept a stranger's blood in transfusion lest it cause their death or at least empower the donor to cause evil to strike them. They believed the very life of a person is in his or her blood.

The Mama Yemo Hospital had re-established the laboratory's blood bank in 1970, and the typing, cross matching, and storage of blood was standard. The problem was in finding donors and, to a much lesser degree, in convincing a patient's family to allow a transfusion of blood. Major surgical procedures and severe trauma often required transfusions, and so did treatment of malaria-infected and severely anemic patients with hemoglobin levels of 2 or 3 grams percent, and we also did exchange transfusions for babies with Rh-factor incompatibility. We had initially relied on family members to donate for their close relatives, but in 1972 this was not sufficient. We tried to get more blood for the bank by requiring a family member to donate a unit of blood before we would schedule elective surgery, even though we did not expect to need blood for the patient. Often if the family donated blood but their relative didn't receive it, they would want it returned to them so they could bury it.

President Mobutu, the "father and guide" of the people, provided a Bantu solution to this Bantu problem. He donated his own blood on television and called on his people to share their blood with their Zairian brothers and sisters by donating to the hospital blood bank. Only a few people responded at first—his cabinet members and the members of his *bureau politique*. Mobutu finally solved the shortage by sending a couple of truckloads of soldiers to have their blood donated to the bank every week. Our needs were met and the problem was solved.

President Mobutu then asked FOMECO to undertake a national program for mother and child health called *Les Enfants Désirables,* meaning "Wanted Children." The program promoted contraceptive techniques and equipment and was violently opposed by the Catholic church and the nuns who ran our hospital's maternity. The promotion of this program was given to our chief of obstetrics and gynecology and a Zairian doctor in that department. Our hospital was delivering almost 150 babies a day by this time and the people of Kinshasa could have benefited from such a program, but contraception was culturally unacceptable to the Zairians.

The president wanted to win stronger popular support from the tribal people in the interior of Zaire, so he asked FOMECO to visit some rural government hospitals to see if the quality of their care could be improved. I was asked to visit and determine the quality of care offered by half a dozen government hospitals in various cities in Zaire, and what would be required to improve them. The government provided me with air transportation to these hospitals. I surveyed them and prepared reports, somewhat like the survey I had done on the emergency rooms of hospitals in Kansas City. The doctors and hospital administrators welcomed me in the hope that my survey would result in action to relieve at least some of their needs. Without exception they said that more money would resolve their problems.

Most of the hospitals lacked adequate medications for even the common diseases, and the patient's family was always expected to buy the medications ordered by the doctor from a pharmacy and bring them to the hospital for administration. Most of the hospitals had an occupancy rate of less than 20 percent, and half of those patients listed as inpatients were actually out on furlough until they brought the medicine to the hospital themselves. Every hospital's condition was similar to what I had found in the Kinshasa General when I arrived in 1970. The problems were overwhelming and the Zairian doctors themselves were part of the problem. They lacked authority and perhaps integrity and were preoccupied with politics. They needed money, medicine, administrators, and discipline. I gave my report and evaluations to Dr. Close, but my effort was an exercise in futility. Nothing was done.

When Bull Elephants Fight

Most of the American doctors in the Mama Yemo Hospital had come on two-year contracts that were completed early in 1973. A new crop of American trained specialists replaced the departing ones. Some of the new ones came hoping to practice their specialty and enjoy an exotic year in the tropics. Many didn't know French or tropical medicine and hadn't worked outside of America before. None of them could understand the enormous effort it had taken to raise the standards to the present level or the work required to maintain the current level.

Bob Williams, my fraternity brother and now a pharmacist, was one of our new staff members in Kinshasa. He had brought his wife and baby with him. In many ways it is more difficult for a black American to live in Zaire than for a white American. Zairians treat whites with more respect and deference than they do blacks. But Winkie and I were delighted to renew our friendship with Bob and to get acquainted with his family. His wife faced the same challenges in caring for her baby that Winkie had with ours, and she had doubts, frustrations, and anxieties, just as Winkie did.

The orientation process for the new staff and their families was a continuous process as the new ones arrived. The new families needed help in buying groceries and getting their children into school, and it fell to the four or five wives who had been in Zaire since 1970 to give this assistance. FOMECO arranged for a bus to transport the children to the American School, and another to take the women shopping each week, and even language lessons were made available.

It was difficult for the new specialists to be enthusiastic about training the Zairian doctors, who had received almost no personal experience in hands-on patient care before their assignment to the Mama Yemo Hospital, and who did not communicate in English. The specialists were eager to use their specialized skills and were frustrated as they were called on to treat and teach diseases outside their specialty. A few of the doctors took their frustrations directly to Dr. Close instead of working through the medical staff's committees. When Dr. Close made exceptions to accommodate one doctor, other doctors sought him for other exceptions until he refused to see them. He told them to work it out with the staff committees.

I could understand the frustration and anger of some of the new doctors and their families, but Zaire and the Mama Yemo Hospital were difficult places to live and work. I became increasingly frustrated and angry and thought some of the new doctors and their families needed to grow up and adapt to a tough situation. The morale of the staff began to fall and their hostilities surfaced. I finally talked to Winkie about it.

She suggested that I try to remember why I had come to Zaire to work with Dr. Close in upgrading this hospital. I acknowledged that it was because I was aware of the terrible condition of medical care in Zaire and I had believed, or at least hoped, that I could make a difference. It had been a challenge. Bill had said he could get the money and political authority to make changes, and I had believed him. Together with Dr. Bazunga we more than met my expectations in that area and we had helped thousands of people, probably millions. And yes, we had trained Zairian doctors. I had come as a response to God's call to treat and teach Zairians. I had come with that mission, I told her.

"Don't you remember when Bill said he wanted American doctors to teach the young Congolese doctors to have compassion?" I asked. "And didn't he say he wanted doctors who had faith in God? And that faith would give the doctors strength and wisdom?"

Winkie was taken aback, and replied sharply, "If you came to encourage faith in God, tell me why you are serving a dictator who steals copper and diamond mines from their legal owners and uses them to enrich himself."

I had expected sympathy, but she reacted with as much frustration and anger as the staff. She went on to say that I was building up the popularity of a dictator who killed the people who opposed him, and who authorized his lackeys to deport or kill foreign businessmen so that he and his cronies could steal their property and their businesses. She said she couldn't understand why I was upset because a couple of doctors complained about not getting the instruments they needed to work. "You seem to have great faith in Dr. Close and President Mobutu, but not in a God of justice," she concluded.

I had not been aware of her pent-up feelings and frustrations. It was certainly true that I hadn't really spent much time listening to her views the past six months. I had thought she understood the value of my work with Dr. Close and the necessity of not complaining about President Mobutu's actions. I suggested that maybe we should just quit and go back to America and abandon the patients. She ignored my sarcasm, but looked resigned.

"That's up to you, Roger. You know I didn't want to come here with FOMECO in the first place. But I'll stay if you stay, and I'll go home when you go. I know you have helped a lot of people and made real changes in the hospital, so don't go over all of that again."

But I did start repeating the values I had clung to at the hospital, until I realized that she wasn't listening. My face must have betrayed my concern and doubts and revealed my confusion.

Winkie smiled sadly and said with a little sarcasm of her own, "You had more time with your patients and better relations with the people you worked with in Sona Bata and Wembo Nyama, even in Kansas City, than you do here."

She was right. And I didn't trust the government and I didn't like administrative work. I had enjoyed working with the young Zairian doctors, especially in the operating room. And I had been even happier when I had taken time to just play with my family. "Maybe I should resign from administrative responsibilities and just try to be a doctor and a teacher. Just be a surgeon," I suggested.

Winkie looked at me with surprise in her eyes and said tentatively, "Maybe you should."

I didn't resign. I didn't change. I felt sorry for myself and resented each complaint aimed my way. One afternoon Dr. Close came into my clinic where I was working at the hospital and told me the American ambassador had suggested we ask the Peace Corps to send us some technicians to help in the lab. The U.S. government would pay their salaries, train them to our specifications, including teaching them French, paying for their transportation, and then putting them in the hospital under our directions. It wouldn't cost FOMECO anything. He asked me to go to Denver, Colorado, and interview fifty or sixty applicants and select the thirty who would be most helpful. "Take Winkie along. Take a little break."

After making arrangements for friends to take care of our children, Winkie and I flew to Kansas City where she met her sister at the airport and went to stay with her and her parents for a few days while I interviewed the Peace Corps candidates in Denver. When I was through in Denver, she flew there and we both went to San Diego to visit my parents in Chula Vista. Dad had been hospitalized for Alzheimer's Disease and was now in a locked ward at the hospital. He had gotten up at night several times before he was hospitalized and wandered away from home, getting on buses and becoming utterly lost. The police had picked him up several times and brought him back home. Mom was distraught and consented to have him stay in the hospital where she visited him three or four times a day.

When Winkie and I arrived at Fredericka Manor Retirement Home, Mom took us directly to the hospital. She was cheerful and upbeat as the three of us walked into the lobby. She was well known to many of the employees and introduced me proudly to many as we walked to the elevator and went to the fourth floor. When we got off the elevator, we were in a small lobby with two doors.

As we paused briefly, a nurse came out one door pushing a wheelchair with an elderly man slumped forward against the sheet around his chest that kept him from falling out of the chair.

"Why, look there, Mr. Eldridge," the nurse said cheerily, "there's Mrs. Youmans. Doesn't she look nice? I bet that's her son that she has told us about."

Mom beamed and nodded, and I said hello and smiled as the nurse wheeled the chair passed us. Mr. Eldridge made no response, and continued leaning against the restraining sheet with spittle dripping from the corner of his mouth. He looked pathetic.

The other door was locked. Mom pressed the buzzer, and I

looked through the small glass window in the door. I saw an old man with a walker shuffling down the corridor toward the door.

When a buzzer sounded, Mom pulled the door open, and led us in. Several more old people were slumped over in wheelchairs in a small day-room ahead of us. All but one looked as if they were asleep, and that one peered up at us with one bleary eye open. I wondered how Mom could stand to come into this ward every day, month after month, to see Dad. It must take enormous emotional strength to see your dearest and closest friend, your lifelong mate and lover, living here among these patients who were slowly dying. A wave of despair swept over me.

Mom led us down the hall. We passed another day-room where two old men and two old women slumped against restraining sheets in four soft chairs. They were pointed toward a television set that was broadcasting some kind of game show. "Your dad is so gentle," Mom said. "It makes me angry the way Mr. Anderson treats him. He's your father's roommate. He takes your father's socks right out of the drawer, and then insists they're his own. One night he began hitting your dad, but the nurse heard the commotion and came and made him quit."

At the end of the hall, Mom led us into a small room. I saw an old man sitting in a chair by the window. He was tied into the chair with a sheet like the others I had seen. His thin white hair had been neatly combed, but the stubble on this face indicated that he had not been shaved for several days. He was wearing a dark blue bathrobe over his hospital gown.

The room was semi-dark with the shade pulled halfway down, blocking most of the late afternoon light. It was as though we were in a cave with an old man, worn out with life, who sat in the dark and stared at the fading day outside. I remembered a poem by Edwin Markham about a man leaning on a hoe, crushed by the injustices of the world. And I could almost see the painting by Millet of a stooped peasant at dusk, leaning on a hoe with an empty expression on his face. Before me in the chair sat a modern version of "The Man With a Hoe," a man without hope or even the memory of hope. It was my dad.

"Thank goodness Mr. Anderson isn't here," Mom said as we walked closer to the man in the chair. The man didn't look at me or

Mom, but stared blankly into space with saliva on his lips and chin. Mom quickly wiped it away with her handkerchief.

"Good evening, Raymond," Mom said loudly but cheerfully. "Roger's here with Winkie. They just came back from Africa." A faint movement, perhaps a smile, flickered on his lips at the sound of Mom's voice, but otherwise his face was blank and passive. He turned his head in the direction of Mom's voice and then looked at me and past me, with no hint of recognition.

Then my dad's animated face emerged from the mist of my memory. His bright blue eyes looked at me from somewhere inside my head and he asked me if the girl I was dating was white or black. Then I saw his tired eyes as he turned away from the notes and books on the make-shift desk and looked at me in response to an awkward question that I had asked about something in a book I had just read. I saw Dad as he officiated at my wedding to Winkie twenty years ago. There had always been a twinkle in his blue eyes, but now those eyes were dull and empty.

I took one of Dad's hands in mine. "Hello, Dad. I'm glad to be here and see you again," but it was a half-truth. I was uncomfortable and a little anxious with this man. Was this Dad? This strange old man didn't recognize me, or anybody, or anything. Whatever Mom's voice had touched in him had faded as quickly as it had occurred. "The children couldn't come with us this time," I said loudly, imitating the way Mom had spoken to him. "But they send you their love."

I thought I saw a little light of recognition in his eye, but it was only a tear. Then he began to shake and make inarticulate grunts and growls. Tears ran down both cheeks. I was rather frightened. I tried to smile, but my face contorted in anguish. Finally I said, "God bless you, Dad." His agitation got worse, with jerking and thrashing motions of one hand, while the other alternately squeezed and relaxed its grip on my hand. Had my voice registered in some deep recess of his memory?

Mom's matter-of-fact voice said firmly, "Where are your socks? Your feet will get cold." She picked up his socks, one by the window and the other from under the chair. "Let me put these socks back on your feet. My goodness, your feet are already cold." She had to hold Dad's leg to keep it still while she pulled the sock over his heel. She gently placed his foot back on the floor and picked up the other sock. Grasping the other leg to hold it still, she pulled his sock on. She stood up for a moment, then bent down and kissed him on his forehead. I remembered how lucid Dad's mind had been and how gentle and intelligent his answers! This is what he had become?

"Dad," I began, "I don't know what to say. Do you know me? You do recognize who I am, don't you?" His face contorted in anguish and he made grunting sounds and continued squeezing my hand and jerking his legs and other arm. Saliva dripped from his mouth. His eyes were confused and bewildered. "I'm Roger, your youngest son, and I've just come back from Africa. I want you to know that I love you. You were always so loving and supportive of me." It was painful, but I struggled on. "I'm not sure that you remember those days, years ago. I remember you, the way you were when I was young. Do you remember?" I tried to ignore his grunts and jerks and the contortions of his face, but I couldn't. "You always had time for me. Remember? You would turn away from the work on your desk to talk to me. Thank you, Dad. Thank you for being my dad. I love you."

Tears streamed down his cheeks and he became increasingly agitated as I talked. I tried again. "We just have to trust God these days. He loves you, and we love you." Tears blurred my vison and the ache in my heart blurred my thoughts. I held his hand while both of us cried.

Mom fussed around with the blankets, adjusted the shade, and then straightened the blankets again. She kissed Dad on the forehead. This was the same man she had married over fifty years ago. For her to believe this man was her husband and sweetheart wasn't an act of faith, she was certain of it. "Tell Roger and Winkie goodbye," Mom said loudly to Dad. "They have to go back to Africa."

We walked out of the room, and with a final glance back, closed the door. "Your father is the sweetest man there ever was," Mom whispered as we walked down the hall toward the locked door.

Winkie and I hardly spoke the next day on the flight to New York.

When we arrived back in Kinshasa, I gave my report and the folders on each of the Peace Corps candidates to Dr. Close. The ones I had selected weren't really what we had hoped for, but he would make the final decision.

Several months later the volunteers arrived and were sent to Rwanda to study French. I wouldn't see them until they arrived at the hospital several months later. By that time most of the candidates had been sent back to the States because of drug abuse, and only four actually worked with us in the hospital. They provided good help and several of them were excellent. I don't think our experience with Peace Corps volunteers in the sixties was typical of their program.

And always there were too many patients to be seen, too many operations to be done, and worst of all, too many meetings to attend. In addition to the care of the patients, the surgery staff had at least one teaching conference each week, and the general surgeons also held weekly teaching rounds with the Zairian doctors. The doctors were working as hard as was humanly possible. We encouraged and supported each other and built a camaraderie of sorts, but we never had enough time.

Dr. Bazunga and I spent hours resolving the differences between the expectations the American doctors brought with them from America and the expectations of the Zairian doctors, nurses, and other employees with whom they worked each day. We often met with Dr. Close to coordinate what the changing politics and financial resources would allow and how employees were responding to the changes. We were motivated by different dreams as step by step we resolved problems and overcame obstacles.

But we were imposing a foreign culture of medical care onto these people, transplanting what had grown in America onto the Zairians. It included information, equipment, and medications, but it was bigger and more subtle than these obvious aspects. It was the *American world view* of the practice of medicine colliding with the *Zairian world view* of health and community. It was in the personal relationships that the differences were most painful for me. The shared goals and efforts that had brought such joy and satisfaction to me at Sona Bata and Wembo Nyama had been sucked away in recent months by administrative hassles that seemed inevitable and irreconcilable.

Winkie eventually got fed up with my complaints again, and one night asked me why I didn't quit doing things I didn't think were important. I protested that Close, Bazunga, and the doctors each had different ideas about what was important. We spent a lot of time reconciling our goals and compromising. We couldn't meet everybody's expectations.

"That's not your problem, Roger," Winkie said firmly. "Your problem is choosing what you will and won't do. Decide what you really want to do, and do it."

I believed I could do that. My job, my goals in Zaire, had changed over the last three years from personally treating sick and powerless people to maintaining hospital standards and teaching young doctors. That was okay, except I couldn't do all of it in the way I wanted with the time and energy available. Better organization didn't seem to me a likely option. My perception of FOMECO's goals was that they had morphed from upgrading the hospital's quality of care into maintaining Mobutu's support for the hospital and running numerous health-related projects in Kinshasa and other parts of Congo.

I wondered if President Mobutu's goals had changed from helping his people to using them for his own personal power and luxury, or had personal power always been his goal? I was not going to affect President Mobutu's goals, and I doubted if I would significantly affect those of FOMECO. But I could deal with my own goals and priorities—to sort out why I was in Zaire and why I was a doctor, and what it all might mean to my family. I could choose what I would do.

Thirty-one
Celebrate

"Weeping may tarry for a night,
But joy comes in the morning."
—Psalms 30:5b RSV

I remembered that morning in Kananga in March of 1966, when Winkie realized I had agreed for us to go to Wembo Nyama without even asking her. She had felt betrayed. I remembered her frightened eyes when I sent her home with the children seven years ago while I stayed in Congo. Worst of all, I remembered how I had pressured her to sign the contract to return to Zaire with me. I knew she now wanted our family to distance ourselves from FOMECO and from Mobutu's patronage. But I still had a vision of medically helping the Zairians and training Zairian doctors. It was a domestic and increasingly serious dilemma.

But I had another serious dilemma. As chief of staff I represented the medical staff and was responsible to them, but they had never elected me. As director of the medical staff I represented Dr. Close and was responsible to him. The essence of the problem was that several members of the medical staff were vocal in their insistence that I was not adequately representing the views of staff to the administration of the hospital and to the Director of FOMECO, Dr. Close. These few doctors wanted to elect their own representative, essentially their own chief of staff, and that seemed reasonable to me.

Dr. Close and Dr. Bazunga reluctantly agreed that the staff could elect a representative to express their views and grievances to our administrative council, which was composed of Dr. Close, Dr. Bazunga and myself. If the staff chose a doctor other than me, I could resign from my administrative responsibilities and have time to teach, see patients, and operate like any other surgeon. At our next regular medical staff meeting, I explained that several doctors had wanted to elect a chief of staff to represent them to the administrative council and that we would hold that election at our regular staff meeting the following month. I appointed three doctors to make the arrangements. I was careful not to claim any real authority for the elected chief of staff, because the only real power regarding the hospital was President Mobutu, who had appointed Dr. Close to carry out his wishes in FOMECO's various responsibilities, including the hospital.

Three weeks later, several days before the staff had their next meeting, Dr. Close asked me to attend a meeting of the *Conseil de Gestion* (the Zairian advisors to Dr. Close whom President Mobutu had appointed). I had never attended a meeting of this *Conseil* before, but Bill said they were going to discuss some policies that he thought I would have an opinion about. When I arrived, Bill was presiding from the front of the room, already filled with twenty Zairians, so I sat down inconspicuously in the back. The discussion was about how much money should be collected from patients for the medical care they received in the hospital. The actual amount of money involved was small, and the discussion was frivolous.

I didn't notice when the discussion moved on to whether foreigners employed by various international assistance agencies in Zaire ought to be charged by the hospital or given free care. The specific question was whether the ATB *(Aide Technique Belge)*, pronounced "ah te be," would be given free medical care at the hospital. I misunderstood the question, and thought it had to do with free care for a case of tuberculosis, which in French would be pronounced "cah te be." When I was abruptly called on to comment, I strongly expressed my opinion that every case of TB should be treated at our hospital, whether the patient could pay for treatment or not. I saw it as a matter of public health.

As I spoke, I could see the confusion on the faces of the men in the room, including Dr. Close. They asked me several questions that were unrelated to tuberculosis. Finally Dr. Close asked me to tell him in English what I wanted to say. After a few exchanges he realized the error I had made and explained to the *Conseil* that I had been talking about "cases of tuberculosis" and not "*Aide Technique Belge.*"

The Zairians and Bill laughed and joked about my mistake for five minutes. I was tired, irritable, and hypersensitive. I mistakenly took their laughter personally and felt ridiculed.

After the meeting I returned to the hospital to continue my duties in the emergency room for the rest of the night. My mood and attitude were ugly and there were several operative cases already waiting for me. When I took a break about 11:00 P.M., Bill was waiting to see me in the changing room. He asked me to come outside and sit in his car and talk for a few minutes.

The first thing he said to me was, "Roger, I want to apologize to you about this evening. I didn't mean to embarrass you there, but I couldn't understand what you meant. I agree that we have to treat tuberculosis patients whether they can pay or not, but that wasn't what we were talking about."

I didn't respond, so he continued, "I know that you are all working your butts off," he said, "and the president knows it too. You can't imagine how pleased he is with the hospital being named after his mother. I just want to thank you, Roger. I'll make it up to you somehow. I just want you to know how sorry I am for embarrassing you."

I had never seen this conciliatory aspect of Dr. Close before and I could hardly believe that he was being so apologetic. I tried to smile, and then I said, "Sure, Bill. It's okay. We're in this together. You and George are doing your part, and I'm just trying to do mine."

"And you're doing far more than your part, Roger." Then he added," If you're through for the night here, I can give you a ride home."

"Thanks, but I'm on duty here all night. Thanks for stopping by."

When Bull Elephants Fight

The nitpicking and complaining among several staff members had not improved as far as I was concerned. I spent the next morning in the operating room and the rest of the day I saw patients in my clinic. A patient of mine in the intensive care unit died in the afternoon. I was exhausted and discouraged, and really wanted to quit everything. I was not able to think clearly.

Winkie was worried about me when I slept twelve hours that night, and she insisted I stay all day Saturday at home with the family. I fell asleep in the late afternoon and awoke early Sunday morning. Winkie wanted to attend a Pentecostal church because an American was going to preach, and she wanted to hear a sermon in English. The kids went with us.

I had never been in a Pentecostal church before and I was upset by the noise and confusion before the service began. The church was packed with about a thousand Zairians who worshiped and prayed out loud. Some of them shouted "hallelujah" and "amen" while others were singing, but they were singing different songs at the same time. Others were beating tambourines and blowing whistles.

The crowd became quiet when announcements were made in Lingala and French. The preacher gave a typical "gospel sermon" in English, waiting between sentences while a Zairian translated it into French and another Zairian translated it into Lingala. He preached the necessity for all of us to confess our sins to God, to believe that Jesus had paid for our sins, and to accept God's forgiveness. I had heard many such sermons like that in the Methodist churches back in America, and in dozens of Zairian churches, too.

When the preacher got to the words "accept God's forgiveness," he added, "And celebrate." I saw myself as weighted down by the cares, frustrations, and worries of the hospital. I thought about my patients and worried about the patient who had died a few weeks earlier. I was plagued by a sense of personal failure to adequately care for my family or take adequate care of my patients, and my inability to raise the medical staff's morale. I recognized my mixed motives in returning to Congo, my resentment toward several of my colleagues, and pride in my achievements. Then I recognized that God already knew me for what I was, and He knew about every failure I could imagine, and yet I knew he loved me anyway. It was an epiphany, an ownership of myself, but covered with God's love, mercy, and forgiveness. I didn't have to carry my self-imposed burdens and guilt-laden self-pity.

When the preacher said, "Celebrate," a sense of relief and joy swept away the guilt and resentments. I was what I was, and I knew it was enough for God. If it was good enough for God, it was good enough for everybody else. I wanted to celebrate.

I'm sure that it was an emotional experience, but it was also a mental and a spiritual one. It was a renewal of what I had known but lost sight of in the stress of work, fatigue, and humiliation. God really did love me just like I was. It was a wonderful feeling! I laughed with relief and celebrated with the crowd of Zairian worshippers.

I woke up Monday morning in a cheerful mood. I didn't know why nor did I care. I went to the hospital as usual, and was happy to just be myself and take care of my patients and my family. Wes Eiseman, the pilot with Missionary Aviation Fellowship who had flown our family out of Wembo Nyama, came by the hospital and asked me to give a little talk at a Zairian prayer meeting Friday evening. "Something simple," he said, and I agreed.

I left the hospital and headed for my car at six o'clock Friday evening to go to the church as Wes had asked. But then I remembered Dr. Mvunu and our talks on the riverboat hospital and thought he might like to go with me. I didn't know where he would be, but when I found him, he wanted to go.

In a few minutes we were driving through the darkening streets of Kinshasa, looking for the little church. Wes had given me the directions and Dr. Mvunu guided me as I related the directions to him. We found the small mud-brick church and there were already about fifty people waiting for us. The Zairian pastor identified himself to us, explaining that Wes had told him we would be coming.

The interior of the little church was dimly lit with two kerosene lanterns in the back, and a larger kerosene pressure lantern with a pump and a mantle, in the front of the church. The large lantern illuminated about a quarter of the room. Without much formality I was introduced as a friend of Wes. The pastor explained that Dr. Mvunu and I were doctors at the Mama Yemo Hospital, and that Dr. Mvunu would translate into Lingala for me.

I stood there in the bright light, looking out into the semi-darkness and I saw a sea of eager eyes and smiles. I had a strange sensation that I was back up at the Wembo Nyama meeting with the workers early that morning seven years ago. I had given a "testimony" that morning and the workers knew me only as the newly arrived doctor who couldn't speak Otetela.

I turned to Dr. Mvunu and said, "You don't have to translate for me if you would rather not."

"I want to," he said. I was surprised because he was usually shy and retiring.

So I began speaking in French, pausing after each sentence until he had translated it. I told them about the experience of trying to communicate that first morning in Wembo Nyama years ago and my frustration in not being able to speak Otetela. Then I read to them from the Bible, John 3:16, about God's love for everybody in the world. After that I just told them as much as I could remember of what the preacher had said in the Pentecostal church on Sunday. Then I told them about the freedom and joy I had experienced in celebrating God's love and power, and in celebrating my forgiveness. They were very quiet and listened intently to what I said and to Dr. Mvunu's translation. I looked out at the expectant faces of the little crowd gathered there in the dark corners of the room, and I invited them to open their hearts and to celebrate God's love and forgiveness.

Immediately the entire group of Zairians in the church began to celebrate. They began to laugh, to pray, to shout, to sing, and to dance. It was a celebration of joy right there where they were. This celebration continued for thirty minutes before I told the pastor that I really had to get back to the hospital. He thanked us for coming, and Dr. Mvunu for translating. We left the people in the church still laughing, singing, and celebrating. We drove back to the hospital. Dr. Mvunu sat silently beside me, staring straight ahead. I glanced sidewise several times as I drove through the dark streets, but Dr. Mvunu's expression didn't change.

Finally he looked over at me, and with wonder in his voice, he said, "Dr. Youmani, I have never seen God bless my people like He did tonight."

I was speechless. But in my heart I was still celebrating.

That night I wrote out two copies of my letter of resignation as director of the medical staff of FOMECO, and I included many of the administrative inconsistencies, compromises, and frustrations that I had experienced. I put one under the door of Dr. Close's office and the other copy under the door of Dr. Bazunga's office. And then I went to bed and slept soundly, unburdened of FOMECO and of the world.

I awoke the next morning euphoric. I had been released from my sense of dependence on circumstances, and from depending on FOMECO, or the hospital, or Dr. Close for my identity. But it was more than that. I felt confident again and free to work hard. I celebrated being alive, free of compulsion or worry. But nobody else at the hospital seemed to notice as I made my rounds.

Monday morning before noon, I received short notes from both Dr. Close and Dr. Bazunga declining my resignation. When we met later that day, they expressed their confidence in me and how important they thought it was for me to continue to lead and direct the medical staff. They asked me to withdraw my letters of resignation. I felt completely free to stand by my resignation, or to withdraw it. I chose at that moment to withdraw the letters. The problem for me had not really been the work and responsibility, but rather my attitude and my assumption that I was responsible for other people's decisions. That's too simple an explanation, of course, but it was a major source of my frustration. Winkie, Dr. Close, the newly arrived American specialists, and President Mobutu were all free to make their own decisions and to express them without my permission or responsibility. What a relief.

At our medical staff meeting the following week I was surprised that the medical staff elected me as their representative and chief. I was affirmed.

A week later my mother wrote a letter stating a need for relief from the daily visits to the hospital to see Dad, and saying that she had always wanted to visit Africa. She had already talked to my brothers, who had encouraged her to go ahead and fulfill one of her lifelong dreams—painting the animals and landscapes of Africa. My brother helped her arrange the tickets and board the plane, but somehow she left without a visa to Zaire. Our director of protocol took me to the airport, then went out to the plane alone to meet her, and there he realized she didn't have a visa. He immediately took her into the VIP lounge to wait for him while he arranged things for her. When I asked him how he had gotten Mom through Immigration without a visa, he just laughed.

Mom seemed oblivious to the politics and the poverty in Kinshasa. She reveled in the picturesque beauty of the tropical flowers and animals. Winkie took her to the president's zoo on Mount Galiema, near the president's house and the paracommando barracks. She saw several of the okapis, the strange animals unique to Zaire that look like a cross between a giraffe and a zebra. Mom painted the lions, leopards, and elephants. She sketched street scenes of sidewalk merchants and beggars. She sketched portraits of people she saw on the sidewalks and streets. She included drawings of our pet dog and cat. She seemed to get younger and more vibrant as the days passed. Winkie took her all over town during the day, and Mom did her best to spoil her grandchildren in the evenings.

Two days before she was scheduled to return to America, Mom tripped over our dog on the outside steps and broke her leg. A cast was applied and the following day a "walking heel" was added. She flew home the next day. She had to change planes three times and the trip took more than twenty-four hours, but the flight attendants gave her special attention all the way because of the cast on her leg.

I hope that I can match her courage and good fortune when I'm eighty years old.

Winkie had more than just my mother to contend with during that last year in Kinshasa. Archie, a son of missionary friends of ours who were stationed deep in the interior of Zaire, had been living in the Methodist hostel while he was finishing his senior year at the American School. He was expelled from the hostel when they found a stash of marijuana in his bedroom. He would be allowed to complete high school only if he agreed to live with a family that would act as his temporary guardian and assure that he stayed off drugs. Winkie and I took him in and he spent the rest of the academic year living with us and our four children. He did well in school, and became a precious part of our family.

Suzanne was an American black woman with a degree in nursing who sought out Winkie at our church in Kinshasa and then spent several months living in our home with our family and Archie. She had married a Zairian whom she had met as a student in Russia, and they had two children. Her husband took some additional wives and expected Suzanne to work like a Zairian woman, a virtual slave, while the other wives took care of her children. She left her husband and two children and fled to Tanzania and later to Angola for several years, but had now returned to Kinshasa. She was bitter, destitute, and desperate when she talked to Winkie one Sunday night. During those next several months we witnessed Susan's metamorphosis as she began working in our household.

The staff of the Mama Yemo Hospital continued to change and a growing number of Zairian doctors became a part of our medical staff. Young Zairian doctors just out of medical school continued to rotate through the hospital for a year before being sent out to work in the hospitals that were so inadequately staffed throughout the interior of Zaire.

The training of Zairian technicians and nurse anesthetists became a larger part of our program. The in-service training of nurses in the emergency room, the intensive care unit, and the clinical and histology laboratories were continuous. The riverboat hospital continued making trips up the Zaire River and its major tributaries each month.

The social and political situation in Zaire rapidly deteriorated even as life at the hospital proceeded apace. In their nationalistic enthusiasm for a return to authentic African values, the Zairian politicians encouraged the confiscation of homes, land, and personal property belonging to citizens of India, Pakistan, Belgium, and other foreign countries. These former property owners were expelled from the country without compensation.

I decided not to renew our contract with FOMECO and began preparing to leave when our contract expired in a few months. I had finally come to agree with Winkie that our continued presence in Zaire would be an endorsement of President Mobutu. He had recently closed the Roman Catholic seminary in Kinshasa, and shut down a Catholic publication because of the church's objection to aspects of the government's "return to authenticity" policies. The church's properties and its very existence were threatened. Mobutu seemed to be trying to replace the institutionalized presence of God in Zaire.

In April I received a telegram from my brother telling me that our father had died, and that Mom now needed the support of all of her children. A memorial service was scheduled in three weeks and he hoped my family and I could attend. Although my contract didn't expire for several more weeks, Dr. Close agreed to let me take my remaining vacation time as a terminal leave and released me from my contract for an early departure for the funeral. I suggested that the Zairian doctor who had been my understudy for a year take my place as director of the medical staff.

Winkie was relieved at this turn of events, but our daughter Grace insisted on finishing her sophmore year in high school with her friends before returning to America.

I remembered the separation of our family after Wembo Nyama in 1967, and fear, like a winter blizzard, chilled my heart. I had promised Winkie that I would never again allow our family to be separated, and here it was about to happen again. Grace was only sixteen, a girl almost entering womanhood. Should I force her to go with us, or allow her to stay? If she stayed and something happened to her, I would never forgive myself.

"Nothing will happen, Dad," Grace said. "Nothing will happen to me."

"You can't be sure of that," I said. But I was the one who wasn't sure. Where is the line between parental control and a sixteen-year-old girl's freedom to grow and make her own decisions? I don't know, but I do know that she, like me, would have to keep growing and learning and taking risks, or something in her soul would die. In the end I put my confidence in Grace and her good judgment. Our family returned to America, and Grace remained in Zaire with our friends. Two months later Grace rejoined us as she had promised.

It would be many years before Winkie and I returned to Zaire.

Epilogue

"Nothing that is worth doing
can be achieved in one lifetime;
Therefore we must be saved by hope.
Nothing which is beautiful or good makes complete
sense in any immediate context of history;
Therefore we must be saved by faith.
Nothing we do, however virtuous,
can be accomplished alone;
Therefore we must be saved by love."
— Rheinhold Niebehr

Fifteen years after we left FOMECO, and twenty-eight years after our first arrival in Kinshasa, Winkie and I returned to Zaire as part of my sabbatical leave from the medical school in America where I was teaching. We stayed in the Union Mission Guest House again, but Tina was no longer the hostess. We used taxis for transportation. Chaos reigned in the Kinshasa streets as vehicles ignored rules and regulations, and every driver did as he pleased.

The Methodist bishop's office was now in Kinshasa instead of

When Bull Elephants Fight

Kananga. In fact, there were now two Methodist bishops, one in Kinshasa supervising the Methodist church in the western part of Zaire, and the other in Lubumbashi supervising the Methodist church in the eastern part of Zaire. Bishop Shungu, whom we had known so well when we were in Wembo Nyama, was now retired, but was still quite active in the Methodist church. Bishop Onema, father of one of Grace's classmates in the American School, was now the bishop of the Methodist church in the western part of Zaire, including Wembo Nyama.

I wanted to visit Wembo Nyama briefly to see how things had changed, but I had not made prior arrangements for our visit. Bishop Onema was gracious as he explained that Wembo Nyama was suffering from a lack of reliable transportation. Repeated political disturbances in the area had resulted in much hunger and sickness.

"The church, the hospital, and the schools are still functioning in Wembo Nyama," the bishop said, "but they are not like they were before independence. You are welcome, but you must not expect too much."

Before we left Kinshasa I visited the Mama Yemo Hospital. The street vendors clogged the entrance area just as they had done in August of 1970. Other Zairians loitered around the entrance, eating peanuts and bananas and discarding the paper containers and banana peels on the street. Garbage had accumulated in small piles against the hospital walls. The buildings looked very much like I had remembered them. But the throngs of people were missing. The noise and frenetic activity was absent. The patients and relatives moved slowly, almost insolently. A resentful hopelessness seemed to have overtaken the hospital.

The emergency room was moderately clean and reasonably busy. I didn't see anyone I had known, and nobody paid any attention to me. What had been our intensive care unit appeared now to be a holding area from the emergency room. The new operating rooms that we had kept so busy were empty except for two cleaners. I asked why there were no operations in progress, and they smiled and said that surgery was done in the morning. One of the operating rooms was now used as a storage room.

A large picture of Dr. Close was on the wall of the laboratory. I got the attention of one of the technicians and asked him in my rusty French about the picture.

"That's the picture of Dr. Close," he told me. "He worked for President Mobutu."

I said I was a friend of Dr. Close and asked where I could find him now. The technician said that he had gone back to America many years ago.

Two other technicians came over and began listening to our conversation. One of them spoke up. "You are a friend of Dr. Close? I met him once." And a proud, happy grin spread across his face.

"Are there any technicians or nurses here today that have been here for a long time? Maybe even twenty years?" I asked.

The three of them looked at each other and then slowly shook their heads. The technician that I had first spoken to then suggested, "Maybe Phillip. He works on the Surgery Pavilion #9. He has been here a long time. Maybe you can go there?"

I looked into the ward in Pavilion #9. An older, somewhat gray-headed Zairian male nurse walked over to me.

"Can I help you, sir?" he asked, staring at me with curiosity.

"Yes, I'm Dr. Youmans, and I just wanted to see how the hospital is getting along."

The nurse's face lit up and a radiant smile expressed his joy. "Dr. Youmani," he said slowly, "it has been a long time. How is your family?"

I was touched again by the personal interest of Zairians in families, and by his having remembered me. "You are Phillip," I said. "My family is well. They send you their greetings. How is your family?"

As we talked, he told me his family was back in Wembo Nyama and that his wife had recently had a new baby. He mentioned that the salaries were not regular after the American doctors left. Phillip had been one of the assistant nurses from Wembo Nyama who came to Kinshasa when he heard that I was the director of the medical staff at this hospital. Several had come looking for work, and Dr. Bazunga had hired them on my recommendation. When he asked if I was coming back here to stay, his eyes began to shine with excitement and anticipation. When I told him no, his face fell and his shoulders slumped forward a little. I was glad that he had such good memories of me and of FOMECO's work, but those days were gone. FOMECO's money had run out, and the political priorities of President Mobutu had changed.

The following day Winkie and I borrowed a car and drove down to Sona Bata. Tata Nsiala, looking much older now, showed me around the hospital. There were no white missionaries, and the young Zairian doctor seemed more knowledgeable than I had remembered most Zairian doctors to be. The hospital was over half full, but otherwise everything looked about as I remembered it.

"Where is Tata Kimpiatu?" I asked.

Nsiala was caught by surprise. "He...he's not here now."

I waited for some explanation, but none was forthcoming. I asked about Kimpiatu's family and was immediately told that Mama Nzuzi was here in Sona Bata and the children were fine. Finally he offered the explanation that Kimpiatu had retired and moved to Kinshasa.

I concluded that something unpleasant or disgraceful had happened to Kimpiatu that Nsiala did not want to tell me. How like the Zairians not to want to deliver bad news. I asked no more questions.

The Cessna landed on the same dirt strip at Wembo Nyama where we had been so wildly and joyfully received years ago. But this time there was no welcoming party. Samuel, my old driver, beamed joyfully when he saw us. *"Moyo, Uwandji!"* he called as he neared the plane.

The buildings on the mission compound were the same, but there were no large crowds at the hospital. There seemed to be a lot of school children on the station. The family of the woman from whom I had removed the huge thyroid goiter under local anesthetic twenty-one years ago was there to thank me again. They still called me *"Uwandji Wechi Koi"* and Winkie, *"Uya Koi"*, and they were still convinced that it was a miracle their mother was still alive after all these years.

The empty beds and the lethargy of the people contrasted with my memory of the hospital. The pharmacy's supply of medicine was still meager, and the X-ray machine nonfunctional. The needs of the people and hospital were enormous, but there was little hope or enthusiasm in the eyes of the nurses or patients. The pastor told me how the people suffered, and how they survived by subsistence farming. They had very little money, and inflation reduced what money they did have. The only paying jobs were with the church and even there pay was low.

Back in Kinshasa, I filled in for several days for Dr. Macpherson in his American clinic. He was the only American doctor from the Mama Yemo Hospital still in Kinshasa. On my third day in the clinic a thirty-year-old American man came in for an HIV/AIDS test.

I started explaining how AIDS was transmitted and how to protect one's self, but he cut me off.

"Don't lecture me, Doc. I'm an AIDS prevention specialist, and I'm over here as a consultant for the control of the epidemic here in Kinshasa."

"You are?" I asked, very much surprised.

"Yes, indeed. We just did an evaluation on that big hospital here in town called Mama Wembo or something like that. We found that over 50% of the women employed there were HIV-positive." He shook his head contemptuously. "So you don't need to tell me about AIDS."

I thought about the blood transfusions we had given patients in the seventies before anybody knew about AIDS. We had given over 5,000 blood transfusions, most of them taken from soldiers. We probably unintentionally spread the disease.

I asked him if he had been exposed to HIV through an accident in the lab with a contaminated needle.

"Hell no, Doc," he said. "I didn't get exposed in any lab. It was one of those damn black women."

I stared at him in disbelief. "Didn't you know...?"

"Doc, it ain't what you know. It's what you do."

Yes, I thought, it's not what you know but how you apply it, whether you're an AIDS worker, a doctor, a soldier, or a preacher. And it doesn't matter whether you're Zairian or American. It's not what you know, but it's what you do with what you know that most certainly determines your future. The path of one's life has many branches, but only one can be chosen and followed at each fork in the path. It is impossible to know where another choice might have led me. I chose a seldom-traveled path that led to Congo, and that has made the difference in my life and the lives I have touched along the way.

I am retired now after five years of private practice, sixteen years of academic surgery in American medical schools, and two visits back to Africa as a visiting professor. Life has not been a picnic in the park for our family. I suffered a heart attack in 1980, and two years later our older son, John, was killed in a car wreck while we were vacationing together in California. He was going to enter college the following week. My wife, Winkie, developed cancer while we were working in Ghana in 1993, and underwent radical surgery here in America, but died the following year. Suffering and death are parts of life, but they are wrenching, traumatic parts that are made both worse and better by the ties of love. Recalling past times of happiness together and supporting each other in times of sorrow, we carve out big places in our hearts that can be filled with love for future needs.

My older daughter, Grace, earned a degree in education at Redlands University in California and taught elementary school in California. She lived in Senegal, West Africa, for a year teaching in a mission school in French. When she returned to America, she earned a masters degree in education focused on teaching English as a second language.

She lives with her husband and two sons in Siloam Springs, Arkansas, and she teaches at John Brown University.

Joy followed in her mother's footsteps, singing at every opportunity. After finishing college, she earned her masters in voice at the University of Southern California. She is married with a seven-year-old son and she sings professionally and teaches in the former Westminster Choir College that is now affiliated with Rider University here in Princeton.

My younger son, Rogé, is now a family practice physician in Siloam Springs, Arkansas. He is married and has five children. He has made several short-term medical trips to Africa, and sometimes his family has accompanied him. He has taken me along occasionally.

In 1997 I married Beverly, a beautiful lady my age whose husband, a neurosurgeon, had died of a heart attack in 1984. I was blessed to inherit two more lovely daughters and another granddaughter. After our marriage Beverly went with me to Ghana for two years, and one daughter and granddaughter visited us there. I now live in Princeton where Beverly has lived for forty years. Currently I serve on several boards for nongovernmental organizations working in developing countries (Health Teams International, Blessings International, and the United Front Against Riverblindness).

It is a small world, and friends and associates from long ago keep coming back into our lives. Dr. Daniel Shungu, the son of Bishop Shungu with whom I worked in Wembo Nyama, is a member of our church in Princeton. He is also chairman of the Riverblindness board and asked me to be his associate executive director. Dr. Bill Close, with whom I worked in Kinshasha, has a place in Big Piney, Wyoming, now where he writes books. We have spent days reminiscing together about Congo. Dr. Otis Simmons, the voice major who touched my life so dramatically when I was in college, has spent his career teaching voice at Alabama State University and was dean of the College of the Arts. He recently asked me to read and make comments about the book-manuscript he has written on the anatomy and training of the voice. He also asked Joy to read it and make suggestions.

Life flows on and we must ride with the current, splashing and laughing, and sometimes being bruised by the rocks as we go. Right now I must get ready for a trip to see my grandson commissioned as an officer in the U.S. Marine Corps, and I must prepare a commencement address for the graduates of John Brown University.

Before Roger L. Youmans, M.D. had completed his surgical residency at the University of Kansas he had already directed a mission hospital in the Democratic Republic of Congo during the early nineteen sixties. Those were turbulent and desperate years for Congo. After finishing his residency and learning tropical medicine and French in Belgium, he took his family back to Congo. He worked over ten years in bush hospitals and in the huge Kinshasa General Hospital, now renamed the Mama Yemo Hospital in honor of President Mobutu's mother. He subsequently had a private practice of surgery in California for five years and taught in three different American medical schools for sixteen years. He was a visiting professor of surgery in both Ghana and Nigeria. He is married and has three living children, eight grandchildren, and now resides in Princeton, New Jersey, having retired from surgical practice.